PRE-COMMERCE

How Companies and Customers Are Transforming Business Together

BOB PEARSON

with

Dan Zehr

JOSSEY-BASS
A Wiley Imprint
www.josseybass.com

Published by Jossey-Bass A
Wiley Imprint
989 Market Street, San Francisco, CA 94103-1741—www.josseybass.com

Jossey-Bass books and products are available through most bookstores. To contact Jossey-Bass directly call our Customer Care Department within the U.S. at 800-956-7739, outside the U.S. at 317-572-3986, or fax 317-572-4002.

Jossey-Bass also publishes its books in a variety of electronic formats. Some content that appears in print may not be available in electronic books.

Library of Congress Cataloging-in-Publication Data

Pearson, Bob, 1962-
    Pre-commerce : how companies and customers are transforming business together / Bob Pearson.
      p. cm.
    Includes bibliographical references and index.
    ISBN 978-0-470-92844-8 (cloth), 978-1-118-02301-3 (ebk), 978-1-118-02302-0 (ebk), 978-1-118-02303-7 (ebk)
      1. Consumer behavior.   2. Social media—Economic aspects.   3. Customer relations—Technological innovations.   4. Internet marketing.   I. Title.
    HF5415.32.P43 2011
    658.8'12—dc22

2010051345

Printed in the United States of America
FIRST EDITION

HB Printing   10 9 8 7 6 5 4 3 2 1

To Donna, Nicole, and Brittany—the story we are writing as a family is our most important one.

CONTENTS

FOREWORD

Mark Addicks, Chief Marketing Officer, General Mills

> *Management is doing things right; leadership*
> *is doing the right things.*
> —PETER F. DRUCKER

About 500,000 people will go online today for the first time in their lives.

Today is just an average day. This pace of change has been going on for several years and will for several more, at the very least.

When you combine the influx of new consumers online with the amazing progress in how consumers utilize technology to learn, have conversations, engage with brands, and purchase products, it's safe to say that we are in new territory.

Consumers today are starting their decision-making process earlier than ever and it is often in places where our companies may not be officially represented. First impressions for our brands are occurring via Google and Bing and Baidu. People are asking their peers for advice before they make a decision. There are many transformative changes occurring in the world of the consumer that require us, as leaders of companies, to also evolve.

Our world is changing for the good. Our best relationships are with our most empowered and passionate brand advocates. It has never been easier for a consumer to learn and build a relationship with us.

The growing power of consumers also keeps us on our toes to always provide the greatest value from our brands. It brings out the best in all of us. It's game day every day online.

The result is that what we have always cherished—building a great long-term relationship with consumers, being highly relevant in their decisions, and sharing our brand loyalty together—is more important today and will be even more important tomorrow.

The big difference is that consumers aren't waiting for that special time to visit us. It's the reverse. It's time for us to excel at visiting them where they hang out and learn and share with their friends. Our goal is to become a relevant peer in their communities.

It is clear to me that we have officially entered the world of pre-commerce, a world where our goal is to form a relationship that is relevant at any point in time in the life of a consumer, as they think, talk, and act related to our brands. We are becoming partners in new ways that are long-lasting and highly valuable.

What I also like about the pre-commerce world is that we already know it well, if we think about it for a minute. Our relationship with our Brand Champions has always been the top priority at General Mills. Nothing has changed. Our Betty Crocker team used to receive and respond individually to approximately 5,000 letters a day back in the 1930s and 1940s: And that is when letters were written long-hand in cursive type. Anyone remember those days?

Betty Crocker was a social brand when *social* meant knocking on the neighbor's door to ask if you could borrow a cup of sugar. We still ask to borrow that cup of sugar today. It's just that we may do it on Facebook. Technology is changing how we communicate, but the core principles are the same. Consumers are consistent. They have always gathered around their passions.

We've all talked about integration for years between offline and online. Now we are doing it. We found that our social media outreach for Fiber

One Chewy bars made a real difference in both the quality of online conversations and our sales. E-Commerce and Pre-Commerce are cousins.

A lot of our best known icons at General Mills don't officially talk online. I'll admit that you don't hear from the Pillsbury Doughboy, Jolly Green Giant, or Betty Crocker via podcast. But these are brands that can—and must—live socially across the digital landscape.

Consumers can develop a deeper understanding of the benefits of our brands by having conversations online with us and with their peers.

When consumers get to know a brand well, it can start to become part of their lifestyle or at least the lifestyle to which they aspire.

The opportunity to educate is of huge value. If we are relevant to our consumers, we don't just want to sell snacks or cereals. We want to describe the health benefits of cholesterol-lowering or why fiber has an important role in one's diet. Partners are willing to teach. Peers share information that is valuable. Companies who will lead in pre-commerce will do both.

We will learn more to improve our products and services if we ask for feedback. We'll learn what is really important if we get to know our consumers well online. We'll get new ideas and new ways of understanding our brands and what they can be in the lives of our Brand Champions. We'll find authentic causes to support and new ways to advocate for social change that matters to our Brand Champions.

It is interesting to realize that most of the answers to how consumers think are right in front of us. With nearly sixty online communities dedicated to Cheerios, for example, we need to become great listeners, so we understand how to be of value.

In today's world, it is more important than ever that we provide a remarkable brand experience to support our top brands. Companies that form relationships with consumers that go beyond the transaction will become relevant peers, and relevant peers are going to be the ones who have the highest brand loyalty and advocacy.

The good news is that leaders of companies have the experience and skills to make this happen. That is not in question. What is needed, however, is a mindset shift to realize that consumers can find everything they need without ever speaking with us. The old days are just that.

So let's all get out there and join with our consumers to build the most remarkable experience possible.

CHAPTER ONE

THE RISE OF PRE-COMMERCE

*In the business world, the rearview mirror is
always clearer than the windshield.*
—WARREN BUFFETT

We all have them. They hit us in the shower, behind the wheel, or at any number of seemingly random moments in our lives—those "Aha!" moments when inspiration, experience, and realization come together in a perfect blend of understanding. Archimedes found his eureka experience in the bathtub. A falling apple triggered Newton's insight into our physical world.

My epiphany certainly won't go down in the annals of scientific research—it arose from an innocuous experience as an everyday consumer—but I'll never forget the first time I'd recognized the most fundamental change in the marketplace since e-commerce took off in 1995. I was preparing for a family vacation in Italy, and I knew I had some driving ahead of me. I know a few phrases of Italian, but not enough to get me around the country without the help of a decent navigation device. So I went on the prowl, starting where pretty much everyone starts their research these days—Google. Now, I'm sure psychologists have studied why the first page of search results carries more

1

weight than all the following pages, but none of that mattered at the time. All I know is I clicked on TomTom because it was one of the first brands I saw listed. And after a few clicks around the subsequent Web sites I realized TomTom's navigation device and its maps would work as well in Europe as they do in the United States.

But that wasn't enough, of course. I still had to find out whether another brand offered a better option. From my time at Dell, I'd become plenty familiar with geek sites that did high-tech product reviews. I chose one of my favorites, CNET, where I found trustworthy reviews of all the decent navigation devices on the market. TomTom scored very well there, so now I knew I was looking at a quality product. The only question left: Was it worth the price? I skipped over to a Web site that compared prices, and found that TomTom not only provided quality, but some of the best value on the market, as well.

I probably was sold at that moment, but sometimes I still take the old-fashioned approach. I hopped in the car and drove out to the local Best Buy, wanting to see the real thing before making a final decision.

To this day, I have no reason to disabuse the salesman of the notion that his little spiel helped me make my purchase that day. He had no clue that I knew as much about that product as he did or more, and he couldn't have known I was going to buy the TomTom device whether he'd delivered his pitch or ignored me entirely. He was just lucky I decided to see it before I bought it. I could have bought the device anywhere online.

It all started to dawn on me as I drove home, and it became even clearer over the subsequent weeks as I pondered the social media strategies I was developing for dozens of Fortune 500 companies while working with some of the leaders in online commerce. I realized neither TomTom nor Best Buy and its salesman had any clue about my decision to buy that specific product in that specific store. Neither company thought to ask how I'd become interested in TomTom's products. Granted, the sale was only a couple hundred dollars, hardly worth pumping serious research dollars into, but I've continued to scour the Web ever since to keep abreast of the latest GPS tools and products. I'll need to upgrade in a year or two, and I don't want to miss a right turn in Tuscany any more than I want to get lost in Texas.

But through no fault of its own—the company and its salesman did everything right, traditionally speaking—Best Buy won't get my next purchase. Worse for them, they might not even realize why. The exploding use of social media channels has fundamentally changed the way customers go about making their purchasing decisions, and very few companies have recognized this remarkable shift. Your customers no longer count on you for information about the products you develop or sell. In fact, they would rather talk to other customers, especially peers who are in the same boat as they are. Like me when I walked into Best Buy, more and more customers will arrive at your doors or come to your Web site with their minds already made up. And if you have no way of reaching them while they're making their decision, there's no way you can convince them to come to your store or your site.

I call this new phenomenon Pre-Commerce. The phrase reminds me of the sci-fi movie *Minority Report*, in which Tom Cruise and the pre-crimes unit can find and arrest criminals before they commit their crime. Companies today have to reach customers long before they commit to their purchases, because customers are making decisions before they arrive at your store or your home page. Ask yourself: How many potential customers are surfing the Web for information about your product—not to mention your competitors' products—at this very moment? What are they finding? And how many of your existing customers are never coming back because they've found a better, more personalized way to research and buy what they need?

Do you know? Do you realize there are ways to find out?

FROM E-COMMERCE TO PRE-COMMERCE

The Internet brought us e-commerce. The rise of social media is giving us Pre-Commerce.

It took only six years from Tim Berners-Lee's initial proposal in 1989 for a World Wide Web until companies started to fiddle with selling online. By the time 1995 rolled around, Dell, Pizza Hut, Cisco, and a handful of other companies had taken the plunge and started selling directly to customers through an online portal. Sites such as Amazon.com and the iTunes store gleaned all those lessons and found new ways to master the world of e-commerce. Online retail in the United States generated more than $155 billion in sales during 2009, according to Forrester Research, and that figure doesn't even include auto, travel, or prescription-drug sales.[1] Add all the business-to-business commerce that streams through Web portals every day, and you start to see why e-commerce is vital to almost every business.

But while e-commerce continued to mushroom throughout the last few years, the advent of social media gave customers a set of new, more-trusted avenues for information and ideas. Customers didn't have to interact directly with the brand. They could independently find and share ideas and information. Virtually no company noticed it at the time, but customers started to shift into a Pre-Commerce world. In that world, the first option for technical support comes from Google, Bing, or an independent forum where virtual neighbors provide troubleshooting tips. In the Pre-Commerce world, ratings and reviews have become ubiquitous, and they're becoming increasingly adaptable to match any customer's specific curiosities. Here, customers can share an idea for a new product and put it to a vote of their peers. And they can learn about your product, suggest ways to improve it and purchase it—all without coming to you for a single shred of information, and maybe not even coming to you for the purchase itself.

Whether you know it yet or not, the Pre-Commerce world ultimately will force your company to interact in a very real way with your customers. The corporation's long-held control over its brand image and message now belongs as much in the hands of the customer, who can reach millions of people with a rave review or a scathing blog post. Your customers are actually shaping the image of your brand in more ways and with more power than your best agency. And that subtle power shift means companies will have to adapt to the things Pre-Commerce customers do very, very well: (1) they share ideas, (2) they share product knowledge, and (3) they provide solutions for one another.

These three drivers of online behavior shape your brand reputation, but they also shape how customers make their purchasing decisions. People share information to help their peers, not to help your company. In the Pre-Commerce world, customers are passionate about helping their virtual friends. You can interact with them if you provide relevant content that helps move the community's conversations forward. Or you can watch as your customers migrate to competitors who help them fulfill their desire to support and interact with their peers. It's your choice to participate, but your customer gets to choose the brand with which they'll participate.

These are deceiving trends for a company that's clicking along in traditional e-commerce mode. To those businesses, customers still look and act very much the way they always did. Yet today, your customers are wired very differently when they walk into your store or come to your home page. The business leader who doesn't understand the way people identify with brands in the Pre-Commerce marketplace will lose customers, brand prestige, and, ultimately, sales.

LET YOUR CUSTOMERS HELP YOU

Marc Benioff, the founder of salesforce.com, rarely looks in the rear-view mirror. If he does, he only sees competitors pushing him to speed down the road ahead. So he has become relentless in trying to understand what his customers want. I've worked with a lot of CEOs in recent years, but none put more emphasis on working *with* customers to develop the next product or service they need. So it came as no surprise when Marc announced the launch of Idea Exchange in September 2006. The forum would allow salesforce.com to get feedback directly from his customers. It was a big hit.

A few months after Idea Exchange went live, Michael Dell called me into a conference room. At the time, I was leading Dell's communities and conversations team, and I knew firsthand the keen interest Michael had taken in all things social media. Already a pioneer in e-commerce, he had started to get a sense of the emerging Pre-Commerce world. He asked me what a Dell version of Idea Exchange would look like. My team and I brainstormed the idea and started to build a proposal. We had roughed out a plan, but we were struggling to come up with a name for the idea. Nothing stuck until Bernie Charland, my colleague at the time, said, "What if we combine brainstorm and ideas together, since that's what we're really doing." And bingo, Dell IdeaStorm was born.

I sent the proposal to Michael on February 10, a Saturday. Anyone who has met Michael Dell knows how intense he is about direct relationships with his customers, and that fire was burning even hotter because he had just returned as CEO. No more than a few hours after sending the proposal, my phone rang. It was Michael, of course. He said he liked everything about the plan except the timeline. It was way too long, he said. We'd planned on three weeks to launch; he wanted it up in two days.

I remember calling Paul Walker, one of our outside consultants on social media, and I told him we had to build and launch this new community in three days. Paul hesitated a bit. It sounded pretty daunting, he said, but we could have it ready to go by Thursday. I laughed and reminded him that "three days" in Michael Dell parlance means seventy-two hours, not three work days. It turns out seventy-two hours can be a long time if you work productively. We soft-launched Dell IdeaStorm on Tuesday, February 13.

We quickly began to understand the power of including customer's ideas in real time. Not only did we start receiving some very interesting ideas within hours—many of which made it into Dell products—we also generated a strong wave of positive buzz throughout the blogosphere. We were meeting customers where they were, and we were giving them a chance to participate with our brand. Within eighteen months, we had more than 11,000 ideas from customers. We launched Employee Storm and other offshoots to get ideas internally, and we generated 4,500 ideas from our own employees. Even more important, though, we'd implemented 325 customer ideas and 140 employee suggestions.

Your customers want to help shape your products, services, and approach to market. Your employees want to help improve your company's operations and morale. All you have to do is ask for their help—and then follow through on it.

About a year after Dell launched IdeaStorm, Michael Dell and Marc Benioff teamed up with Starbucks CEO Howard Schultz to launch mystarbucksidea.com. "It [Dell IdeaStorm] was absolutely fascinating to watch, and for Dell, it has opened a new chapter for a terrific brand," Benioff said. "Michael was kind enough to share his experience with Howard Schultz at Starbucks, and then we helped them build mystarbucksidea.com."

Case Study

"Ho'olu komo la kaua" ("Please join us")

Marc Benioff, Chairman and CEO, salesforce.com

Marc Benioff sees trends inside today's corporations before most other people do. He thinks in terms of how to free up capital and how to improve collaboration inside a company. He constantly gathers customer insight and puts it to use in ways that improve current products and create new successes. With perspective and insight like his, game-changing ideas emerge on a regular basis. Like in 1999, when Marc and his team first launched salesforce.com, and again with their subsequent introduction of a "platform as a service," called Force.com, his ideas have helped make "cloud computing" one of the hottest technology trends going today.

We live in a different world from when we started salesforce.com more than a decade ago, but the importance of Pre-Commerce is something we've seen since our earliest days. Salesforce.com offers a service delivered over the Internet, which means the Internet itself has always been one of the most important members of our sales team. In fact, in the beginning we didn't even have salespeople; we just relied on our Web site. A prospect could log onto our site, learn everything about our service, and sign up for free. It created an unusual sales phenomenon: Most prospective customers were using our service before they ever heard from someone at salesforce.com.

We hired our first dedicated salesperson several months later to help make paying customers out of our many beta users (at the time, we called this group our "design partners" because they gave us feedback on our products and services). However, at that point the heavy lifting had already been done. Customers had researched, investigated, and explored the product on their own—both on our Web site and through the infinite amount of information available on the rest of the Web. They relied on discussions they had with their colleagues and peers, and they made a decision about our service before we even knew they were thinking about us.

This might sound unusual, and it is a definite departure from the old way of doing business. But it's not something to fear—it's something to leverage. At salesforce.com, we embrace the fact that our most essential sales tool is the Internet, and our most effective strategy is turning every customer into an evangelist for our brand. Customers will talk about us whether we like it or not, so we know we have to find ways to make them love us. And we've seen the effectiveness of this: According to an independent study by CustomerStat, 94 percent of customers said they would refer someone to our service and 74 percent already had—twice the rate most on-premise software vendors were seeing.

We feel especially excited about the evolution we've seen on the Web over the past decade. The emergence of social media, cloud computing, and conversation allows us to get closer to our community of customers and partners. For example, we feature an online marketplace called AppExchange, which *BusinessWeek* called the "eBay for business software" and Forbes described as the "iTunes of business software." Much like eBay and iTunes, AppExchange works because communities work best within a market dynamic. Like any thriving marketplace, both online and offline, we provide a site where customers can find what they want, test it, and discuss it with other like-minded peers. The exchange now provides an incredible customer base for developers who upload their applications—and a fantastic opportunity for salesforce.com to engage with our customers.

Today we have relationships with more than 260,000 developers. They've built more than 160,000 custom applications on Force.com, each addressing a specific business need. There's no way we could've built that many on our own. But our partners have. They've developed innovative ideas for accounting, human resources, and areas of business we didn't even know existed. And our ability to share those ideas makes us stickier with current customers and more attractive to new ones.

The recipe for success is in how you partner. With AppExchange, we provide the fuel—developer environments, resources, tools, content, etcetera—and our developers reciprocate with amazing ideas that often lead to the formation of new companies. When you partner well, you help create an ecosystem that works together to build success for the long-term. A real ecosystem is a community that enjoys being together. Gone are the days of closed communities that develop products or innovate. The best ideas come from the constant iterations, innovations, and improvements that result from the collaboration of many viewpoints.

We've seen the power of capturing the collective intelligence of the "crowd" to develop the best next ideas. There are approximately two billion people online; consider the opportunities that arise if you tap into everything they know. Calling upon crowd sourcing models and Web sites like Digg, which allow users to share, discover, and vote on content, we built a service called IdeaExchange, which gave our community the option to vote on ideas and share their insights. This community was a first for a corporation and served as the inspiration for Dell's IdeaStorm, which led to successful product launches, including notebooks and desktops with Linux pre-installed. It also led to MyStarbucksIdea, which helped CEO Howard Schultz establish what he called "a seeing culture."

We're in a very exciting time for the technology industry. Cloud computing is at a tipping point. The Gartner Group predicted that cloud computing services will continue to be a top strategic priority for enterprise technology managers through 2014. The research firm estimated that cloud services revenue will approach $150 billion by then.[2]

Driven by sites like Facebook, Twitter, and YouTube and relayed anywhere, anytime on mobile devices like the iPhone, and iPad, consumers and employees are moving into new uses of the cloud that enable more collaboration, mobility, and real-time information flow. Instead of corresponding with one person, we now correspond with entire networks in real time. With these new social models, which are based on groups and feeds, there is a way to immediately leverage the knowledge of an organization. People with expertise and relevance are instantly looped in, can participate in the conversation, collaborate, and make contributions more simply than ever before.

People in every industry spend an inordinate amount of time talking about innovation. We seek innovation like it's the Holy Grail. But innovation isn't necessarily "easy" or "difficult." It doesn't even come from within. Many of our best ideas have emerged from our customers, including one request from a customer that led us to transform our offering from an application to a Web-based platform—the key to what we've become today. The secret to innovation is an intense and unrelenting focus on what customers really need, even if that need has never been spoken, and then combining it with our expertise in the capabilities that technologies can deliver.

One of the primary mantras at salesforce.com is to "Make Everyone Successful." We started in a rented, one-bedroom apartment. Today, in 2010, we have 5,000 employees, and, according to *Fortune* magazine, we're one of the fastest growing companies in the world. Every step of the way, we succeeded by eliciting the feedback of customers and prospects and constantly using their insight to keep improving our products and services. I still give everyone my e-mail address, and I always respond when they send a note. But we now have much better tools to create a feedback loop, and we need those new tools in this new Pre-Commerce era. Finding innovative and effective technologies that allow you to listen to the needs of customers—and convert them into evangelists—will keep us competitive, innovative, and relevant.

Case Study

A TECTONIC SHIFT

Modern science hasn't figured out how to predict earthquakes, but we have all the evidence we need to prepare. We can clearly identify the fault line. We know it's bound to happen sooner or later. And we know the steps we can take to be ready for the tremor when it inevitably arrives. Even if we can't predict the moment it happens, we're prepared nonetheless.

Business has operated on the same wavelength for centuries. In the early 1900s, industrialists adopted Frederick Taylor's theories of "scientific management" to revamp their operations and generate huge gains in efficiency. By the start of the twenty-first century, hundreds of companies had taken hints from Toyota's lean manufacturing methods and Dell's direct model to further streamline the production and delivery of goods. Marketing has made significant shifts as well, and the ability to mass market products now has been tailored down to our own living rooms and PCs.

But every now and then, business doesn't see the fault lines of a new shift. We can't see any predictive evidence of a tectonic shift in the marketplace, and it catches us off guard. Pre-Commerce changed how commerce is conducted online, and we're only starting to recognize it after the fact. It's much harder to identify the 500,000 people around the world who come online for the first time each day. We didn't see the individual cell phone purchases accumulate as an entire generation skipped landlines in emerging countries, and now mobile phones outnumber laptop computers by a three-to-one margin. Today, we're only starting to fully comprehend the massive amount of data being stored effortlessly in remote data centers—in the "cloud," as it were—a change that will make it seamless to store, access, and share files from anywhere on virtually any device. And in the emerging Pre-Commerce world, companies just aren't there as millions of customers make friends with people around the globe, interacting through connections on forums, Facebook, blogs, and other social media.

THE MOST IMPORTANT OPPORTUNITY OF ALL: COLLABORATION

Michael Dell, Founder, Chairman, and CEO, Dell Inc.

Michael Dell was a Pre-Commerce leader before the concept existed. He has been innovating in how companies build relationships directly with customers since 1984, when he founded Dell with $1,000 and an unprecedented idea. Whether it was figuring out how to build the best supply chain in the world or becoming one of the first companies to sell directly online or enabling customers to give their ideas directly to the company to help build new products and services, Michael continually innovates in ways that are pragmatic and meaningful for organizations of all sizes. He has instilled in me how important it is to listen, learn, and adapt to what customers need every day.

It may have taken a few decades, but the Internet is now unlocking the most important opportunity of all for individuals, businesses, governments, and organizations of all types. We have entered the era of ubiquitous collaboration.

The concept is not new, but the means to truly collaborate, exchange ideas, and activate the collective potential of every bright mind has finally gone mainstream. And it will forever change the way we work, live, and interact with each other.

When I was a teenager, about thirty years ago, I used what we then called an electronic bulletin board system to connect with other early adopters. We shared code, posted messages to one another, exchanged news, and formed connections—all through a dial-up modem. The ability to connect with people I'd never met through my computer in my room at home changed the way I viewed technology. Those experiences ultimately became a big catalyst for why I started Dell years later.

Today, entire generations are growing up with online collaboration. Power collaborators are connecting anywhere, anytime via the social network and the device of their choice. They believe in a fundamental assumption that we all are meant to share, learn, and collaborate from each other online any way we like. Entire populations of young adults don't know any other way. After all, the best answer might be 3,000 miles away, in a whole other place and time.

The power of online collaboration is also changing the way we work. We're finally tapping into the knowledge housed in the world's greatest operating system in the world—the Web—and unleashing the potential of billions of creative minds to work together in ways we've never seen before.

Geography is irrelevant. Title is irrelevant. Knowledge applied to the right situation each and every time will create the advantage that many companies have yet to experience. It will also change the way business works, and the way society works. We'll continue to see more rapidly self-organizing groups, and I think we're going to rewrite the standard definition of how work gets done in the next ten years.

It's easy to say this. It's much harder to change how we collaborate—so that the smartest teams answer the call, not the available teams. We want ideas as quickly from our colleagues in Xiamen, Chennai, and Round Rock as we do from our customers.

This requires a shift in mindset for most businesses. We need to embrace the social network, even the aspects of it we can't always control. When Dell launched IdeaStorm to create a two-way conversation with our customers, we couldn't be sure what the nature of those conversations would be. Hundreds of customer-inspired innovations later, it's clear that the leap of faith was well worth it. Customers are out there talking about you and me, and it's critical that we participate and engage.

Giving team members around the globe the tools to ignite this collaboration is equally vital. While micro-blogging tools behind the firewall are typically the preferred internal collaboration tools, the reality is that your sharpest team members are often innovating out in the open, in the realm of the social web. Brainstorming and idea generation in environments like Twitter and Facebook are the new reality, and we need to embrace it and even encourage it.

When collaboration is genuine, we are capable of creating solutions that would have never occurred otherwise. When you no longer wonder about where an idea came from, forget about time zones, and know that you have accessed the best thinking from anywhere on the planet every time, then you are truly leveraging collaboration.

We will see dozens of applications and software platforms that promise to change our lives. Ultimately, they won't. It's true that technology will be the great enabler, but each of us will drive the success of collaboration. What is important is combining the best technology infrastructure with a culture that embraces the sharing of ideas, insights, and expertise freely amongst team members, customers, and influencers.

Technology has always been about enabling human potential, and there's never been a more exciting time to be human.

The pace of social media change that's happening below the surface is blazing at revolutionary speeds. The pace of change within corporations is glacial. Your customers are redefining your brand and your company before your eyes. But because it's happening in a Pre-Commerce world, few companies even realize it's happening, let alone understand and have a plan for it. The company that moves into the Pre-Commerce world will engender more brand loyalty and fuel greater sales, and it just might put slower competitors on the defensive for years to come.

"Word of mouth has always been the essential secret ingredient," said Andy Sernovitz, CEO of SocialMedia.org and author of *Word of Mouth Marketing*, one of the seminal books about the way social media is changing business. "A company that gets customers for free through word of mouth can always beat one that is paying for it. But here's what's new: First, word of mouth (luck) became word of mouth marketing—a measurable, plannable marketing function. The necessary toolset and awareness took off in 2004–2006, and smart companies started growing with it . . . and then social media hit in 2008 to give it a mass scale. Companies could now encourage and learn from word of mouth at a level that made it practical for a big company, and it gave our fans and critics the scale to force us to pay attention."

THE FOUR As

Companies today use what I call Cave Man marketing. We scratch out the pictures on the wall, then step back and watch how people react. We've been trained for decades to think that awareness leads to action. I can hear my own little "ooga booga" soundtrack every time I watch a company create an ad campaign that consists of little more than an advertisement in the Sunday paper. Forget the obvious fact that fewer and fewer people actually take the analog copy of the newspaper. Customers learn in entirely new ways now. They no longer rely on ads to raise awareness; they use search engines and social media tools—as I did when I needed a GPS device.

Back in the old days, meaning a few years ago, customers made a choice to stay in constant touch with the brands they cared about. But because of all the information available at their fingertips today, customers can easily and efficiently research broader topics and product categories on an ongoing basis. Someone who likes to travel can read and learn about vacation spots, airfare, and hotels 365 days a year. Customers can get feedback and get new tips on products at any time, not during the one or two times they're actually ready to conduct the transaction. Yet companies gear all their resources toward that one transactional moment.

To put this in greater perspective, we spend less than 1 percent of our entire lives online making transactions, and our companies spend close to 100 percent of our funding against that 1 percent.

The result is a split, one that is leaving companies on the wrong side of a widening fault line.

I've spent much of the past five years studying the shift to Pre-Commerce and why businesses have failed to see a change that, at least now, has become glaringly obvious. I'm convinced that our training has a lot to do with our inaction. For better or worse, we're programmed in school and corporate training to learn "The Way We Do Business Here"—and, gosh darn it, we're going to do it better than anyone else. The rest of the world doesn't work like that, of course. Our customers don't really care what we think or how we are trained.

Take the classic and famous Four Ps of marketing—price, product, place, and promotion. The Four Ps have been a staple of marketing instruction for years, ever since E. Jerome McCarthy, a Michigan State business professor, coined them in 1960. I learned the Four Ps were the bee's knees when it comes to commercialization, and it was all true when I joined my first large company in 1986. Very powerful people make big decisions for and about their customers. They decided on everything— and that's precisely the problem. The Four Ps are completely company-driven. Every decision comes from a conference room. You decide on the price. You build the product. You determine where to distribute it, and you make every call on how to promote it. You base that on tons of market research and the advice of highly paid consultants, of course, but interaction *with* the customer is all but unheard of. The Four Ps can't comprehend a customer with power of his or her own.

The Pre-Commerce world demands a new interpretation of the Four Ps, one that understands how social media changes the way customers make purchasing decisions and gives those same customers a far-reaching influence over brand image. We've developed a new model that follows these Four As – awareness, assessment, action, and ambassadors. It is driven by customers, not corporations. The customers will decide when they listen, what they'll discuss on the Internet, where they'll research their purchases, and where they'll make them. Brand loyalty won't come from the cave-wall paintings, it will come from persistent, positive interaction between a company, its brand, and its customers.

- *Awareness*—A company must understand when and how to penetrate the market's noise to reach customers and create awareness for its brand. This only can happen effectively with active listening to what customers say online. You want to raise awareness with the right influencers in the right sites using the right content.

- *Assessment*—The customers are not on board yet, but they are committed to learning more. A company must supply content that customers can download, view, read, and act upon, and it needs to provide that content where customers will access it.

- *Action*—Simply put, this is the point at which the customer is making a decision that shows they are on board, ranging from the most obvious, a purchasing decision, to a surrogate, such as clicking on a coupon to print out.

- *Assessment*—No social media interaction is perfect. A company has to review and re-assess its approach to identify potential improvements and understand your share of conversation that is pro, con, and neutral. Measuring positive share of conversation is easy. Negative share of conversation is diluting your message. And neutral or flat experiences can actually be the death of a brand. You need to understand the dynamics for all three.

- *Ambassadors*—Every business has customers who are uncommonly loyal to its brand. A company has to know and build relationships with these loyalists, keep them informed, and give them every opportunity to help spread the word. These are folks who write a few thousand forum posts a year, write a hundred blog posts, or do fifty videos. They live for your brand.

I realize I have listed five As here, but I do so only to stress the importance of assessment. The interaction and learning should never stop in the Pre-Commerce world, because the environment is constantly and rapidly changing. In fact, we have to look at the entire list of the Four As as a cycle. Awareness will help a company identify its ambassadors. Assessment will produce more fruitful action. And ambassadors can help a company find the right places to break through the clutter and into the next awareness phase.

Ultimately, the Four As represent a sea-change in the way companies approach and interact with their customers. As such, they raise some significant questions for forward-thinking executives. Companies will have to generate a whole new level of insight about their customer base, the type of knowledge that can come only from relationships with customers themselves.

ARE YOU READY FOR THE FOUR AS?

The Four As raise significant questions that executives will have to answer if they expect to engage customers in a Pre-Commerce world. These questions can provide a quick guide to help gauge your company's or business unit's readiness:

(Continued)

- Do you know the behaviors of your customers so well that you can cut through the clutter to reach them? If yes, what are the top fifty locations where they have conversations today?
- Do you know when, where, and how people assess your brand and learn about it? If yes, what is their favorite way to learn? Vlog? Podcast? How does the media mix change by topic?
- Do you know when, where, and how customers make decisions to act, whether in affinity with your brand or that of your competitors? What do they say in decision-making mode?
- Do you know how your customers react if they like or don't like something about your brand? Do you actively try to shift opinion your way customer by customer?
- Do you know how your customer feels about their experience with your brand and how their interactions and reactions change when those experiences occur online?
- Do you know your most passionate brand advocates, and do you know them all by first and last name? When is the last time you spoke with them?

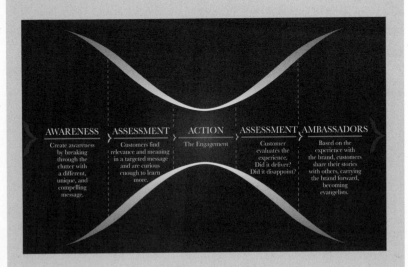

AWARENESS | ASSESSMENT | ACTION | ASSESSMENT | AMBASSADORS

Create awareness by breaking through the clutter with a different, unique, and compelling message.

Customers find relevance and meaning in a targeted message and are curious enough to learn more.

The Engagement

Customer evaluates the experience. Did it deliver? Did it disappoint?

Based on the experience with the brand, customers share their stories with others, carrying the brand forward, becoming evangelists.

The tools exist to answer all these questions, and you'll find that your customers are more than willing to help if you reach out to them. Even so, these straightforward questions stump the vast majority of executives today.

KEEP IT SIMPLE

Common sense rules the day in the Pre-Commerce economy. The sexy social media campaigns we see from consumer-products companies make a big splash, and everyone has heard about some of the more successful consumer campaigns. But the biggest opportunities often exist between two brick-and-mortar companies who simply agree to open a window between their operations and improve their interactions.

Imagine working for a company with 50,000 employees. You want to reach a key customer with 100,000 employees. If you're the leader of a Pre-Commerce company, you'll encourage your account leader to find ways to open up the world between his team and the customer. You might consider creating a private, business-to-business community between the key people on both sides of the wall. Employees on both sides could blog, share ideas, review processes, and discuss ways to improve products, processes, services, or support. With today's ever-improving social media tools, your account manager can monitor and guide these discussions seamlessly and efficiently. You end up with robust, business-specific information you can use to improve your company. You can share solutions in real time. And you'll build a deeper relationship that can redefine how you and your customers conduct online commerce.

This is the direction Pre-Commerce will take business. It abandons fancy models that collect loads of data but have limited insight. In fact, companies far too often confuse listening with the collection and analysis of voluminous troves of data. Pre-Commerce will empower customers and give them the ability to help filter insight from the data companies collect. The rapid innovation spawned by social media developers will produce new technologies that help separate the wheat from the chaff. The interactive world will provide the bridge between a customer's big idea and the engineers and developers who can integrate it into your next product. In the e-commerce world, we still create endless PowerPoint decks to make our case and then we eventually cascade these insights to the troops. Pre-Commerce will remove the middleman, his PowerPoint deck, and all the confusion in between. It will simplify the process by connecting your customers directly with your teams.

I've seen these connections produce powerful results. I'd gotten up early one morning in March 2007 for Dell's quarterly meeting of vice presidents and directors, and I was looking forward to what Michael Dell would say about IdeaStorm. My team had launched the site a month earlier, and already customers had flooded the site with ideas, votes, and comments. In that short period, the open-source community supportive of free Linux software had made their wishes clear: Dell should pre-load and certify a Linux-based operating system on its consumer PCs. The only problem was, we had no plan to do this. If we dismissed the most-discussed idea our customers offered us, would this great community experiment lose credibility before it really took off?

Michael delivered his usual motivating talk, and we moved on to the Q&A. One of my colleagues raised his hand, stood up, and asked: "I see that the top idea on IdeaStorm is about Linux becoming available on consumer systems. What are we really going to do?" In retrospect, I was probably cynical, but it felt to me like the question expected a "Let's do nothing" sort of response. But it was a legitimate question. IdeaStorm was one month old and our customer's top idea was an offering we did not even consider in our product roadmap. Michael looked straight at the questioner and said: "You are going to talk with our customers, find out what they want, and deliver it."

Right then and there, I knew the game had changed at Dell. In a matter of seconds, we went from a company that might have dismissed this request to a company on a mission to figure out how to incorporate our customers' online feedback. It was 100 percent driven by our customers' ability to tell us, through social media, what they wanted in a product. Our consumer team went to work and two months later took the idea from nowhere to production. On May 24, 2007, we started selling three computer systems with the Ubuntu 7.04 operating system pre-installed.

I'm still amazed at our team's speed to market and the energy and passion with which they did it. I would dare say they actually enjoyed it. It was an example of the new model, and we knew we were on the front edge of something big. We realized the pursuit of knowledge will lead to our success. It might not happen every single time you step up to the plate. But if you consistently interact with customers and work with them to deliver the content and products they want, you'll differentiate your company and discover new breakthroughs your competitors can't match.

THE FIRST STEP

At WCG, we use a series of inquiries to help companies determine their readiness for a Pre-Commerce world. They're a good first step for determining the right path for your company.

(Continued)

- Where do you get your new ideas for new products and services? In other words, who drives innovation for you? If the answer is a clear "Department X is in charge of innovation," you know you're heading down a misleading path. Your customer is your co-driver. Consider instead how your teams can learn directly from customers, analyzing feedback and assessing insights to develop a co-created product—a customer-driven product.
- How recent is your customer-insight data and how rapidly is it aging? Do you have real-time data gathered 24 hours a day from millions of customers, or are you looking at highly processed, already outdated results? Processed results are as good for you as processed food; find the fresh stuff.
- When was the last time your executives or your reports talked with a customer? Every company has a collection of bright, passionate leaders, but all their enthusiasm is wasted if they don't know how to interact with customers in a persistent, positive manner.
- Do you have a list of your top 100 customers? Do you know who your most passionate and loyal customers are? Do you know them by name? Brand ambassadors often carry a lot of weight in the Pre-Commerce world. You have to know them and the influence they wield. Can you pick up the phone and call them right now?

If you can't do these things yet, here's the good news. Your competitors haven't figured it out yet, either. But know this—the company that figures out how to make itself relevant to the Pre-Commerce customer will build a strategic advantage at the expense of its slow-footed rivals. The race has started.

IT'S NOT AS HARD AS IT MIGHT SEEM

Human beings are creatures of habit. If we had to pore through an endless stream of constantly changing data, we'd have no hope of reaping any real customer insights. But we don't. Because humans work in patterns, we can study how people interact online, and from that we can draw increasingly clear guidelines about how customers assess, learn, decide, and advocate for a brand. Similarly, we can become very familiar with our competitors' proclivities by identifying their most common moves, another approach that can lead to new insights for your brands.

While social media inherently involve a range of content—from text to podcasts to YouTube videos—most insight comes in word form. Invariably, your customers will use their own language to communicate. We use fancy terms to describe the analysis of all this, tossing around ideas like "keyword dictionaries" and "search engine optimization" to put a complex and high-minded terminology on what, ultimately, comes down to nothing but words. Words remain the primary currency at the foundation of Pre-Commerce. In the e-commerce world, we used keywords as a guide for our advertising. But future leaders will begin to learn the natural language their customers use in the Pre-Commerce arena.

Consider what your teams could achieve if they could identify the exact language people use when they're studying your products. Then imagine how you could use that recognition to scrape all those conversations into a folder your salespeople could use to reach out to those customers in real time. These tools already exist.

But social media is, by definition, social. The company that doesn't participate actively in these discussions will find itself left with half-answers and partial data. Newspapers have struggled in recent years, but they still offer a good example of how to provide content customers demand. The best newspapers have a knack for knowing what news we want to read. They know how to find it, report it, and distribute it in a manner that makes us want to read more every day. Meanwhile, almost none of the Fortune 1000 companies provide a dynamic body of content on their Web pages or through their nascent social media efforts. It's like putting out the same issue of the *New York Times* every day of the week.

It doesn't have to be that way. Companies such as Networked Insights in Madison, Wisconsin, have built an algorithm to identify the emerging trends for a given topic. Their products can identify emerging subjects of highest interest and show you which topics are trending toward that point. With that information in hand, the Pre-Commerce Company can provide relevant content that customers actually want to see.

I can hear you now: "We're not in the content business." But in the Pre-Commerce world, you have to be. You have an opportunity to reach your customers each and every day with relevant information, to establish a connection that will forge stronger relationships. Or you can ignore it all and repel them with your own version of a week-old *New York Times*. Your customers won't tell you your content is outdated; they'll simply stop visiting your site.

LEADERS OF THE PRE-COMMERCE COMPANY

The Pre-Commerce world impacts every corner of your business, and taking a piecemeal or segmented approach is bound to limit your success. I've worked closely with C-suite executives who recognize that competitive advantage is not built without the support and oversight from the top. We've heard many Internet experts suggest that companies ought to create an executive-level social media guru. We couldn't agree more, but we'd stress that every C-suite executive has to play his or her part in bringing a traditional company into the Pre-Commerce world. It starts with the CEO at the top, but it goes nowhere unless each executive instills the mindset throughout his or her business group.

So in the following chapters, I'll show you how high-level executives can implement the pre-commerce approach throughout their organization. This isn't the nitty-gritty guide to social media, nor is it the high-minded academic's guide to a new world of commerce. There are plenty of books for that already. This is pragmatic guidance for the C-suite, for the executive who wants to understand how social media has changed the marketplace—and how he or she can reshape a company to win in the Pre-Commerce world.

CHAPTER TWO

THE EVOLUTION OF
E-COMMERCE

Trends, like horses, are easier to ride in the direction they are going.
—JOHN NAISBITT, AUTHOR OF *MEGATRENDS*

As a young man growing up in New Jersey, I never gave much thought to the way things work in Korea, France, or Brazil. Words like *ni hao, shukran,* or *aufwiedersehen* weren't foreign words, they were simply foreign. But by the time my job started pulling me around the world, I couldn't afford to be a Jersey-born stranger in a strange land. I disciplined myself into a new routine before every trip to a new country: I would read a book or two on the history of its people to gain a better understanding of their culture and their perspective. We're all influenced by our history, and mixing a look at where we came from with where we are gives me a better understanding of the people with whom I'm about to do business.

The online world might seem commonplace by now; it's certainly taken over so many aspects of our lives. But corporate and organizational use of the Internet, particularly social media channels, remains stuck in an odd sort of infancy. For many companies and executives, their next foray into social media will be their first. Others have been exploring it for years, but even these practiced social companies are still surveying a newfound landscape. We're still struggling to get a handle on the culture of this nascent and constantly evolving society. Like reading a few books before heading to a new country, it's worth taking a few minutes to think of how we've progressed in terms of e-commerce and online habits. A little history lesson, when applied to our real-time learning, will allow a richer understanding—and in turn, a more successful approach to the Pre-Commerce customer.

The roots of e-commerce run deeper than the Internet, silicon microchips, and vacuum tubes. Go back 4,000 years ago, give or take a few decades, when the idea of currency was born. Our ancestors decided that your word might be well and good, but a bona fide receipt of your intentions was even better. If you were hanging out in Mesopotamia around 2000 B.C., chances are you weren't reading much of anything. You probably passed the time with your crops or livestock. You might have trusted your buddy when he delivered some grain, but the king's henchmen didn't. They wanted a form of receipt to match the grain put in the king's storehouses. They didn't have anything against you or your buddy—or maybe they did, it's your imagination. Either way, that was the emerging form of business exchange.

Turns out bosses haven't changed much over the millennia, and neither has that fundamental attribute of commerce. So let's jump forward, about 3,970 years and a couple technological advances later, as we finally start figuring out how to order online. It's 1982, and the French agency that would become France Telecom introduces an ingenious little idea it called Minitel. I was working for Rhone-Poulenc Rorer in Paris at the time, and the revolutionary idea struck me immediately. Now, I could book travel via this little electronic box with glowing green characters on the screen. I doubt anyone realized it then—I certainly didn't—but the emergence of Minitel ushered us into modern-day e-commerce.

By today's standards, Minitel was crude. The high-tech explosion throughout the 1990s introduced new security protocols, expanded bandwidth dramatically, and made it easier and cheaper to own computing technologies. Without any of these key trends, we would have stayed in experimental mode forever—ordering tickets off a green-screen Minitel box. But with massive leaps in online security, bandwidth, and personal computing, by 1994 we could buy pizza at PizzaHut.com. It wasn't a radical leap forward but, damn, it was cool. Of course, e-commerce wasn't exactly ubiquitous at the time, but it got a huge jumpstart over the next two years. In that time, Amazon.com started selling products online, a small auction Web site called eBay went live, and Manish Mehta helped launch what now has become one of the world's three largest e-commerce sites—Dell.com.

"The analogs to today are pretty striking," said Mehta, Dell's vice president of social media and community. "We are absolutely convinced, as we were in the early days of e-commerce, that if we embed the use of the social Web across the fabric of our business, then we constantly become a better business and deliver technology that works harder for our customers," he said. Many of today's corporate leaders are struggling to figure out how they can use social media to advance their business strategies. In that sense, they're much like yesterday's corporate leaders, who struggled to integrate e-commerce into their strategies.

But social media shouldn't serve as a means to advance a strategy, Mehta told me, it should help determine it. It's a fundamental way to run a customer-driven company, harkening back to the mom-and-pop shops of old. "Customers and the businesses valued those relationships because 'Mom and Pop' offered convenience," Mehta explained. "They listened to their customers and used their suggestions to improve the business. They provided great service and found ways to thank their clientele. Social media is really nothing more than the simple application of these business practices in a digital form."

It's that simple, but it's just as hard to let go of our old ways.

THE INFLUX OF NEW CUSTOMERS ONLINE

Through our research at Dell, we found that more than 500,000 people went online for the first time each day. That translates to six people each second and more than 180 million people each year—none of whom had seen your brand online before. Every year, a population larger than that of Pakistan, the sixth-largest country on the planet, could see your online branding for the very first time. And every year, your company could miss that many potential Pre-Commerce customers. But because this is happening incrementally, spread over more than 170 countries, few people even pay attention.

Facebook has more than 600 million customers, a population much larger than the United States. Yet we tend to see Facebook's users as a single community, not a massive collection of people in different nations, cities, towns, and neighborhoods—all of whom go online and, increasingly, go there to find information about your products. The Pre-Commerce customer is forming his or her first impression of your brand without you. Your current customers are deciding what is important about your brand via their own research and questions of their friends and colleagues. And your online marketing—or lack thereof—will form more first impressions than you realize, because it's all happening outside your Web site and your traditional advertising and marketing campaigns.

Ask yourself, "Where do my customers go today to learn about my brand?" Do they visit Slideshare.net, the leading community for data sharing? Do they prefer iTunes for podcasts on their favorite topic? Or do they ask questions of their peers on a specialized community forum?

DO YOU EVEN KNOW?

If not, you're not alone. Just remember one important fact—you have a chance to build a brand new relationship with nearly six new people

WCG

Influence Areas	Trend	Relevance
Audio	Favorite of sales force; customers on the go.	Podcasts of all types, plus audio tracks of video segments, are an undefined area of online, yet have growing utility.
Blogs	>200MM; trend is to have multiple blogs, multiple languages.	We should know the top influencers by topic who drive relevant share of voice. The numbers of influencers are small; precision is key.
Data/Slides	30MM uniques at SlideShare.	A great location to share all public presentations.
Forums	The engine of conversations online; often patient driven.	Knowing who is driving conversation in forums is key. We should treat high-volume moderators with the same respect as we do journalists.
Images	Is all content tagged to impact natural search?	Companies often forget to tag all content in the ten languages that reach 90% of the online population.
Micro Blogging	An effective way to alert influencers; help propel news cycles.	A great opportunity to build a network of influencers who want to share your news in real time. Twitter is a prime example.
Search	Yes, Google is #1, but YouTube is #2.	We need to know the influencers on the first screen for our brand and key topics. We also need to understand where people are taken when they search.
Social Networks	The communities that are often our "first place" to go online.	Our day often starts and ends with Facebook or MySpace or Orkut or other depending where we live.
Video	Consumption habits are starting to favor video vs. copy.	There are over fifty video sites to analyze, which sometimes house ratings and reviews of our products.
Wikis	Free online peer edited online encyclopedia.	Nearly every topic has a Wikipedia entry, which means it could be the first information a consumer finds on any topic they are seeking information about.

Top Ten Online Influence Areas

every second. Since 1995, the combination of improved security, increased bandwidth, and ubiquitous computing brought e-commerce to the mainstream. But the meteoric rise of social media tools is taking e-commerce to an entirely new world—the world of Pre-Commerce. Understanding the people, culture, and habits of this land requires a whole new mindset.

Your customers, whether they are business-to-business or business-to-consumer, utilize ten areas of online influence, each of which entails a rich network of sites.

BECOME A STUDENT OF PRE-COMMERCE

I like to think of Andy Sernovitz as a serial entrepreneur. Rather than developing new widgets or gizmos, Andy creates organizations that help companies learn. But when my phone rang and I heard him on the other end of the line, I had no clue that I'd become part of a novel new group he was piecing together. He had just left as leader of the Word of Mouth Marketing Association (WOMMA), and he said he was looking forward to getting a much-needed rest and doing a little consulting work. I think we both knew that wouldn't last very long, especially once I asked him for a little advice on something I'd been churning in my mind for a couple months.

Corporations needed a person and an organization that could help coalesce the thinking on blogging. A growing number of large enterprises had started blogs with mixed success, but we were going at it blind. Most companies had moved into it with an open mind and an adventurous spirit, but we clearly were novices at social media. I asked Andy if he could help. He liked the idea, so he discussed it with friends at Procter & Gamble, Cisco, and Wells Fargo. Within weeks, Andy had formed the Blog Council. Now called SocialMedia.org, the group in 2010 included members from more than 150 of the Fortune 1000 companies.

It brings influencers from those companies together to share their ideas and learn from one another.

Andy always had an innate sense that companies would have to build a discipline around social media. So as a brilliant quirk, he included a council provision that allows members to invite six colleagues and one corporate attorney to join as well. The provision was a remarkable shift in the way social media groups operated—especially bringing in a lawyer—but Andy realized that fully implementing ideas in the corporate world would require a remarkable shift in the way people operate, both inside and outside the company's halls.

Internally, executives have to help change the way their employees learn, so workers can start to expand beyond the limitation of habits they've formed throughout their careers. To change how your employees do business, you need to change how they learn. As business leaders, we make this mistake over and over and over again. We become enamored of a new concept, so we introduce it once, hold an internal webinar, and then return to work. Weeks later, we might stop to wonder why nothing happened—if we stop to notice anything at all. Employees might remember what you said, but their mindset hasn't moved an inch. Only when it continuously seeks to teach and learn in new ways does a company really change its long-term perspective. Take a minute here to think about your own company. How many times have you tried to teach a new concept (or reinforce a key idea) in the past year? How many times have you tried that idea once or twice, only to finally abandon it and throw up your hands in frustration? It happens more than any of us would like to admit, and I see it on far too regular a basis when I ask companies about their social media efforts.

Companies, from the board room to the call center, have to learn a new way of learning. They have to become students of Pre-Commerce. It starts with no small bit of honesty. First, we admit that we've been conditioned by mass media marketing, the traditional Four Ps of marketing, and all the other approaches and models that make it sound easy to move the needle. It feels right because it's what we've always known. Many times, it even works, but you'll see its success bottom out as Pre-Commerce continues its inevitable rise.

Having realized the groove we enjoyed for so long now has become a rut, we have to move on. Enough of that; we now become students, open to new ways of gaining insight into social media. We'll learn to understand how markets are maturing. We'll know what broadband penetration and mobile phone-to-laptop ratios mean for our business. We'll learn to track the ways our customers consume content, whether in text, audio, or video formats. And we'll learn how social media have changed the ways customers research, buy, and grow loyal to a brand.

Make no mistake: This education won't happen in a meeting room. As a Pre-Commerce company, your customers will walk your halls. Those of you who learn how to learn from your virtual visitors will discover new and powerful ways to sharpen and focus the selling, customer service, and marketing fundamentals you've always used.

Walking Your Halls

Over the past twenty-five years, I've been exposed to every type of customer expert, analyst, and consultant on the planet. You name 'em, I've seen 'em—the market scientists, C-Sat analysts, proponents of net promoter scores, and all the countless agencies and firms who walk corporate hallways these days. They bring their sheaves of primary and secondary research, match it with insight from multiple-regression analyses and Bayesian interpretation of probability, and offer you a nice PowerPoint of action items. These people can help you reach customers; in fact, they've built a lucrative business on doing exactly that. But to reach the Pre-Commerce customer, you have to unleash them, and that will require a new direction that breaks from today's corporate-consultant inertia.

If you're anything like me, here's what you end up doing most of the time. No doubt you're late for the next meeting, because your day is packed. You pull out the Blackberry on the way to the next meeting and mutter a yes or no to the person walking beside you, to whom you're only half-listening. You sit down in a conference room and listen as the expert du jour goes through a carefully crafted package of slides that chronicle how far you've progressed since his or her last report. Month to month, quarter to quarter, year to year—it all marches past us in lockstep with prior presentations. Any new ideas challenge your established thinking about as much as a dead fish would. But this is what companies do, even though customers couldn't care less.

It's usually around this point I realized I'm bored, annoyed, or both. A presenter intent on showing you insights he knows you'll accept immediately limits the scope of his analysis. And you sit there thinking, "This looks like last quarter's deck," as you covertly start checking e-mails under the table. You're busy. You don't want to be impolite. So you endure, learn next to nothing, and truck on over to your next meeting.

Here's what I want you to do next time this happens: Stop the meeting and turn off the projector. The shock value should be enough to jolt everyone out of their stupor. Now start a discussion about how the company can build a competitive advantage by knowing its customers better than anyone else, including that paid expert who's still trying to figure out what to do without his PowerPoint slides.

Now take it one more step. Demand that you and everyone in the room have access to all customer data in real time on your computers. If you want to know who has influence, how they're assessing your brand, and what they do or don't like, you *must* have the information you need to take action as close to real time as possible. You have to be able to take action as close to real-time as possible because you're about to start speaking to these influencers on a regular basis. Your customers are about to start walking your hallways, and they're going to be present, albeit virtually, in every decision you make. The conference room and all those monotonous meetings? Gone. You'll be talking to Jim Franklin from Boise, and Francois Brisson from Paris, and Shekhar Patel from New Delhi. They're going to tell you something you've never heard before, because what they tell you concerns them and the products they want to buy from you, not your company's bureaucracy and its horde of consultants.

The most persuasive person in the conference room will no longer win. The customer will win, every time. Each person in that conference room will become an expert, so you won't have to rely on a packaged presentation to assess your market. That yawn-inducing data is history, completely irrelevant to the experience your customers are having right now. "Businesses will line up for customers instead of customers lining up for businesses," said Marcel LeBrun, chief executive of Radian6, a global leader in research, monitoring, and analysis of social media. "The social web is reversing the line-up. You might have well-designed queues and forms to fill out on your website or phone system, but customers are gathering and discussing your brand, competitors or industry wherever they feel like it. Smart brands are meeting their customers at their point of need."

Traditional communications channels reach customers in an established time or place, leaving almost all conversation and interaction feeling transactional. The social web expands what LeBrun likes to call the "field of listening," allowing companies to learn more about their industry, their competitors, and themselves. Your Pre-Commerce team will define a new, interactive relationship between your customers and your brand. If you want the deepest possible insights that will move your business forward, your Pre-Commerce team will gather it from your customers. They will bring a new power to listen to and converse with a broader set of customers, delivering insights at an ever more granular level. You no longer hear the phrase, "This isn't possible." You only hear: "I know what our customers really want."

Let's not beat around the bush anymore: If you don't do this—and many leaders won't—your inaction will speak with an unbelievable power. You will tell your organization that going through the motions is more important than knowing what customers say and what customers do. "Hey, that's just how we roll at this company," you'll say, as you get back to work making the same old products that the same old customers want to buy. So much for growth; you've just implied that customers are more a distraction than a driver. And every employee will read you loud and clear.

That's old school, and that ain't you anymore.

Word of Mouth Has Changed

You'll learn new things now that you bump into a customer every time you walk around the office. With your customers walking the halls, one of the first things that should hit you is how dramatically the brand–customer relationship has changed. The shift has caught most companies, probably including yours, completely off-guard.

I've worked and walked the halls of some of the largest companies in the world. I can't count how many times I'd hear things like, "We need to do a better job of profiling and targeting" or "Let's focus on increasing our call center efficiency." Some of my personal favorites were "How we are doing on upsell opportunities?" and "Let's get our lead generation into swing." Nothing topped "We need to get these people in our database and reach one million total." People said these things with such gravitas, as if they'd just unlocked the solution to all their companies' woes.

Run a quick grammatical exercise on each of these statements. Every one of them implies an action the company will perform *on* or *to* its customers to sell more products or services. These actions put the company in a position, at some point, to dictate its message to the customer. I'll let you in on the most obvious secret in corporate history: Customers don't care. Really, when was the last time you bragged to your friends that Company X dropped you into their database today? So why did the corporate world become so control-oriented while the world was getting more and more decentralized?

It wasn't that long ago companies controlled the ability to learn about products, and from a corporate perspective it was a lot easier that way. Thousands of years ago, we learned how to tell our story visually or textually. Our ancestors moved from painting on rock walls to textual conversation. Anthropologists have identified actual commercial messages in the ruins of Pompeii. Our methods of communication evolved, especially as more people learned how to read and write. Paintings on cave walls lost their effectiveness, drowned out by town criers. Socrates bemoaned the advent of the written word, saying it would lead to a loss of oral history and communication. Fortunately, he drank his hemlock long before the printing press arrived. No telling what he would have thought once someone had the bright idea of creating a daily printed news update and ushered in the newspaper era.

With all this newsprint space available to reach potential customers, it didn't take long for the first paid advertising, and the first advertising agencies, to launch into business. Newspapers realized they could lower their prices and still generate a larger stream of revenue, while business owners could avail themselves of a single, easy-to-use channel through which they could touch thousands of customers. France's *La Presse* took the first paid advertisement in 1836.

Fast forward to the twentieth century and we took marketing and advertising one giant step further. The age of mass media dawned in the 1920s with the advent of commercial radio, and it took a giant step forward when NBC and CBS launched wide-ranging radio networks in 1926 and 1927. A couple of decades later, both media companies had pushed into broadcast television, bringing video and a whole new sophistication to the way companies could spread their messages. And by 1963, companies had started using ZIP codes in the United States to send direct mail to targeted groups of customers. Each media revolution opened up broad new audiences, and with each step companies developed increasingly effective ways to draw customers through advertising.

But at the core of each medium, the essence of advertising and marketing never really changed: The company always controlled the message, and in a manner, it hoped, that connected with its target audience. From rock walls to billboards, from commercial messages in Pompeii to commercial messages on your flat-screen TV, the company delivered the message and the consumer, well, consumed it. When done properly, it was quite effective, but it never really changed the way customers interacted with a brand. When companies controlled the experience through a small number of channels, thus limiting the customer's options, it wasn't important to know everything the customer cared about. They'd be back. What else could they do?

The Internet and the explosion of social media use have fundamentally changed the notion of corporate control over its brand messaging. Customers still own the power of word of mouth—and let's face it, strong word of mouth always meant more to individual customers than any advertisement did. Only now, those same customers have a forum on which they can reach as many potential customers as any company can. You can ignore it and let the conversation happen on its own—and believe me, it will. Or, as Scott Anderson has done at Hewlett-Packard, you can find new ways to engage your customers. Anderson, vice president of customer communications for HP's enterprise business, spent a lot of time with his colleagues considering how and why the company would launch a blog platform, its initial foray into social media. That introspection proved invaluable, he said, because they realized they needed to take a very pure approach. "Business conversations, if effective, tend toward relationships that lead to ongoing business. It's been that way since the dawn of time," he said. "The social media tool-set that continues to evolve so rapidly offers a great platform to amplify and extend business conversations between HP employees and the audience we'd like to do business with."

Online word of mouth reaches customers in ways we don't fully understand yet. What's clear, though, is that the Pre-Commerce world lives and breathes communication and interaction. You can either participate in these communities and learn how they work, or you can be ignored by them.

THE NEW PEER INFLUENCE

Social media has turned peer influence on its head. That one, never-satisfied customer now can influence hundreds, thousands, or millions of potential customers. Jeff Jarvis is a sharp thinker and a fantastic writer, but there's nothing unique about him that would suggest he alone should influence millions of people. Yet that's what he did when he had trouble with his Dell computer. Jeff started writing about his personal "Dell Hell" on his blog, BuzzMachine.com. Soon enough, dozens of other customers had commented or blogged about their own, similar problems. The criticism spread like a wildfire across the Internet, and nothing we did at Dell would quench it—until, finally, we went online and joined the conversation. We took our lumps, but only once we'd started our corporate blog and started reaching out to the people blogging and posting video about their problems did we start to change the online sentiment in our favor.

We finally started to realize how radically social media had empowered and changed the notion of peer influence in the dawning age of Pre-Commerce. And to get there, we had to stop and really think about influencers such as Jeff Jarvis. Who, what, where, why, and how are influencers playing in the Pre-Commerce world?

Who is influencing your customers? This involves the overt group of people who influence a customer, but also the covert influencers of the Internet. Let's start with the latter. If you go to Techmeme.com and look at the Techmeme Leaderboard, you'll find a list of the top 100 most influential technology news-sharing outlets. The amazing part is that approximately three of every four top technology outlets in the world today are blogs. Traditional media outlets make up only a quarter of the top influencers.

And this gets to the first important conclusion about peer influence. Customers don't care where the news comes from. They merely want interesting, informative content, and they want to share it with all their friends. It can come from a traditional news outlet such as the *New York Times,* Bloomberg, or Reuters. It can come from an online-only entity such as Engadget, Gizmodo, or the Huffington Post. Either way, the top original-content producers (the outlets high on a Techmeme Leaderboard search about your company or industry) will have the greatest influence on your customers. Do you know the top influencers who are shaping the conversation around your brand?

What is influencing your customers? Most people like a little help making a decision. They want to make sure they're not getting ripped off, so you'll often hear how "ratings and reviews" have considerable influence on customers these days. They certainly do, but this sort of influence tends to come at the later stages of a purchasing decision. The most important influence typically comes at the moment of first impression, when a potential customer has his or her first real interaction with your brand. It often comes through something as basic as an Internet search experience. What pops up on the first screen of Google, Bing, or Yahoo search results when you type in the name of your company? Do you know what Baidu looks like, and how its search results make your company look to millions of Chinese consumers? For each link on the first page of search results, someone out there has exerted some sort of influence on your brand. Customers often have an open mind before they even consider going to your Web site, and what they see on that initial search will have an outsized impact on the beliefs they form about your brand.

Where is this influence occurring? The easy answer is to just say "online, with peers," but it gets much more complex and intriguing. Consider a few of the key dynamics that occur when customers start forming their opinion of a brand. In a June 2010 survey by Harris Interactive, 71 percent of respondents said reviews from friends and family members exerted a "great deal" or a "fair amount" of influence on their decision to use or avoid a particular company, brand, or product.[1] Not only do 90 percent of consumers online trust recommendations from people they know, according to a July 2009 report by the Nielsen Global Online Consumer Survey, but a remarkable 70 percent of the respondents said they trust opinions from users they don't know.[2] In my observations over the past five years, I've found that at least three-quarters of e-commerce customers turn to peer reviews, blogs, forums, and other social media channels before completing an online transaction.

"With the incredible popularity of micro-blogging via Twitter and Facebook in the past several years, many analysts speculated that blogging had peaked, but that's just not the case," said Richard Jalichandra, CEO of Technorati, the top blog search engine. "We see much more blogging activity than ever before, and checks with the top blogging platforms validate that. . . . Blogging has gone completely mainstream. Show me the Web presence of any 'mainstream media' property, and they probably not only have a blogging component but also feature blogging. From a pure activity-measurement standpoint, blogging is more robust than ever and doesn't appear to be slowing."

Second, social media have changed the definition of peer group for today's customers. I started to realize the extent of this evolution while watching how customers behaved online across dozens of countries and multiple years. I discovered that customers unconsciously behave like a "liquid network." Similar to a river, where the water constantly moves downstream, customers continually move toward the content that provides them the best answers. They are loyal to great content, period, and they will flow wherever they can find it. Companies used to building dams—"capturing leads" and sending their messages to the captive audience—will find this river flowing right over them.

Why is it so powerful? The answer is pretty simple: People don't trust companies and organizations. Companies have done themselves no favors by holding on to mass media models and bombarding their customers with catalogs, e-mails, and direct mail, none of which does anything more than ask us to buy something. Every one of those messages that show up in a mailbox, inbox, or voicemail erodes trust just a little bit more. In the Pre-Commerce world, customers won't take it anymore. They can research on their own, add that to the recommendations of other, similar customers, and make their own decision, thank you. But social media also give companies a channel through which they can interact with customers in a very transparent and timely manner—interactions that improve not only customer service, but also the level of trust between company and customer, said Mickey Mantas, the former manager of digital and social media for Sears Holding Corp. Better customer service and a tighter bond of trust already work in a company's best interest, Mantas said, but the potential for building closer relationships can generate even greater, previously unthinkable opportunities to innovate and test new ideas.

"Customers' needs change over time, and a willingness to hear and respond accordingly is a new expectation," she said. "As a social media-savvy consumer, I use Twitter, Facebook, and YouTube to better understand what's behind a company's marketing message. Think of it with a 'constructivist's view'—we construct only as much as we want to learn by snacking on accessible content. Offering multiple variations and placement of a consistent message is becoming essential."

How do you become part of your customer's peer group? Companies that act like a peer, not a parent, will do well. Like any peer relationship, a company must convince its customers to remain loyal to its products and services, and that only happens through the right actions and behaviors. Personality plays a role. Customer service plays a role. Every interaction with a company must align with a quality relationship between peers, not random parts of it. You can't get customer service right and then send countless e-mails to the same customer and declare victory. When you're not consistently looking out for the customers' interests, they sense it immediately—and they'll penalize you for it just as quickly.

REACHING THE PRE-COMMERCE CUSTOMER

Few executives truly understand how much their companies have abused the customer's trust. All the consultants, research, and slick PowerPoint presentations in the world might suggest that trust in your brand has eroded, but none of it will give you a full understanding of how deep the rift has grown. Read one angry customer's blog, and you'll understand you can't just repair this with a coupon for 50 percent off. Let's be clear, though: Putting your virtual arm around a customer's virtual shoulder and having an honest conversation doesn't mean you'll restore his or her trust and loyalty. However, if you don't do any of that—if you continue to act the patron instead of the peer—I guarantee you'll alienate the customer further.

The only way to start rebuilding trust and brand loyalty with the Pre-Commerce customer is to become an effective peer. An effective peer is one who provides the right information at the right place and at the right time. An effective peer doesn't look for ways to avoid blame or responsibility. He or she corrects problems swiftly and to the satisfaction of the person wronged. And an effective peer constantly works to improve the relationship. That last step, the constant work on the relationship, is the most rigorous and the one we'll focus on here. It requires that companies develop a deeper understanding of their customers and how they interact and make decisions in the Pre-Commerce world. Like anything else, it starts with a first impression and evolves over time.

Ray Kerins figured this out early in the evolution of the Pre-Commerce world. Like his father, a New York City homicide detective, Ray can piece together evidence of a trend and see the answers long before most people even begin to take notice. It serves him well at Pfizer, where he's vice president of communications and leads the pharmaceutical company's social media outreach. To build an effective and fruitful relationship with customers, a company has to respond with speed and sympathy, he told me. "We have a twenty-four-hour rule," he said. "Basically, you have twenty-four hours to get a crisis under control before you lose control of it. But getting control of a crisis takes more than a quick reaction. You have to display true humility and heartfelt engagement, including from senior leaders. The words 'I'm sorry' really resonate if they're true."

As companies increase their interactions through social media channels, they attract more and more scrutiny from regulators, legislators, and consumers. And that makes many executives gun-shy. But, Ray said, if a company shows it understands the importance and significance of an issue—and takes a similarly earnest approach to solving the problem—the scrutiny becomes an opportunity for the firm to display its regard for its customers.

An Open Letter to the Corporate Bigwig

Dear Corporate Bigwig:

We don't really know you. You don't come online where we hang out, and we don't much care about the old fashioned garbage you keep trying to force down our throats. But your products have an impact on our lives, so we thought we might give you a little advice. You didn't ask for it, but since you have no idea how to reach us we thought we'd just send you our Top Ten:

1. *You're welcome to join us.* No offense, but we don't need companies anymore, at least like we used to. We're part of a "liquid network" and we're loyal to great content, which we can easily get online. We go to a lot of places that don't show up on your media buying plan.

2. *Save the e-mails and trees.* We don't really respond to catalogs anymore, and we're tired of promotional e-mails that preach at us like Big Brother. We love when companies speak directly with us. We can get to know each other, and that makes us more likely to buy from you.

3. *There are 365 days in a year.* We might buy something from you once or twice a year, but we like your brand. We might think about your product on a regular basis, but not always with the intention to make a purchase. Surely you can find a way to make your brand relevant to us even when we're not ready to purchase. And don't worry, we can give you a few ideas if you're stuck.

4. *Video rocks.* We like to learn much more via video than text. It's one of the reasons YouTube is now the second-largest search engine in the world. You might want to consider this a more important channel for your brand. We're there waiting.

5. *Personalize search.* Why do we always have to go to a destination site to begin a search? It's so annoying. Can you please help

integrate Google or Bing into our favorite community—or into your online community?

6. *Ratings and reviews.* A lot of you have started doing this already. Thank you. But there's one problem: Now we have too many of them, and we're starting to tune out. So let's make it easier to find out what our peers think—and by peers I mean customers like me, not my grandfather. We seek out peer advice before purchasing 75 percent of the time. The better the advice, the better the conversion.

7. *Technical support.* Forget the "company leaders don't do technical support" crap and just do what you can to improve our experience with your brand. More than 90 percent of us will never call you this year, but we'll still have problems. We'll figure it out on our own or with help from our own technical support team— our peers. You're welcome to come out and help and save both of us the hassle of that frustrating phone call.

8. *Languages.* We live all over the world, so why do you speak only English? We make important decisions in our native language, just like you, so at least learn to speak the ten languages that reach 90 percent of the world's population.

9. *Our phones.* We love our phones, and they're becoming a primary device alongside our laptops. Any reason most of you don't offer SMS alerts or make mobile apps that fit the way we live and interact? With a few billion phones and ubiquitous data connections covering much of the world, you might want to move this up the priority list.

10. *Your role.* We don't even know each other, yet you still want to create our experiences with your brand? We don't expect a personal handshake every time we buy something, but at least remember we're outside your building whenever you're done flipping through your PowerPoint slides. Come on out sometime. We won't bite.

Yours truly,
The Pre-Commerce customer

THE START OF THE JOURNEY

Earlier this chapter, we ended our brief journey through advertising history with the advent of television and direct mail. Let's pick it up again in 1998. Our friends at Google have emerged with a new way to learn and tell your story. At the time, it didn't change much of anything in the corporate world, but you'd be hard pressed to find a company that's not impacted in some way today by the world's Titan of Search. But since business philosophies can change at a glacial pace, many companies still cling to the notion that advertising remains the most effective way to tell their story to help customers learn about their brands. One more billboard . . . one more Super Bowl ad . . . one more catchphrase . . . and customers will flock to our doors.

In reality, the importance of advertising has shifted. It hasn't disappeared, but it works in a much different way. No longer does it provide an effective platform to tell your brand's entire story. Customers put much more trust in their peers than your clever (or not) TV commercial. More people form their first impressions of a brand through an Internet search. They solidify first impressions with ratings and reviews. They confirm their suspicions, good or bad, with YouTube videos that show your products and services in action. They search for information about your product—more than 10 billion searchers per month on Google sites alone. Across the Internet and through its myriad social media channels, your customers are telling your brand's story for you—only now, it's their story too.

So rather than telling the story, advertising has become the catalyst that begins the story. It's the introduction that sets the whole tale in motion, the "Once upon a time, there was a company that had a cool new product." Done properly, it will prompt customers to learn, interact, share, and ultimately decide what they'll do in the future. Anyone who spends a lot of money on advertising, e-mail marketing, or other forms of traditional promotion can see this change already. Some future leaders in marketing will have started using advertising strategically, to start conversations or to shift them. It will happen more and more in the future. The successful Pre-Commerce marketing team won't expect an ad to answer all the questions, to drive sales growth, or to get a customer to act on the company's schedule. They'll make the advertisement a more integrated piece of the broader marketing campaign, a campaign that will include the company's interaction with any customer inquiries, searches, and conversations its ads generate. Ads will become more focused and, thankfully, we'll see less "drip advertising."

The key lies in what the people who buy your brands do when your advertisement triggers their awareness. Their actions might come immediately. (I saw this cool commercial, and I had to go online and find out more.) Or they might not react for weeks and months, long after you wanted them to move. (I didn't click on this banner ad atop my favorite Web site, but now I'm in the market for that product.) Either way, a successful advertising campaign will spur some action, and we're already starting to see how all of this plays out in the Pre-Commerce world.

- Display ads have an impact. A 2009 study conducted by the Online Publishers Association and the research firm comScore found that one in five people who merely viewed an online display ad visited the advertiser's Web site, and they spent 50 percent more time on the site than the average visitor. These visits occurred up to thirty days after the visitors had viewed the ad, the study found.[3]
- According to a 2009 survey from Performics and ROI Research, 48 percent of Twitter users who saw an ad via Twitter said they conducted an online search for additional information about the brand.[4]

Advertising sparks the search to learn more, and I mean "search" literally. But in the Pre-Commerce world, advertising that integrates social media can add rocket fuel to that spark. Consider a recent survey conducted by GroupM Search, a unit of the global marketing giant WPP. The study showed that customers exposed to both social media and paid-search programs were almost three times more likely to search for that brand's products compared with people who saw only the paid-search campaign.[5]

Your customers might start their journey toward a purchase when they see your paid search program. They might start it when they run across a blog post you had nothing to do with. They're much more likely to start their journey when they see both. Regardless, they're going to start that journey, and they're going to take it whether you come along or not.

OUT WITH THE OLD, IN WITH THE NEW

It's time to clean the garage. Most of us, if we clean the garage at all, do it grudgingly. At some point, though, all those old items we needed years ago—or, like that wagon wheel coffee table, never needed at all—simply have to go. So we block out a Saturday afternoon and go to work. A quick trip to the Goodwill donation center, and we feel a little better about ourselves. (Of course, our sense of accomplishment is only aided by the fact that we can park the car in the garage again.)

Keep this allegory in mind when you think about how your company tracks the ways customers make decisions about your brand. Most companies have a bunch of old metrics cluttering their garage. They count Web site visitors, how long customers stay on the site, or how many click-throughs they take. But none of these have any use for you anymore. In fact, you could build a terrible Web site that would increase time on site and click-throughs because it's so unclear. Those measurements would only mislead you. Instead, get out in your garage, clean it up, and start to focus on new metrics.

Your new metrics need to measure the online reactions your potential customers have to your brand and your marketing. New tools can help you measure your marketing campaign's ability to spark online reactions—searches, recommendations, and discussions—and can track those outcomes in real time so you can adjust on the fly. The new metrics will help you measure the lingering effectiveness of your campaigns, tracking whether these online discussions stop immediately when the program concludes or continue under their own power. The new tools you will put in your garage will allow you to create the right learning environment for your customers, blending your Web site and search with other social media sites and even with offline experiences. They will help you craft a campaign that helps you better understand how customers interact, and you can use that intelligence to build a lasting communications model that works for both company and customer.

I shake my head every time someone tells me how many unique visitors their Web site gets. They're missing the point. Worse yet, they're missing the Pre-Commerce customer, the person who developed an opinion about their brand long before becoming another "unique" visitor. The tools you need in your marketing garage let you follow the conversation wherever it's happening. They give you the information you need to confidently invest more in a program, or to pull the plug on it. You know success or failure in days, and with the feedback you receive you can craft more flexible programs. Imagine if your media buying plan was based on results, not long-term buying commitments, and you'd have those results so quickly you could switch your program on and off within days or even hours.

Mass media thrived on a marketplace with limited options. In fact, mass media *needed* a marketplace with limited options—just look at the mainstream media's struggles today. When customers have options they vote with their feet or with a click of the mouse. They let us know loudly and clearly via their actions. Your company can do the same with its marketing programs. Clean out the garage and get the tools that can help you take advantage of the options you have.

GET OUT OF THE STORE

Your customers don't ask peers for advice because they haven't anything better to do. They don't research a purchase for weeks or months because they're bored. Customers of every stripe want to know they're getting value for their money. More than anything else, they want to make sure they're not getting ripped off. Back when brick-and-mortar was the only shopping option, customers could put their five senses to work. They could touch, feel, see, and try for themselves—take it for a test run and make sure it lives up to expectations. But with more and more commerce moving online, your customers give up that visceral chance to satisfy their concerns. They do so willingly, for the sake of convenience, but they still feel compelled to compensate for the lack of first-hand experience. So they do the next best thing. They research and explore online. They search out similar people and ask for their advice. They visit trusted communities to learn more. They go to Yahoo! Answers, or Mahalo and see what other people have said. Because social media tools make it so easy to do so, customers keep gathering troves of information until they feel certain the product won't let them down. Only then do they pull the trigger.

In the Pre-Commerce world, customers substitute the sensory-rich offline experience with a deep, thorough online exploration and interaction. And this shift is leaving most marketing professionals in the dark. Despite their protestations to the contrary, very few marketing professionals can say when, where, how, or why their customers decided to pull the trigger on that purchase. For most companies, e-commerce hasn't changed anything. They play the same old retailer, stationed behind their virtual counter and patiently waiting for customers to click their way into the store. Gumballs: 5 cents each.

The leaders of the Pre-Commerce era will find ways to purposefully interact with customers before they make their decisions. They will integrate community into their e-commerce sites, and actively work to engage with communities outside their company's infrastructure. They will allow a customer's experience outside the company's online presence to continue within their virtual boundaries. They will become a valid and trusted partner in the Pre-Commerce journey.

It's easy enough to write these platitudes, but let's not kid ourselves. Companies have a long, long way to go to rebuild trust with customers. The divide has become so wide, the same few companies that bridge the divide keep popping up as examples of how to do it right: Zappos.com and Trader Joe's, for example. For the rest of us, rebuilding trust will require a radical transformation in the way we think about our customers. In today's world, control of the brand image and message no longer lies in the hands of the company; it's shared between company and customer. Executives have to act accordingly if they expect customers to invite them on a Pre-Commerce journey. But this is precisely what I love about the evolution of the Web, and why you should see Pre-Commerce as an incredible opportunity. Business leaders who learn how to adapt their approach and put their knowledge to work in new ways will engage with their customers like never before.

Every time we think we've figured out how to do e-commerce and social media, we realize we've just taken one of our first steps. One mistake won't doom anyone, just as one success won't guarantee another. It's a constant change, a continuous education, and an ongoing business evolution. If the pace of change seems overwhelming at times, remember the fundamentals. The basics you learned in business school and on the job haven't disappeared; they've just changed a little.

MY PRE-COMMERCE JOURNEY CHANGED MY LIFE

Jim Weiss, CEO and founder of WCG

If I was a lineman for the San Francisco 49ers, I would've been just another big guy, but I was a forty-two-year-old father of two who was trying to keep up with his kids on the ski slopes of Tahoe. It wasn't working for me. My doctor had told me to lose weight or put myself at greater risk of death—something I knew all too well after twenty years of trying every diet known to man. I was "pre-diabetic," weighed 320 pounds, wore size-48 pants and size-56 jacket. I could fill a room, and I knew I had to make a change.

My primary care doctor kept directing me to Weight Watchers and other less invasive programs that didn't work for me in the past, and he kept up a steady drumbeat about the risks and dangers of surgery. The record was stuck, and it kept playing the same song. If I didn't figure out my own solution, no one would do it for me. I was determined to educate myself and find the right solution, and it was here that I started my own Pre-Commerce journey.

My search soon led me to Lapband.com, and through it I discovered a site run by two local bariatric surgeons, Dr. Paul Cirangle and Dr. Gregg Jossart (lapsf.com). The same site came up repeatedly as I searched for my personal solution, and it became a constant gateway to more and more of the information I needed. As time passed, I started to realize that a great Pre-Commerce experience involves listening to peers, experts you trust, and your own intuition. It's not one-way. It's how you integrate what you learn so you can make the right decisions over time—and now I was trying to decide whether I wanted to try surgery to help control my weight.

So I kept going online to educate myself about my options. I researched the track records of the surgeons I would consider. The more I learned, the more confidence I had to go directly to surgeons I found online and learn from them. I signed up for regular e-mails from LapBand, which kept this option atop my mind. I read positive stories and testimonials of peers who had taken the surgical route, including how they dealt with side effects, complications, and other difficulties. And I worked with other doctors to ensure I could sustain the weight loss by addressing psychological factors to eating.

Armed and ready, I took the plunge on March 4, 2008. I ultimately chose laproscopic vertical gastrectomy (VG), a bit more of an invasive and permanent approach. Although VG was a new and more experimental procedure at that time, I never looked back or regretted my decision. I was in and out of the hospital in about a day and back at work within about three days of surgery. They filmed my surgery in high definition with my permission and posted it on their YouTube channel to educate other surgeons about the VG procedure.

I lost 47 pounds in the first month and 110 pounds over a 14–18 month period. My pants size dropped from 48 to 36 inches, and my suit went to size 44 from size 56. I was back to my normal and natural state, and I felt great in my role leading an independent communications company with many health care clients. I was walking the talk, not just talking the talk.

Now, three years later, I eat a somewhat restricted diet and have to take vitamin supplements for the rest of my life. But these are small tradeoffs given the far better and sustained results. I can keep up with my kids on the slopes and I'm off all medications other than vitamins and Lipitor, which I take to control my cholesterol.

This year, my twin sister joined me and had the same surgery. She already has lost 90 pounds and transformed her physical and emotional well-being—just as I had done. It's amazing what we can do when we take control of our lives. It's equally amazing how easy it is to learn online and educate ourselves to make the right decisions. I've become an ambassador in the truest sense of the word, recommending my surgeons and their Web site to dozens of potential patients.

The Pre-Commerce journey isn't just about selling more products. It can be life-changing in a very real way.

Case Study

REMEMBER THE BASICS

Almost twenty-five years later, I can still picture Joe Papa striding into the conference room at CIBA-GEIGY. A lot has changed since then. CIBA-GEIGY only exists as a part of Novartis now. I've gone through a handful of employers in a couple of countries since then. But none of the changes dulled my memory of the high energy and high focus that instantly infused that room in Summit, New Jersey, when Joe walked in.

We'd gathered to discuss the upcoming launch of Estraderm, a product that in 1986 would become the first skin patch treatment for menopausal symptoms in the United States. When Joe walked in, we knew we were going to win with this product. In Joe's world, anything less was inconceivable. Sporting a bushy mustache, this hockey-playing MBA from Kellogg exhibited an intensity and passion for business I'd never seen. Joe was all about the Four Ps. He wanted to know the exact sensitivity on pricing. He obsessed over every detail of the product, from how it was packaged to how it was presented. He seemed to know every detail about the competitors as well as he knew our plan. Joe was playing chess when most people were still playing checkers. He had no cracks in his armor.

For me, it was an awakening. All of those blurry days of college courses now started to become clear to me. Joe had this aura about him that demanded we focus as keenly as he did, and it worked—at least with me. I became equally obsessed with understanding every aspect of how marketing and sales worked. I was hooked. The classes I had taken and were continuing to take as an MBA student at night were now making sense. The Four Ps now meant something. We needed to master every detail of this model, and so we did.

Estraderm was a huge success for us. And it's no surprise that Joe today serves as CEO of Perrigo, the world's largest manufacturer of over-the-counter pharmaceutical and nutritional products for the store-brand market. You could see his future success decades away. But without an intensity and focus like Joe's, the Four Ps can easily become a routine part of our market plans. They've become such an integral part of what we do, we hardly stop to think about them anymore. Given the fundamental way in which Pre-Commerce is transforming the business world, we might do well to pause and focus on them in this new context.

Product—We always want the product to match customer demands. So we gather insight, add customer support, guarantees, special deals, and more. But do you know exactly what your customers want, and how do you find out in the Pre-Commerce era?

Pricing—We've built decades of science around pricing. But value, the key concern for Pre-Commerce customers, means much more than price. What value does your company provide online customers who can't take your product for a test run? And what new abilities does the Internet and social media give you to add value for customers and gain their trust?

Place—To some extent, the Internet has turned the concept of place on its head. We still have a sense of place offline, but "place" can be anywhere online. Executives in the Pre-Commerce world will define place as anywhere their potential customers might go to glean information or advice about a purchase. Does your company limit the places customers can access your brand? Perhaps it makes sense to do so—you might not want your information showing up on a pejorative forum—but do you have a clear rationale for your limits?

Promotion—Companies keep throwing more and more money at the transaction and the call to action, yet the most powerful form of promotion occurs when real people express their real desire for your brand. Personal selling might make us think of sales reps, but it also involves customers who are passionate about your brand and want to tell others about it. In the Pre-Commerce world, customers can do as much quality promotion—and probably even more—than the company itself. How do you help them spread the good word for you?

The rules are the same, but with a new twist. As always, you need to identify the decision maker for every sale, but now you also need to learn how and where that person formulates his or her decision. (Hint: They're getting more information from sources you don't control, or perhaps even know about.) While you need to explain the value of your product, as always, you also need to know how your value message stacks up against the online community's version of your value message. (Hint: Customers share ownership of your message now.) You need to know when they will make the purchase, but to get repeat sales you also need to follow their reaction to your product. (Hint: A lot of customers will share their experiences with anyone who will listen.)

The twists will work their way throughout your organization. You might have to open the kimono a bit wider to satiate your customers' desire to be involved. You might have to track your competitors in altogether novel ways, perhaps to get an advantage that closes a sale. In fact, the online community might tip you off to a competitor you never even knew you had (or one you previously downplayed as a novelty). But if you allow your organization the flexibility to twist with the Pre-Commerce world, you'll find it becoming much more open and interactive. Be direct. Contribute more than the product to the relationship. Answer all the customers' questions as completely as possible. Always say thank you. Don't say negative things about competitors. Be available for question-and-answer conversations.

To be sure, the Four Ps still play an integral role in marketing in this new environment. But they also have to flex and twist. Executives need to understand how the application of these principles applies to the Pre-Commerce marketplace. But hey, not to worry, you've done this for most of your career. As new markets opened up and the competitive landscape changed, you adjusted the Four Ps to fit each new situation. It seems so different this time because your customers' purchasing habits are undergoing a dramatic, fundamental shift. So let's start at the heart of the matter—the drivers of online behavior.

At a foundational level, Pre-Commerce customers want to support a brand in one of three ways: (1) they want to provide ideas to improve a product or service, (2) they want to share product knowledge because they have experience with the product, or (3) they want to help solve problems. In each case, customers want to help their peers first and foremost. If that happens to support a company and brand they like, all the better. But make no mistake: The Pre-Commerce world is peer-driven.

You can see some powerful examples of this from the two idea communities formed by Dell and Starbucks (www.ideastorm.com and www.mystarbucksidea.com). Each site provides customers a forum where they can voice their opinions—whether praise or grievance—and they allow peers a chance to weigh in on each topic. Some topics generate more interest than others, and as such provide a de facto guide for customer sentiment. Other topics don't gather the same interest but offer clues to customer demands or, in some cases, customer behaviors. But in every case, the forums allow customers an opportunity to feed what drives them, whether that's a need to improve a product, share their knowledge, or solve a problem. In fact, one of the inherent beauties of these sites is that they accommodate all three key drivers of Pre-Commerce participation.

Without the proper forum to participate on their terms, customers might never visit your Web site or consider any of your brand messaging. They might form an opinion—and a rather informed opinion—without you ever knowing it. Don't fall into the trap of downplaying other information, the stuff you deem "unofficial." The information usually carries as much or more weight than any "official" information you share. And because of your hubris, customers will leave and never come back—long before you even had a chance to say hello. I hate to say it, but within the past week you almost certainly lost dozens of customers you never met.

It's high time you abandon the typical beliefs about the health of your customer relationships. Don't fall back on the typical business-to-business excuse: "Our customers are B2B, so they don't really go online." Give up the "We know our customers, since we have a database of five million people with whom we regularly interact." Don't fall into the trap of "We know exactly how many people visit our site and what they do when they're there." You can cling to those excuses and do a decent business today. But your competitor, who just decided to let go of those old beliefs and reach out to the Pre-Commerce customer, will be eating your lunch tomorrow.

UNANTICIPATED LEARNING

Paul von Autenried spent time as a systems engineer for Hewlett-Packard. He eventually moved on to Kraft Foods for awhile before taking his current role as vice president and chief information officer for Bristol-Myers Squibb. Needless to say, Paul speaks like someone who has straddled a few of the world's most influential industries.

We sat together one quiet morning in the BMS cafeteria in Princeton, N.J., talking about the importance of becoming a learning organization, when Paul brought up the idea of "unanticipated learning." I'd never thought of learning in those terms before. But in his position, Paul's thinking ranges from advanced analytics that compare drug effectiveness to new ways he can improve collaboration by opening the walls between BMS and its partners. He started to describe a world where "emerging market innovation may directly influence developed markets," rather than the opposite.

Look at General Electric's MAC 800 heart monitor, he suggested. GE had developed a heart monitor in India and China and launched it in emerging markets. Soon enough, the innovation that occurred in the far reaches of the globe started influencing demand in developed markets. People in richer countries saw a really interesting product in an emerging market, and they wanted it too. If we stay focused on what the customer wants, Paul said, the days of mature markets always leading are increasingly irrelevant.

In an announcement saying it would import the innovative MAC 800 heart monitor to the United States, GE Healthcare called it a "new phase in its globalization strategy." One of America's bellwether companies listened to its engineers in Bangalore, put them in partnership with other colleagues in Beijing, and together the teams developed a portable diagnostic tool that physicians could easily carry into the Indian or Chinese countryside. This is what happens when you listen and innovate close to your customer. You get a product that weighs seven pounds, yet can match GE's standard sixty-five-pound electrocardiogram machines. Better yet, it costs 80 percent less than GE's current comparable equipment. And now it's being introduced in the United States and Europe as a disruptive, innovative product.

"When data becomes available, you'll have to know the data's potential full impact in real time," Paul said that morning. "R&D data will be adjacent to sales and marketing data." Having all the available insights at your fingertips—and imagining all the different ways you can apply that data—will lead you to better decisions. You can't do this unless you, like GE, choose to embrace "unanticipated learning," and then do something about it.

THE FOUR As

The Procter & Gamble Digital Advisory Board filed into the break area one overcast morning in the spring of 2009 to have a discussion with Alessandro Tosolini, P&G's head of e-commerce, a passionate guy to say the least. He asked the board about the future of e-commerce.

Now fully energized by Alessandro's passion, I raised my hand and threw out the idea that just bored itself into my brain: "Alessandro, it's not about the transaction or e-commerce as much as it is about Pre-Commerce. We need to be experts about what happens before the transaction. We need to be the experts on how the decision is made, often without us." Well, we immediately figured someone ought to buy the URL for PreCommerce.com. I'd been trying to say exactly that for years, but I couldn't put the words to my thoughts. I have to thank Alessandro for finally pulling it through my thick skull.

It was all well and good to have this notion of Pre-Commerce, but it didn't mean a damn thing without some sort of skeleton on which companies could hang the muscle of their business. My colleagues Paulo Simas, Paul Dyer, and I struggled to come up with a framework that would explain how companies could turn the idea of Pre-Commerce into a driving force for their business. It had to be simple, obvious, and repeatable—like the Four Ps, we realized.

Paulo Simas is the mile-a-minute guy, the type of colleague who, no matter how long you work with him, still blows you away with his creativity. He's a baseball dad with four boys, but also a surfer with jet-black hair and a pair of earrings. No barriers stand between him and a good wave, nor between him and a good idea. Paul Dyer is the whiz kid. He made money in college playing video games for other people so they could gain levels of expertise without the monotonous work of doing so. He's the kind of guy who figures out a way to squeeze 30 hours into every day. As for me, well, I'm that guy—the Fortune 500 executive who has met every agency, traveled to all corners of the globe, and sat through every type of PowerPoint presentation you can think of. When we think together, good things usually happen.

The three of us brought different perspectives to a singular challenge: Show our clients how significantly their customers' experience and behavior had changed with the onset of Pre-Commerce. We saw it every day through our analysis of more than one hundred brands under our purview, but it would take us too long to explain the urgency of the transformation we were seeing firsthand. We needed a new model, so we started to play around with some ideas, building off the Pre-Commerce inspiration we'd gotten from Alessandro at P&G.

At first, nothing came. Until one day Paulo, more out of frustration than anything else, blurted this into the phone: "They're just doing caveman marketing. They put all of their money into awareness to get you to take an action. That's not right." I immediately thought of Pavlov's dog. As consumers, we'd all become hooked on the reinforcement bred and fed by mass media. We had no one to feed us but the corporate world, with their usual fare of TV commercials, print advertisements, and direct mail or e-mail campaigns. It didn't make sense to me anymore, because now I could go online and enjoy a conversation with one of my peers anytime about anything. The Internet let me choose my own dog food. I realized I didn't need to salivate every time a company put food in my bowl. I could eat any time I wanted to, and moreover I could eat *anything* I wanted to—whether these companies dished it out or not. In fact, the dog food I preferred came from people like me, and almost never from the corporate world.

So out comes the nerdy executive in me. I got Paulo and Paul thinking about this, and we started to ponder how this new "Pavlov's dog" might think about the Four Ps that dominate the marketing profession. The Ps were always there in one form or another. Sure, people debated the merits of one "P" over another or argued about how they worked in harmony or discordance, but they were still the overarching guide to marketing. So what were the Four Xs of the Pre-Commerce world?

We came up with the Four As. In the midst of working up a client presentation, Paul described the rise of search terms, customer conversations, and e-commerce outcomes with the phrase "awareness, assessment, action, and ambassador." As soon as I saw it I knew. Paulo immediately grabbed it and whipped together a visual display of what it might look like, and we all started in on the debate. We wondered if we should add more As. We played it out with dozens of brands to look for holes in the model. We looked for all kinds of ways we could break it apart. But in the end, we ended up with a customer-driven model that's as simple and robust as the Four Ps were when Michigan State University Professor E. Jerome McCarthy introduced them in 1960. Awareness, assessment, action, and ambassadors . . .

We realized *awareness* isn't simply about raising it. In the Pre-Commerce environment, awareness means knowing your marketplace well enough to find the holes in the clutter so you can raise the right awareness with the right influencers in the right places to penetrate the din of the market. None of this happens without the best analytics/ listening model available.

We discovered that *assessment* relates to the myriad new ways we can learn about the marketplace. The customer might not praise your brand, but they will download, share, view, and discuss everything your brand is about. We found different degrees of assessment—some obvious, such as a product review, and some more subtle, such as searching for information on a semi-related topic.

We already knew *action* refers to decisions you want customers to make. But when looking at the Pre-Commerce environment, we quickly realized action also refers to decisions you won't like or might not even know about. Companies have to learn how and where customers make purchasing decisions if they hope to participate in the process.

That requires transparency and a willingness to learn what any action—whether positive, negative, or neutral—conveys about both the customer and your brand.

And we have brand *ambassadors,* customers who passionately support the brands they like and admire. They want to tell the world about your product, and they'll do it with or without your help. You have to build a tighter relationship with them, because they have the ability to cut through the Web's clutter and raise awareness for your brand. If you give them the access they crave, they can exert a major influence on other customers in the midst of the decision-making process. If you don't know your ambassadors by first and last name, you should.

Since developing the Four As, we've presented them hundreds of times to dozens of major companies. In the presence of some of the brightest marketing minds in the world, we've seen new lights come on. We've debated them, parsed through them, and had them picked over by some brilliant people. But in the end, virtually every company has started to integrate some version of this model into their marketing—or at least consider the impact of the Four As on their business. They've started to become pre-commerce companies.

WELCOME TO THE ENGAGEMENT SPAN

Paulo Simas, Chief Creative Officer, WCG

The Four As map out a vital framework your company needs to interact and learn from Pre-Commerce customers. It helps define how you listen, learn, and engage throughout every stage of interaction, and it can help you gain a better understanding of your customer's mindset at every stop along the way. We all want to positively influence

(Continued)

the customer's mindset, help shape a positive brand experience that engenders deeper loyalty, and spawn a generation of loyal advocates. To do this, companies need to move from the blueprint provided by the Four As to the nuts and bolts of putting it into practice. At WCG, we call this the Engagement Span.

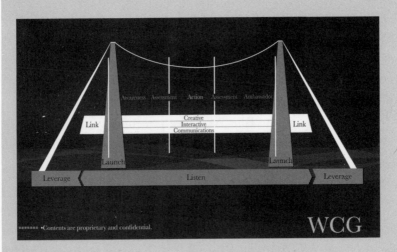

The Engagement Span: Building Connections

The Engagement Span takes the Four As and the ideas of Pre-Commerce and makes them a real part of everyday business operations. This happens through four interrelated steps called the Four Ls—*leverage, listen, launch,* and *link*. The Engagement Span starts by *listening* to customers. It then *leverages* the resulting insight to formulate and *launch* big ideas. And after launching that creative content, it *links* individuals to bring them closer to one another and closer to the brands with which they choose to engage. This process continues every hour of every day, and it covers all the social media channels through which brand influencers interact. To ensure the integrity of the whole program, the Engagement Span requires constant stress tests to reinforce or debunk each strategy and to make sure the program is positioned across all key communications channels.

In the Pre-Commerce marketplace, companies have no choice but to strengthen relationships between their brand and their customers, no matter where they are or when they want to engage. The best way to do that is through an integrated model, whereby the philosophy of the Four As marries the reality of the Engagement Span and its Four Ls. Think of it as a superhighway: We use the Four Ls to build new Engagement Spans, each of which connects to the myriad online and offline highways that customers travel. We pave a smoother, faster road that draws more traffic (i.e., market share), enhances the brand experience, and guides our most loyal customers to ambassadorship.

Of course, the bridge collapses if it's not built on a solid foundation. The most important part of the Four As of customer engagement is to understand how people make decisions. Knowing how *and* why customers engage with a brand determines the type of bridge we build; it dictates how we communicate with them. That knowledge begins with awareness and assessment. Today's business leaders have to look beyond ways to deliver a compelling message. They have to deliver a compelling message that's relevant and that meets customers where they live. It's not about just reaching out to grab attention and build awareness—anyone can build awareness. It's about *listening* to the customer and *leveraging* their insights to build a full messaging platform that's creative and properly positioned to reach customers. It's *launching* a creative message with an authentic voice, kicking that back into the market with just the right mix of spice—something that surprises and engages customers and moves them to action. And it's about *linking* those customers to one another and to your brand.

(Continued)

The creative content is the spark, the ignition for the story and the catalyst for action. The creativity breaks down invisible walls. The relevance penetrates the customer consciousness. And the combination compels customers to go from a full stop to 100 mph on the road toward ambassadorship. In the Pre-Commerce marketplace, companies must create a unique voice that makes customers an equal partner in the engagement—to identify themselves as part of the brand. They will expect to hear something relevant, something meaningful, and something that really matters. If you do that well, you have the customer saying, "I'm in. I'm willing to jump in and take action. I'm going to engage in the experience that you promised." When you have a lot of customers saying, "Dude, check this out," you've hit the jackpot.

Remember that speed matters. Your competitors can get all the same insights and inspiration. You have an opportunity to engage your current and future customers and shepherd them effectively to ambassadorship for your brand. The Engagement Span is the bridge to get them there.

Time to start building. . . .

BECOMING THE PRE-COMMERCE COMPANY

With his company's reputation crumbling in the blogosphere, it didn't take Michael Dell long to realize how little we understood about how dramatically social media were changing commerce. And once that sunk in, it took even less time for him and then-CEO Kevin Rollins to kick us into gear. Customers were demanding that we move faster—and in new directions—so Dell and Rollins shot that sense of urgency into the rest of the company.

Manish Mehta and I created a group we called Web 2.0 and designed the forum in a way that would eliminate barriers to brainstorming and inspire future innovation. We invited colleagues from across the company—IT, marketing, communications, customer support, and e-commerce—but from the start we knew we couldn't accomplish much via the typical meeting process. The fine folks at Dell can get an impressive amount of work done in a single meeting. But like most companies, too many people would arrive at meetings with reasons for how something *can't* be done. Too few came with the imagination and the mindset to spur something truly new and creative. So we set a few ground rules that would rule the Web 2.0 forum over the years to follow:

1. Anyone in the company was invited to join.
2. You could talk only about the future.
3. You could only discuss how to solve problems or create opportunities.
4. No one was allowed to be negative or update us on current work.

Those who strayed outside the rules immediately earned the label "antibodies." When discussing innovation, we found most people think first about what can't be done. That's especially true when the customer, not the company, drives the idea. It shorts the circuits if you're not careful, so we took a sort of Zen approach: acknowledge it, have fun with it, and move on to what we really need to get done. Anytime someone said, "That's an interesting idea, but . . ." I cut them off with, "You're being an antibody!" Soon enough, it became sort of cool to call out an antibody.

We stunned a lot of new members, but soon enough they were the ones having the most fun nailing me to the wall for being an antibody on someone else's idea. Even Mehta and I would slip from time to time, but now we had a group of people who wanted to look at social media, reject the corporate inertia and see the opportunities for what they were: new, exciting, and virtually limitless. What started with Michael Dell and Kevin Rollins had trickled down through the rank and file, and everyone was starting to buy into it. Dell had become a Pre-Commerce company.

We were blessed to have full support from the top when we started in 2006. But without the support of the people who make the machine run, we couldn't move fast enough to identify disgruntled customers, start a new blog, or create a video-sharing site. Their support doesn't just happen at the snap of your fingers. I can toss out a few examples of innovation and a theory or two, but that doesn't do anything to change your culture. You need to get all of your 500, 5,000, or 50,000 employees focused on listening to customers more effectively. At Dell, it worked very well to start with an open forum for learning and a new focus on our customer relationships. We'll get into some other examples and suggestions as the book progresses, but remember that a good idea for one company might not work at yours. That said, I've talked about this with dozens of companies, including some of the largest in the world, and I've found one universal phenomenon: Once employees become students of Pre-Commerce, the cultural change spreads faster than any executive could mandate.

CHAPTER THREE

THE MOVE FROM MARKET RESEARCH TO CUSTOMER INSIGHTS

*I skate to where the puck is going to be,
not where it has been.*

—WAYNE GRETZKY

G lenn Neland and Brett Hurt come from vastly different business backgrounds, but I never would have understood the emerging Pre-Commerce marketplace if I hadn't had the chance to learn from both of them.

Glenn spent twenty years at Texas Instruments before leaving in 1997 to become senior vice president of procurement at Dell. He lived in the world of large enterprise, working like a wizard with supply chains and like a white knight for the customer. Glenn took over Dell's customer-experience team in 2006 and set off to do what leaders at big companies do. He assembled a team of people with the best customer-experience chops, and he asked them to overhaul the company's interactions with customers. We didn't realize it at the time, but Glenn was nudging Dell into the Pre-Commerce world.

"Customer support is a very broad term," he said. "We touch the customer in a number of ways and every time we touch them it affects their experience and perceptions of our business." In most cases, business leaders think of customer support as solving a problem, whether technical, logistical, or business-related. Those are critical issues to address, and all the more difficult to master for a large, multinational operation with millions of customers scattered across the globe. "Providing support to such a large set of geographically diverse customers on a consistent and timely basis requires well-defined processes and tools," Glenn said. "Without that definition of how to classify and respond to specific problems we end up with a diverse set of solutions for the customer, all of which become confusing and frustrating."

Glenn taught me that a Pre-Commerce company needs a disciplined process to govern its customer experience programs. Brett Hurt taught me how the flexibility and power of social media could turbocharge that process. Brett is the techie whiz kid to Glenn's brilliant corporate manager. He started computer programming at seven years old, around the time most of us still harbor dreams of a Major League Baseball career. When he was ten, he launched a bulletin board system on a 110-baud modem. He created one of the first Web-based multiplayer games in 1990. Then he got a little more serious. In 1999, he launched his first major company, called Coremetrics. It eventually became one of the leading marketing-analytics services for the global e-commerce industry, and today its products help optimize online marketing for more than two thousand business Web sites. (IBM acquired Coremetrics in 2010.) If there was any question Brett had a nose for Pre-Commerce opportunities, he answered it with BazaarVoice. Since founding BazaarVoice in 2005, Brett has grown the Austin-based startup into the leading global platform for customers who want to share and learn about products through reviews, ratings, Q&As, and more.

The confluence of Glenn's initiatives at Dell and the meteoric rise of Brett and his colleagues at BazaarVoice really jolted me. I realized the marketplace had changed, and I realized I hadn't changed with it. I felt as though the business world had left me behind, and I spent the next few days in a mild panic. A tuna sandwich and a customer-satisfaction survey zapped me back to my senses. I was flipping through the results of the survey while eating lunch in my cubicle. As I pored over all the green, yellow, and red bars, I realized what I really wanted to know simply wasn't there. I asked my colleagues in the company's research department. I asked the executives with whom I worked. No one could tell me what this survey could tell us about the millions of customers who hadn't responded to it.

Just a few days earlier I thought the business world had all but passed me by. Now I realized virtually no one really understood the tectonic shift that Pre-Commerce had sent rippling through the commercial landscape. For Dell and most other companies, surveying customer satisfaction had become knee-jerk. We rarely considered the world beyond the pool of survey respondents. We gathered more and more data all the time, but we never really accumulated the insight we needed to attract new customers and grow our businesses. Glenn and Brett, each in their own way, had showed us how we could do both. Now, rather than panicked, I was jazzed about the opportunities.

THE CUSTOMERS WHO DON'T TALK TO YOU

Stop for a second and try to picture the entire span of your customer population. If you're like most companies, fewer than 10 percent of those people will visit your Web site or call you in any given year. (In fact, the actual number is probably less than 5 percent for many companies.) Yet we consistently base our thinking on these small fractions of our customer pool who feel motivated—for reasons good or bad—to reach out to us. We use that miniscule sample to decide whether our work is up to snuff. Yikes!

Around the time my eyes glazed over that Dell survey, I realized the new-school answer was right in front of us. If we wanted feedback from more than 10 percent of our customers, we needed to use all the information at our disposal. We would have to comb through both online and offline channels. We had to go online and study the behavior and indirect feedback provided by the millions of customers who never talk directly to us yet still wielded an immense influence on our customer base. And we needed to figure out how to separate those with real influence from those who screamed much ado about nothing.

We had to extend the same thinking across all our market research. Why limit our insight to a pool of people we predefine? Why not get feedback from every customer or potential customer we can find, whether offline or on? Every time I asked myself another question, I flashed back to my days stuck in conference rooms at Grey and Novartis. I could still hear echoes of the terms our marketing gurus would rattle off—"demand estimation . . . net promoter score . . . concept testing . . . copy testing . . . ad tracking . . . focus groups . . . commercial eye tracking . . . segmentation research." Almost every company does the same thing. So we're all complicit in repeating it, even when we know this data shows a picture both partial and out of the past. As the great Wayne Gretzky would say, we were skating to the place the puck had already come and gone.

At Dell, we had a great team of employees who spent hours interacting with customers every day in the blogosphere or through our customer resolution team. We could identify what our customers were saying, even when they didn't call or visit our Web sites. We had all the ingredients for a more successful recipe in front of us, but we spent our time ignoring the sugar and adding yet another cup of flour. We had gotten closer to our customers, but we weren't doing anything with what we'd learned.

In the Pre-Commerce marketplace companies have no choice but to get closer to their customers, Lukas Cudrigh told me. As Microsoft's senior director for digital solutions, Lukas has seen how tighter interactions can generate more and more relevant posts and higher-quality discussions. But as I learned at Dell, he knows none of that matters if companies don't act on this information. Technology tools can help parse through all this consumer information, shape it into a finely tuned media campaign, execute it across a range of digital platforms, and optimize it as part of a holistic (e.g., online and offline) marketing program, Lukas told me. And as interest-based marketing evolves, he said, this well-structured customer data will become an increasingly vital asset to run more effective campaigns.

"To process this overwhelming influx of data and media formats into integrated and efficient campaigns, innovative companies are starting to build out systems that automate the planning, execution, and monitoring of digital campaigns across brand, commerce, advertising, and social media channels," Lukas said. "These systems will have the capability to capture campaign goals, generate media plans, and coordinate campaign activities on all channels against a predefined flight plan. I see this as a critical capability, especially for larger companies or sophisticated marketers."

Today's model for market research needs the sort of immediate transformation Lukas talks about. But that sort of breakthrough change only occurs when companies—from the CEO down to the new hire—willingly abandon the current model. Companies that expect to build a competitive advantage and maximize the value for their brands have to start by gathering deeper customer insights. And that means looking beyond the 10 percent of customers who come to you.

THE TRANSFORMATION OF MARKET RESEARCH

The advent of Pre-Commerce has done nothing less than flip the market research process 180 degrees. And it has left virtually every company working backward, starting with the usual market research in a vain attempt to gain insights about customer behavior. We need to turn that around. Thanks to all the customer activity on the Internet and through social media channels, companies now have an unprecedented ability to harness customer insights first, and then use that knowledge to conduct targeted market research that refines their understanding of the customer, the industry, and the market.

For example, consider the annual *Business Week* survey of the top 100 brands. Just one of these well-known global companies can have 5,000 to 10,000 conversations occurring about its brands on any given day, most likely in English alone. If you include the top ten online languages (see Figure 3.1) that reach approximately 90 percent of the world's Internet users, we can assume the number at least doubles. These conversations have become a massive and still-expanding influence on your brand reputation. People you don't know are helping potential customers decide if your brand matters, and their conversations have far more influence than your advertising. And in some cases, their silence has even greater influence. Perhaps nothing poses a greater risk to a top brand than silence. Silence and the lack of passion are close cousins. If you're not intimately aware of what your customers are saying about your brand every day—or what they're not saying—then you've effectively decided to outsource your brand reputation management to the public. In essence, by doing nothing you already made a key leadership decision, albeit a passive one.

For the proactive executive who wants to participate in the public shaping of his or her brand, social media channels are the best place

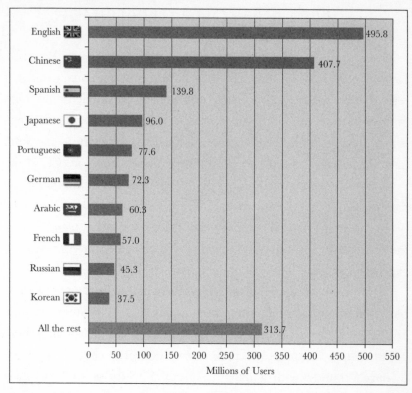

Figure 3.1. Top Ten Languages on the Internet (in millions of users) in 2010

to start. With some basic research tools and a little thought, a company can gather insight from its customers online, use that information to craft a focused and effective research program, and apply the combined knowledge to forge a competitive advantage. Most companies won't do this, because they've pumped so many resources and so much time into traditional primary research. Over the years, we've come to trust primary research with its correlation and causation, its means and modes, random sampling, and other data points. But today that groove has become a rut. You search and search for new information, when the answers to many of your questions are publicly available and sitting right in front of you.

THINK LIKE YOUR CUSTOMER, NOT A COMMITTEE

Do you ever feel a bit intimidated when someone presents a research report? The experts in the room will debate the influence of high outliers on the mean, or they'll argue whether the statistical significance is truly meaningful in the particular sample at hand. Most people don't have the specific expertise to contribute to these conversations, so the experts in the conference room—the people just smart enough to be dangerous—drive the entire debate. Every company needs all the smart people it can get, but no company can thrive when smart people usurp the conversation over an esoteric point. No company thrives when the experts speak more loudly than the customer.

Your market research team can perform heroic feats for your company, but only if you help them accommodate the customer's impact on the Pre-Commerce environment. The company that makes these adjustments will supplement their research experts—still great people to have around—with a dynamic group of experts who can find and process the key insights gleaned from its entire customer base. And the more employees a company has interacting with customers, the more information it gleans and the more intimate its customer relationships. Set your market research team loose, and they can do this for you.

It doesn't have to be difficult or technical, either. Newell Rubbermaid took a no-nonsense approach when it set out to create a social media strategy to support its Graco brand of baby products. Bert Dumars and his team simply went out and asked mothers what they wanted to see online from Graco. "We started in the late summer of 2007 by going out and meeting new moms and influential mom bloggers," said Dumars, the company's vice president of e-business and interactive marketing. "We asked two simple questions: What would you want to see from

Graco if it entered into the online conversation? And what would you not want to see Graco do in the social media space?"

They asked those two simple questions at events across the country. They gathered some of their existing research that helped guide the way. They consulted with most of the popular online influencers for baby products and moms. And when they processed all that information they came up with Graco's "Heart to Heart" blog (blog.gracobaby .com), its Twitter ID (twitter.com/gracobaby), and its Flickr page (flickr.com/photos/gracobaby). The Flickr page and the blog were immediately successful because of the sites' focus on children, parents, and parenting—exactly what mothers had said they wanted all along. The strategy worked so well, in fact, that the company extended the formula to its Rubbermaid and Sharpie brands as well, Dumars said.

The Pre-Commerce market never stops shifting, though, and since launching the company's social media program Dumars has continued to analyze the feedback and data the sites generate. He uses online measurement tools. He keeps tabs on the sites' followers and visits their blogs, Facebook pages, and Twitter feeds. "We analyze where they are in the parenting lifecycle—new parents, parents with children in the Graco purchase lifecycle, parents with older children but still focused on parenting of younger children, etc.," Dumars explained. "The Graco brand has enjoyed high awareness and has had strong word-of-mouth for a long time, and we are using social media marketing to continue supporting this area."

Unfortunately, the approach that works for Graco today might not work for your company tomorrow. The good news is that every business leader can craft a workable strategy using three basic steps. The first step focuses on the development of your online expertise and perspective—you have to know what you're doing. The second step focuses on your customers and what they do over time (i.e., their online journey with your brand). The final step focuses on bringing the necessary rigor to your research, as Dumars did, by developing the direct insights and behavioral analytics you need to turn data into knowledge. Let's take a closer look at each step.

VIRUS CHECK

Before we get to how to do this, let's address how these same market research teams will push back on change. It's human nature. Everyone does this and I can already tell you what they will say. I call them the "antibodies" in a company, because they embrace change intellectually but are unwilling to act on it physically. You might call it other things, such as passive-aggressive behavior. All that matters is that you don't let it prevent change from occurring.

Here is what you will hear from your teams as you ask for change.

This is really secondary data that is unpredictable.
We can't match it up with our primary research.
We can't control sample size over time.
The population sample is unclear.
The response rates vary greatly, so we can't plan ahead.
We're not using tried-and-true survey tools to gather data.

The list goes on. It's an antibody response and it's OK. Let people get it out of their system as you help your team completely transform from "market research" to "customer insights."

STEP ONE: DEVELOP YOUR ONLINE PERSPECTIVE AND EXPERTISE

It helps to think about the Pre-Commerce landscape in terms of the Earth's tectonic plates. They shift slowly, and only with the onset of massively disruptive occasions (read: earthquakes) do they enter mainstream conversation. The same happens routinely online and through social media. A major disruption that rumbles through your industry might reveal itself suddenly and overnight, but no doubt the pressure had built up through dozens of pressure points over the preceding weeks, months, or even years. No company can fully comprehend the myriad pressure points that have developed with the emergence of Pre-Commerce. Very few companies have bothered to start searching for them today.

I have a favorite exercise I use with executives I meet. I have them Google their brand and look through the links on the first screen. Of the results on the first page, I ask them, "How many do you know personally?" After all, the people behind these links create the first impression of your brand for most of your potential customers. When I ask how many they know, I usually get silence.

The fact is these people have as much or more influence on your brand image as you do. And since facts like these represent reality, I like using them as much as possible. Nothing slaps you awake like a cold, hard dose of reality. You can do the same for your teams. Share the facts of the online world with your team, and you'll start instilling a social mindset throughout your company. Ask your teams, in turn, to become students of the online marketplace so they can spread awareness throughout the company.

Your teams need to learn about the tectonic plates that impact your industry. Some are universal, including the three ACE plates—access, commerce, and experience—which I regularly share with clients.

Access

Each day since 2006, about 500,000 people have gone online for the first time in their lives, according to research we conducted at Dell, and I don't see any evidence to suggest this trend will slow in the next four years. Most of the new users come from developing markets, primarily in Asia, Eastern Europe, and Latin America. If you're a global company, you need to know as much about Tudou as you do about YouTube.

The company that knows how many people use each site has taken a smart first step. But to find the Pre-Commerce pressure points, companies have to understand how Tudou, by letting users watch full-length movies and TV shows, will change factors such as user experience and intellectual property rights in a way that YouTube won't touch. The company that tracks high-speed Internet penetration in emerging markets is ahead of most competitors. But the real advantage comes when you know the actual bandwidth in those markets and how that impacts how customers can interact with your e-commerce and social media channels.

People today use a range of devices to connect. We too often cast the rest of the world in light of our own experience in our home country. Most U.S. executives picture e-commerce zipping through a monitor or laptop computer. Only with the rise of the iPhone and its smartphone competitors has that popular view changed, yet outside North America the cell phone already dominates many of the world's markets. It isn't Nathan B. Stubblefield's wireless phone anymore. In 1979, NTT in Japan introduced the first generation of cellular phone technology. The Finns at Radiolinja introduced 2G in 1991; NTT DoCoMo came back with 3G in 2001. Today we have 4G, with speeds, capacity, and abilities Stubblefield never could have imagined. In many countries, entire generations have bypassed landlines. By the end of 2010, the world's wireless telecom companies will have sold more than five billion subscriptions, according to the International Telecommunication Union.[1]

People don't care about the old rules you live by. They create their own. They will access your brand from new places and new devices, redefining the experience they want to have.

Commerce

As we noted when discussing the Four As, a company has to know where Pre-Commerce customers make their decisions. Otherwise, it has no chance of exerting any influence on the process.

Imagine a fantastic day at work. Your boss walks into your office and announces she just promoted you to country manager for Canada. It's a brand new market for you and your colleagues, and she wants you to establish a presence for your company. You might call your spouse and share the good news first, but you soon will ask for all the market research you can get your hands on. You'll start assembling a sales force, complete a strategic plan for the next three to five years, and identify your product offering. Your approach might vary some, but the basics are there.

Now imagine a twist on that theme: Your boss walks in and says, "I've promoted you to manage our third-largest market." No offense to my fine friends from Canada, but that's a huge jump. You already started thinking about exotic trips to a new country when your boss says, "Do you have a Facebook account already?" Behind China and India, Facebook is the third-largest market in the world. And while it's a virtual community, you need to treat this assignment with the same respect and preparation. The Pre-Commerce customer demands nothing less.

You soon come to find that half of Facebook's members visit their page every day, and people who access Facebook through their smart phone are twice as active as others. The new marketing professional will analyze these communities just as he or she appraises the marketplace for yogurt or fitness equipment. What is the Facebook equivalent of a state, city, or village where your brand fits? Who has the most influence on your brand image and your messaging? How will you reach people in the more than seventy languages Facebook offers today?

Your company doesn't have decades of historical data on a hard drive somewhere. But even a quick survey of the Facebook ecosystem will prove your competitors don't either. If you dig in faster and further than your rivals, you can unearth rich data, process it into customer insight, and produce a significant competitive advantage in the world's largest virtual marketplace.

You know what you would do in "real life." Facebook, Tudou, Orkut, and dozens of other virtual communities are "real life" in today's Pre-Commerce environment. The fifteen- to twenty-nine-year-old age group lives in an SMS world. E-mail is for their parents. Television is just video they get whenever they feel like it. Peers have had the highest influence on them for almost all their lives. Will they care about your e-mail marketing campaign? Will they pay attention to your TV commercial or use the DVR to fast forward through the breaks?

In the Pre-Commerce world, the real and virtual worlds are inseparable.

Experience

You've pondered the ways customers access your brand. You've thought about the new worlds in which commerce takes place. Consider now the experience you provide customers in these new marketplaces. Your customer's interactions at every point along your "supply chain of experience" will flavor their opinion of your brand. Companies have conducted online surveys for years, asking customers how they feel about the brand. All these surveys consider a single point of contact, yet customers today experience your brand through dozens of social media and Internet avenues—many of which you don't own. How does your customer experience rate across all those channels?

A few companies have stumbled across this very powerful realization. Your supply chain of experience has no common tie. Different silos house different parts of your customers' experience, and rarely do those silos interact. Making matters tougher, no one has quite figured out how to get their firm's silos working hand-in-hand with the social media channels they don't own. Larger companies send out completely uncoordinated messages from their multiple brands. In simple terms, companies have told customers in no uncertain terms that they care only about the transaction, not the experience.

Is it any wonder customers increasingly turn to their peers—to those social media channels you don't control—in an attempt to sort their way through the confusion? Companies frustrate customers with their lack of efficiency and insight, and frustrated customers don't buy.

THE CUSTOMER EXPERIENCE

Here are some of the key elements of this supply chain.

The introduction—we send out catalogs, buy e-mail lists, and advertise to let people know we are ready to sell to them.

The captive audience—a person registers in our database and we reciprocate by e-mailing them on a regular basis with offers and news.

The purchase experience—we sell our product.

The upsell post-purchase—we ask days or weeks after the purchase if you would like to buy related products or warranties or services.

The first issue—the customer has an important issue and is counting on you for the answer.

The second purchase—the life of the brand purchased is now complete and it is time for a repeat or new purchase.

Make it easy on yourself. Take out a piece of paper and write down each agency and each team that is involved with each area. That will be enough to convince you that your team is not coordinated in the most effective manner.

STEP TWO: YOUR CUSTOMER'S ONLINE JOURNEY

I like to think of a customer's journey as an actual hike. Their trek never really ends, but at the end of each day's walk your customers make a purchase. And each day they pack up camp and start off for their next destination, not necessarily knowing where they'll camp next. Companies, of course, wanted to guide hikers to their campsites. Traditionally, each company would reach out to customers at the beginning of the day and hope they would meet them again that evening. Eventually, the smart company started to identify the major forks in the trail and set up signs to guide hikers its way.

Today, millions of Pre-Commerce hikers are walking the same paths. When they reach a fork in the trail and see the dozens of signs—none of which really tell them what they want to know—they simply ask their fellow wanderers. The customers choose their path long before they have any contact with the company, and rarely does the company have any influence on their choices. This is your customer's online journey.

People have become highly desensitized to the typical approaches companies use to introduce and tout their brands. The average conversion rate for untargeted broadcast e-mails hovers around 1 percent, according to a 2006 study by Jupiter Research (now part of Forrester Research). That's 99 percent of customers who don't convert—99 percent. Out of one million people, only ten thousand decided to buy. Celebrating the few who buy is a short-term view, at best. When you start to think about where the other 990,000 spend their time, you start to understand there's gold in them thar hills.

Even the most technology-illiterate executive knows the amount of information customers receive through social media has exploded over the past decade. Not as many realize the rate at which that information prompts further action. It doesn't have to be a complex message to spur movement. In the last chapter, I mentioned research about Twitter that shows 48 percent of its users introduced to a new brand went on to search for additional information about that company. Those little 140-character snippets of conversation prompted almost half the Twitter users who got the message to search for more information. About 44 percent of the users surveyed said they had recommended a product in a tweet, and 39 percent said they'd discussed different products on Twitter.[2]

Recall for a moment Figure 2.1 in Chapter Two that lists the top ten online influence areas. They include blogs, audio, video, and forums, among other channels. As an executive concerned about your brand image and messaging, you have to understand how your customers use these areas of key influence. You need to study the journey your customers take, where and from whom they learn about your brand, and how they spread the word to other potential customers. They're learning about your brand from a range of sources, with every step along the trail. You can't greet them at the start or end of the day's hike and truly understand how they got from Point A (consideration) to Point B (purchase). At some point, you have to put on your virtual hiking boots and take a walk down the same trails your customers use.

Here's the first path to take: search engines. Learn the top five questions asked by your customers on Google, Bing, YouTube, and other popular search sites. Keep a constant vigil over the rising search terms for your brand. Track the search behavior of your customers when you launch a new marketing campaign to see if their habits change.

As you're walking, pay close attention to all the peer influence on the trail. Of course it happens at the major intersections along the path, but it also occurs when two hikers walk side-by-side for a while. You can track peer influence in many ways, including through analyses of rating and review sites, Yahoo! Answers, community forums, and other sites where peers drive the conversation. At these points along the way, you'll discover which hikers have the most influence on your potential customers. You'll find that about 1 percent of these virtual hikers actually generate content; 9 percent of them share that content with others; and the last 90 percent just soak it in and learn from it. The ratios vary from topic to topic, but 1–9–90 works as a good rule of thumb. Most customers are just hiking, but they have their eyes and ears open to everyone around them.

One word of caution as you get started: Don't let all your hiking go to waste. As you walk, map out your customers' Pre-Commerce experiences. I prepare a little chart I call a "conversation blueprint" (see The New Top Ten box in the next section). It shows the top places customers visit via their online searches. It lists the top forums, blogs, and social media sites they visit. It includes the top questions people ask when they search. You have to constantly update this map, but having it will prove invaluable when you want to reach the vast majority of customers who don't come to you for their information.

STEP THREE: DIRECT INSIGHTS AND BEHAVIORAL ANALYTICS

Having mapped out a blueprint of the customer's online journey, now you have to build the bridge to them. Those smart people who took over your meetings in the past? Now that you have them refocused on the customer, bring them back into the room. Like any other marketing process at your company, you have to build some rigor and develop some consistent processes that will help you understand the Pre-Commerce customer over the long haul. You have to know how and where your customers learn about your brand. You need to have some idea of how they are likely to react to the tsunami of information the Web pushes their way. And you have to comb through all your incoming information to find real customer insights—the knowledge you need to craft a marketing plan that becomes a relevant part of their decision-making process.

At its core, this approach merely brings the rigor of traditional marketing to the Pre-Commerce marketplace. But few companies think to adjust their thinking, and those that do find themselves at a loss for where to look. Again, the key pressure points in these shifting tectonic plates change from industry to industry and company to company. But if you've taken the time to complete steps one and two—if you've developed some online expertise and studied your customers' online journey—some of the pressure points for your company will become more and more obvious. Here are a few to consider at the outset:

- The specific features about your brand that are (or aren't) popular in reviews, and why.
- As customers share more about your product online, do your inquiries and returns increase or decrease?
- Of the sites your customers visit before jumping to yours, which lead to the highest conversion rates?
- How is your natural search position improving due to customers sharing more content and views about your brand? Will any improvement lessen your need for paid search?

This list will apply to most companies, but by no means should a marketing professional consider it at all comprehensive. For example, attentive companies use available social media diagnostic tools to track actual patterns of influence. Customers learn about your brand on YouTube, Flickr, Twitter, SlideShare, Google, iTunes, and dozens of other search and social media sites. In each case, you can track the top influencers who drive "share of conversation" at each site. You can identify the forums that shape your brand image and message in the mind of the greatest number of current and potential customers. And across it all, you can judge how your marketing campaigns impact the same conversations.

For most business-minded people I meet, the toughest part of all this is the realization that some insights will arise from something other than cold, hard data. The qualitative nature of behavioral analytics often reveals more to you than the quantitative factors alone. Video is a prime example. A study led by Dr. Wei Ji Ma, an assistant professor of neuroscience at the Baylor College of Medicine, proved that visual information can improve our understanding as much as six-fold over the spoken word alone.[3] The brain naturally uses images to clarify ideas and thoughts. But we can't yet quantify the impact video has on a brand, whether it's customers posting do-it-yourself fixes or an analyst's demonstration of how to use an old product in new and interesting ways. What's clear, though, is that thoughtful and well-crafted video can have a powerful influence on your customer base.

That said, the speed at which we can see trends ripple though social media and the Web can help offset a company's unease with qualitative data. For example, a quick look at consumption patterns will show you that prime time for most industries runs between 9 P.M. and 1 A.M. It makes complete sense; we've finished up work and put the kids to bed.

Successful Pre-Commerce companies will leverage the power of online analytics and flavor it with qualitative observation, producing more-effective advertising campaigns and increasing the agility of their media buys. But today, most companies launch their campaign, measure the traffic to their Web site, and declare victory if the number looks at all impressive (and any number can look impressive in the absence of any real comparison). In the future, successful campaigns will change the attitude and behavior of customers toward your brand. They will incorporate flexible media buys based more closely on real-time need. And they will prompt customers to take the short- or long-term action in which you've invested.

The Pre-Commerce company will measure how search habits change, how proactively customers are recommending their brand, and whether potential customers are seeking more information. They'll know that silence means the campaign isn't working, and they'll have Plan B ready to fire out within days because they're not locked into a long and expensive media-buy plan.

Remember the old tongue-in-cheek saying, "You know half of your marketing budget is working, you just don't know what half"? Well, now you do.

THE NEW TOP TEN

Traditional marketing meetings often felt like an ode to PowerPoint. The speaker droned on, the Blackberrys came out, and half the group started thinking about their weekend barbecue. That ends in the Pre-Commerce era. Any discussion of important brand influences requires immediate data from everyone present, because everyone is part of the market research team now. Better yet, you have just one slide to deal with—ten questions to debate based on the data and insights everyone has on their PCs and at their fingertips.

1. How do we build a richer relationship with the top fifty influencers who drive share of conversation for our brand?
2. Why did one particular feature of our product drive an increase in online reviews, and why is that online comment volume more (or less) than what our competitors receive?
3. How do we incorporate the five interesting product-development ideas that our customers just suggested online?

(*Continued*)

4. How do we optimize our marketing to take advantage of the ten new keywords that are driving customer search?

5. What are the top questions customers are asking our product-support teams, and how do we feature them on our customer-support Web site to save time and frustration for everyone?

6. How much of the "supply chain of experience" have we integrated into our Pre-Commerce marketing strategy, and how soon can we make that 100 percent?

7. How do we increase our presence in the online and social media channels customers most often use to learn about our brand?

8. Why is the word-of-mouth buzz about our brand increasing/decreasing/static on social media sites, such as Twitter, and how do we keep it energized?

9. How do we double the length of news cycles based on our Pre-Commerce customer insight?

10. What languages do our customers speak, and which one should we add next so we can relate with influencers and customers in their own words?

A MARKETING RESET

As you lead your company through these three steps, you'll start to see your marketing team identify new forms of competitive advantage you never contemplated before. You'll develop a more agile media-spend program to help reduce your marketing costs while increasing the effectiveness of each campaign. You'll start making targeted online investments that feed positively into the online discussions about your brand, and you'll give your brand ambassadors the information they crave to help spread the word.

It can seem daunting—like that brief moment of panic when you realize the world has changed around you—but no need to fret. Without even knowing it, you already spent years experimenting with these programs. Most companies have conducted in-home and in-store observation to understand how shoppers act and react. We know shoppers almost always walk to the right when they enter a store, and we have a pretty good idea of how customers use our products once they get them home. In the Pre-Commerce environment, you have to move a greater chunk of your research online, where customers are making almost all the information you need available on a constantly updated basis. Rather than completely overhaul everything you do, simply redefine the key market-research programs we use.

For starters, you probably will want to add these programs:

- *Crowd-sourcing ideas.* Customers will participate when they have the option to provide input (e.g., voting on ideas), discuss them with peers, and hear directly from the company.
- *Human preference networks.* No one brags about the number of databases they're in. Customers want to engage in a network that understands their preferences—including how best to contact them (e.g., e-mail, SMS, Twitter), and what information they want to receive (e.g., product news, customer support).
- *Referrals.* Companies don't need net promoter scores if they can track exactly how many referrals and recommendations their brand receives in real-time online.
- *Beta communities.* Companies ask their top customers for advice on a regular basis, whether in public or in private beta communities. These communities are your most important research asset, and the participants are true partners for your brand.
- *Data connections.* Because the social media landscape is young and rapidly evolving, companies must continually seek new streams of

online data. What leads you to new customer insights today might disappear tomorrow. And the data sources that do survive for the long haul will constantly pump out real-time data, which reveal new trends and insights. It never ends.

And you probably should get rid of these, which have outlived their usefulness:

- *In person qualitative surveys.* Today's customers are too busy, and we already see their unaided advice on our community sites.
- *Online panels.* Gone are the days of asking linear questions to customers who never get to see the actual results. Crowd-sourcing provides far more powerful knowledge, with greater insight for both company and customer.
- *CYA research.* Research used to "cover your ass" or justify someone's pet project won't work. Even if no one inside your company will stand up and say it's a bad idea, the online community definitely will.
- *Satisfaction studies.* Strong online analytics and monitoring will deliver all this information to you already. Why waste resources on redundancy?
- *Focus groups.* Ten people at a time? Are you serious? Through idea communities, forums, and other social media tools, we can get 10,000 people at a time, every day and for months on end.

Ultimately, you have to refocus your market research on the ways people share information, influence customer attitudes, and make decisions about your brand. It's no secret—all the data you need to turn market research into customer insight is there on the Web. It's flowing through social media channels and revealing itself in Internet-search trends right now, and it's evolving and changing in real time. The Web is the greatest research tool ever built. It's high time you start using it to its fullest potential.

_____

CHAPTER FOUR

MEET THE NEW INFLUENCERS

You don't have to be a "person of influence" to be influential.
In fact, the most influential people in my life are probably
not even aware of the things they've taught me.

—SCOTT ADAMS, AMERICAN CARTOONIST
AND THE CREATOR OF *DILBERT*

I grew up in a *real* baseball family. We didn't just like the sport; my dad, the elder Bob Pearson, played shortstop in the New York Yankees farm system in the late-1940s and early-1950s. He was pretty good, too. In 1952, he and Crash Davis, the middle infielders for the Raleigh Capitals, set a Carolinas League record for double plays in a season. The real Crash Davis was a second baseman, not a catcher like Kevin Costner's character in *Bull Durham*. (Apparently, the Bob Pearson character was left on the cutting-room floor. Worse yet, dad said no one like Susan Sarandon ever hung around the Raleigh Capitals. *C'est la vie*.)

Baseball engrained itself in my DNA like a glorious mutation. I bathed in box scores and statistics, and dusted up with friends in endless debates on which player was better and why. My friend Dave Judge was the statistics whiz. He could tell you the weather in Anchorage the day Pete Rose got his two thousandth hit against Charlie Williams in

San Francisco on June 19, 1973. But as much as baseball lends itself to endless statistics, it inevitably leads to myriad ways to interpret the very same numbers. Dave could tell you that Al Kaline had more home runs than Johnny Bench. But on our weekly Saturday afternoon trek to the local 7-Eleven for a Slurpee, none of Dave's statistics could convince us that anyone was a better power hitter in the clutch than Reggie Jackson.

Even so, the way statistics gave Dave an edge always intrigued me. As I grew older, it seemed all the more businesslike and obvious to rely on statistics. But it wasn't until 2003, when Michael Lewis released his widely popular book *Moneyball,* that it all came together for me. The common sense of Oakland Athletics general manager Billy Beane's data-driven theories resonated with the businessman in me. Beane was a new kind of data hound, but his ideas were really quite straight-forward. He developed a more effective way through baseball's statistical clutter, figuring out how to place his bets more effectively than his peers. His decision making became very precise and aligned with his larger strategy.

By carefully studying the factors that really made the difference between a victory or defeat, Beane figured out which players would have the most influence on winning the game. He identified hidden talents of ballplayers who didn't always make headlines but had high potential. Who you were, how much money you made, or how many endorsements you pitched had no bearing on his decisions. Data ruled, so he would go after players who got on base more often instead of the person who had a nice batting average but didn't have a great on-base percentage, for example.

But he didn't stop there. He looked more holistically at the combination of skills a team needed to succeed. He selected players based on how their talent fit within the team. The adage suggests that necessity is the mother of invention—it fits for Beane. He put his system together because the A's had far less money to play with than other teams. He had to outsmart rival general managers, and he routinely did. Beane compiled a 976–804 (.548) record in his first eleven seasons as GM of the A's (through 2008), the third-best record in the American League.

Like every business person I know, Beane wanted to create a competitive edge that was meaningful. He didn't care about the noise surrounding it—just get an edge on the competition, thank you. It all made sense to me, both as a baseball fan and a businessman. But it took a kickboxing CEO to finally hammer it through my thick skull.

THE POWER OF THE CUSTOMER'S WORD

About a year after *Moneyball* hit the shelves, Novartis CEO Thomas Ebeling walked into our bi-weekly global communications meeting in Basel, Switzerland. Technically, it was my meeting, but Thomas is as direct an executive you could meet, a fact I really appreciated when I worked for him. (Thomas currently is CEO at ProSiebenSat.1 Group, a leading media company in Europe.) You always knew where you stood with him, and anything that even hinted at the status quo got him riled. Everyone in the room and on the phone that day knew precisely whose meeting it really was.

We started discussing the latest measurements about our brand stories and how well they were reaching potential customers in key global markets. Thomas had a way of flashing a half-grin and a searing stare at the same time. He flashed that look across the boardroom table at us and said: "I want to know exactly which product message matters to people in France. I want to know exactly how it stands out versus our competitor's message. I don't want to know about every single one of our messages; I want to know which one is working, where it's working, and why it's working."

An awkward silence fell. We all knew he was dead on, but we hadn't drilled that deeply into the data. We realized it didn't matter how much noise we created. Reaching the right people, with the right message, at the right time mattered. Prompting customers to buy our product mattered. All the rest of the buzz was distraction—for customers, potential customers, and us. We cut that meeting short and went right back to the drawing board to figure it out. It took about four months to generate the insight we needed, but we got it.

That meeting happened in 2004, but long before then companies knew they needed to reach the right influencers with their brand stories. That very fact has become a staple of marketing programs for as many years as I've been in business. It's like breathing for marketing professionals. But the advent of Pre-Commerce has sent a disruptive shockwave through the influencer landscape. The Internet and social media have transformed the company–influencer relationship in a very fundamental way. *Your story is no longer the most important message. What matters is how your audience discusses and validates your story.*

The future leaders in a Pre-Commerce era will do the best job of ensuring their customers do the talking for them. And to do that, companies have to understand, identify, and build relationships with the new influencers—the people who validate your brand's value.

CULLING THE HERD

The whiteboard in my "double-wide" cubicle probably never communicated all that much to my Dell colleagues. A psychologist might have found the clutter of blue, green, and red marker a better gauge of the way I think than the way I really try to get across a point. It was my doodle pad, a physical manifestation of my stream of consciousness. I was scrawling away one morning in early 2006, when I started to think about how we, as company leaders, could get more out of our people involved in our emerging crusade to reach more and more customers online. The more I scrawled away, the more I felt like Don Quixote, tilting with markers at a whiteboard windmill.

A bit exasperated, I finally stepped back and looked more closely at the numbers—and there I found our new influencers. With a little basic research I realized that 5,000 to 10,000 conversations about the Dell brand occurred each day in online communities, but we didn't participate in more than a handful of them. We let customers shape our brand image. By default, we had decided to outsource our reputation management to people we didn't even know. Worse, we had no idea what most of them were saying about us, whether good or bad.

I stuffed that and a lot of other data together in a presentation, but I could have used one slide with this one data point. It was more than I needed to focus people's attention on the issue. And to Dell's credit—especially Michael Dell and Kevin Rollins—the company displayed an ever-increasing intensity to become a relevant part of those conversations. I've left Dell since, but that push continues today.

I still felt a little Quixotic, though. Now that we'd decided to join the conversation, did we really have to talk to 10,000 people every day? Would it really be that much work? I couldn't see how we could manage it without hiring dozens of new employees, not something that would go over well in Dell's very cost-conscious environment.

Back to the whiteboard I went, and scrawl after scrawl later my brain finally returned to what it long had known. I quickly erased the board and started pondering what lessons we had learned from traditional media about the new Pre-Commerce market. I'd spent years consulting with and leading teams whose responsibilities included media relations. At Novartis, for example, we had more than 300 people in communications who regularly interacted with reporters and known influencers on any given day. At GCI, we dealt with everything from anthrax attacks and mad cow disease to support for AFLAC and its now-famous duck commercials. Understanding how media works is second nature for me.

While at Novartis, I realized that, in any country, fewer than fifteen journalists really drove the company's image. You probably can tick off a handful of reporters you read on a regular basis, whether they cover your industry or your hobbies. In the larger countries, such as the United States, about a dozen reporters drove the majority of stories about Novartis. In smaller markets such as Canada, the number dropped to five or fewer. And when I added all of them up, I had less than three hundred people across the globe that my teams and I needed to know very well. We couldn't ignore everyone else, of course, but we knew this group would have the greatest influence on our brand. We knew this because we'd done the quantitative analysis. We knew most other reporters wrote stories based on an article published by one of the three hundred.

I'd scribbled this train of thought on the whiteboard, stepped back, and immediately thought of *Moneyball.* Everything I was doing fit with Billy Beane's strategy to find the right people who fit the right framework of influence. Our traditional media experience told us we could identify a relatively small group of people who had an outsize influence on our customers. And we knew we couldn't just ignore the big, name-brand media experts. But we realized we didn't need to waste all our time fretting about them. They were obvious enough already, akin to the superstar baseball players with giant contracts. We needed to focus the bulk of our energy on people who had their own blogs or answered everyone's questions on the tech-support forum. We had to reach out to the people who influenced huge swaths of customers but did so from a lesser-known platform. Like Beane did with the Oakland A's, we needed to find the lesser-known players who do what it takes to win but don't get the huge contracts and the headliner endorsements.

In the years since, we've built and tested this theory dozens of times with leading companies across a variety of industries. It's been a home run every time.

THE NEW INFLUENCERS

You might not know your new influencers yet, but they have a significant impact on the choices your customers make. In fact, they probably have more influence than the people you read on a regular basis. For the most part, they're not professional writers, analysts, or MBA recipients. They're schoolteachers, emergency technicians, technology managers, and Starbucks baristas. But they all have one thing in common: They care deeply about the topic at hand, and they regularly channel that passion into engaging content that draws an audience.

Over time, the combination of their passion, their content, and their audience lends them a credibility that rings truer than any press release or ad you put out. They become trusted peers for your customers. In the Pre-Commerce ecosystem, a company has to understand the value of this peer influence, why a topic carries more weight than its brand ever can, and how it can find its new influencers.

Peer Influence

By now, you've heard all about the outsize influence peers have on e-commerce (or any decision made online, for that matter), but few of today's business leaders understand why.

We briefly discussed the primary answer in Chapter Three: the 1–9–90 rule. It's pivotal to understanding how online influence works, so let's revisit it here. We grew up hearing about the 80/20 rule, where 20 percent of the people do 80 percent of the work. It doesn't happen that way online. On the Web, we find that 1 percent of the population are the *original content producers.* About 9 percent of the people are the *content distributors,* sharing links and their take on the ideas forwarded by those original content generators. The remaining 90 percent are the *lurk-and-learn* crowd, who read, watch or listen to a wide range of content as they research purchases and come to a decision.

It works as a good rule of thumb, but understand that the actual numbers for any given market will vary, sometimes significantly. If you are looking at laptops, you have an active market that may tip higher toward the content generators. If you are in markets geared toward older customers, you often see a remarkably low number of generators but a massive lurk-and-learn population. With a little research, a company can get a good picture of the ratio for their business or industry. One easy way to test this is to look at the monthly searches conducted about a topic and compare that with the number of conversations about it. I recall one example for glaucoma that generated more than 400,000 searches in one month but sparked just a few hundred conversations. Don't let a lack of conversation fool you into thinking nothing is going on.

Don't overthink it all, either. It's human nature to share information about things we care about. It's natural that we allow sources we trust to influence our decisions. If my friend, Dave Judge, sends me an update on the New York Yankees' star shortstop Derek Jeter and his march to 3,000 hits, I'll probably share it with friends. After all, I have a passion for the sport, I like Derek Jeter, and I trust Dave's judgment on baseball matters. If the Yankees sent me the same information, I'd read it but probably wouldn't share it.

The bloggers who write about your company do the same thing when they look for their next post. They're not always interested in what you have to say. It's the topic that matters to them, not the company.

The Topic Is More Important Than the Brand

Business leaders spend so much time inside the company walls, carefully crafting a rich story about their brands. They come up with a list of key messages, supporting materials, and special spokespeople. We like to think our customers want to hear from us more often. It's hard to wrap our heads around the fact that the topic matters, not the company, as a source of information. Customers don't care about your carefully crafted story; they care about the one piece of it that interests them. The topic is where influence happens.

If you think like a traditional company leader, you overlay that mindset on the Pre-Commerce world and start to think customers want to talk about your brand. You reinforce that with every mention of the company, even if the posting only discusses a miniscule fraction of your story. With all the conversations occurring each day online, it's awfully easy to create your own self-fulfilling prophecy.

Given the Pre-Commerce transformation under way, you have to proactively remind yourself that real influence centers on the topics about which customers have a passion. Consider, for example, cholesterol. A company that develops a treatment for high cholesterol does a survey of the online activity about its new product. It studies the Pre-Commerce landscape for mentions of high cholesterol, and of course finds dozens of conversations and influencers. But without a careful, deeper search—a search that considers the topics instead of the brand—this company could overlook the dozens of subtopics that are driving the conversation about its brand. Customers don't think about high cholesterol and leave it at that. They're searching topics such as diet, nutrition, symptoms, HDL, LDL, treatments, side effects, and on and on. In each one of those topics, an influencer is driving the conversation and swaying your potential customers toward you or your competitor. Each company might have ten very valuable subgroups to consider, or many more.

You need to know who drives influence for each topic that's important to your brand.

David Witt, senior manager of social engagement at General Mills, knew he found an influencer the first time he discovered "Hungry Girl," a Web site (hungry-girl.com) and free daily e-mail created by Lisa Lillien. Witt said he met Lillien in early 2006 through e-mail, when she had about 100,000 consumers on her e-mail list. Today, he said, more than one million people receive her free daily e-mail, she has three best-selling books to her name, and she just started taping her own television show. She has become a media property in her own right, with a reach that rivals many brand-name media outlets—and she did it in four years with minimal resources.

"She is a great writer with a unique and fun voice," Witt said. "She has excellent taste buds. She has a clear definition of her niche, she sticks to it and she writes about weight management that tastes good (my words, not hers). . . . She creates something that is bite-sized for a lot of people, not something really large for a few people." Her rising popularity has made her a go-to influencer for many of General Mills brands. When the company launched its Fiber One chewy bars, Witt said, the marketing teams made sure Lillien had tried them and had all the information she needed to write about them. The Hungry Girl endorsement sparked online word of mouth, which helped drive early sales, he said. General Mills went back to her with its Progresso light soup and its Yoplait Fiber One yogurt.

The amazing thing is how there are passionate ambassadors with major influence for any product. If you are interested in cameras, you will find experts on film formats, accessories, camera designs, the mechanics of a camera, image galleries, and antique plate cameras. Experts focus on what they know. Communities coalesce around experts they trust and who add value to their lives. Communities intuitively know that no one person is an expert on everything, so they listen closely to the people who know what they're talking about.

How to Find the Influencers

In the technology world, we have one of the best examples right in front of us every day. If you want to know the hottest stories at anytime, day or night, you go to www.techmeme.com, which lists the most widely shared stories. And if you look at the Leaderboard, which shows you who drives each story, you'll find about three of every four outlets are blogs.

There's a reason for the bloggers' considerable influence. People will follow someone who comes up with something new and intelligent to say about a topic they enjoy. They will follow the 1 percent—the *original content producers*—and read just about anything of interest they produce. It's just that simple: If you write original content people care about, you'll have influence. People will read your post and forward it. They'll download your video and send the link to like-minded friends. They'll friend you on Facebook and follow you on Twitter. And more often than not, they'll take your advice and act accordingly. If you are simply repackaging news, it doesn't matter what brand name you work for. But if you produce worthwhile content, it doesn't matter what your URL says. People will find you.

Life doesn't happen that neatly, of course, and neither does Pre-Commerce. Some journalists continue to hold tremendous online sway. People never really get to know a lot of community forum leaders. As for most of the world's bloggers, they post their daily feed for an audience of friends—their community. Today, companies have to make sense of all this. They need to develop a way to separate the wheat from the chaff—to group the influential name-brand journalists with the unknown community forum leader and the largely unknown blogger.

Mainstream media always kept a close watch on the pharmaceutical industry. I saw it during my days at CIBA-GEIGY, but Ray Kerins and his colleagues at Pfizer have seen more of the external scrutiny shift steadily to social media. Ray points to Scott Hensley, who pioneered new ways to cover the industry for the *Wall Street Journal* Health Blog and now is transforming the way National Public Radio covers health care and the pharmaceutical industry. The news cycle now runs 24/7, and journalists like Hensley are becoming more and more like bloggers and other social media participants. Ray has tweaked his communications teams at Pfizer to accommodate this changing form of journalism—but also to accommodate the way bloggers are becoming more and more like journalists.

"I knew we had to have a blogger strategy in place," he said. "So we focused on the top twenty bloggers for our industry and started treating them like we do our top-tier press. We had no choice. Their content syndication is so impressive, and their deadlines aren't tied to a printing press. The 3 P.M. call might come at 11 P.M. now, and we have to be ready for that. There might not be any editorial oversight, because the emphasis now is time to market and bloggers are putting out a lot of news."

THE BRAND MEME

At WCG, we made *Moneyball* come alive. In the summer of 2009, I asked Paul Dyer, our head of social media for North America, to help us build an algorithm that would identify the core influencers of virtually any brand. Paul came up with an algorithm that weighs twenty-seven measurements of online influence. It might sound complicated, but the underlying premise is remarkably simple: If someone posts something relevant and potentially influential, what they say will be shared and indexed in search engines. People will find ways to subscribe to their content, follow them online, and "friend" them at networking sites. We identified twenty-seven ways the other 99 percent—the *content distributors* and *lurk-and-learn* crowd—access and share influential content. And this, of course, leads us back to the influencers themselves.

We couldn't work the other way. First, there are far too many original content producers to follow what each one said on any given day. More important, we had to make sure we know how influence flowed, not just its source. We couldn't just find the spring and understand where and how people drank its waters. We had to chart the entire river as well. We started thinking about the idea of a "brand meme," following on the notion of online memes—the topics and ideas that spread across the Web through shared writing, speech, rituals, and other ways people convey a concept. A meme spreads not only because the online community wants to share content, it spreads because people care how and where the point is made. Ever see a Lolcat online (http://icanhascheezburger .com)? They have no purpose other than simple humor, but because so many people find them funny, they've become one of the most enduring memes out there. Most business leaders would kill to have a brand meme with the online staying power of the Lolcats.

The point is, we knew we couldn't just identify the influencers and call it a day. We had to identify the patterns of influence, and we had to understand how and where influence happened. People care when someone they consider influential suggests something to check out or do. In most cases, we have already decided this person is influential, because we follow their Tweets, have an RSS feed from their blog, or connected with them on LinkedIn. And we create our own rituals for each community. If John Battelle, the CEO of Federated Media, writes about something I find interesting, I'll see it on my Facebook page because I don't look for John's stuff in other places. I read *The White Tiger,* by Aravind Adiga, because John posted a recommendation on Facebook. As expected, I enjoyed the book, too, so I went right back to Facebook and recommended it to my friends.

Customers make the call on whether they'll share what they learn with their peers. They'll choose who they trust and who they'll learn from, and it's a choice they often make subconsciously. *Your customers live in a meme-driven world. If you don't identify and research your own brand memes, you'll never really know who's influencing your customers and how.* Your company needs to capture more than content; it needs to navigate the entire river of influence. Only then can you understand who holds sway in the Pre-Commerce world.

We crafted our brand meme algorithm to search for content producers, whether an individual or an outlet, and track their reach, relevance, and ability to syndicate content on a particular topic. (Remember, topics matter more to customers than brands, and as much or more than individual influencers.) We built in metrics that look at the number of fans and followers a content producer has on social media sites. It tracks the number of times a search engine indexes a content producer's headlines on the topic at hand. It factors in the number of topical search results we find for each content producer, the number of bloggers who link to their Web site, and the percentage of their Tweets that mention a brand, a key topic, or more. This way, we can track both the influencers and the path of their influence.

We then scrape all the available information online—basically everything that is public—and whittle the results down to a list of the top forty or fifty people who have the most influence for a specific brand or category of interest. There's no guesswork; each influencer is quantitatively ranked. We know their exact online network—where they blog, who sees their Tweets, where customers take their original content and share it with even more friends, and on and on and on. We make sure we know how to reach each influencer, and we make sure we know their ecosystem.

I can't say we have a bulletproof algorithm. No one does. But this type of process will take care of 90 percent of the job that seemed so overwhelming earlier. And now you can narrow your research to find the online influencers who don't show up in your brand meme. Combine both channels of research, and you will have a precise map that shows who is driving the share of conversation about your brand. You will know who to call. You will have the invite list for your meetings and events. You'll identify your ambassadors, your critics, and the influencers who don't care either way (the people with whom you can engage in hopes of fostering more brand interest). You know exactly who has influence and how they wield it. Now it's just a matter of acting on your knowledge.

BUILDING A REAL RELATIONSHIP

Dr. Kevin Pho—or Kevin MD, as he's known online—consistently shows up as one of the top influencers for health care companies, yet most of those firms have never met or spoken with him. Kevin has an internal medicine practice in Nashua, New Hampshire, but he also has a huge following on Twitter, Facebook, and through RSS feeds from his Web site (www.kevinmd.com). In fact, his Web site has more traffic and influence than most health care company sites. The mainstream media realized Kevin's influence could add value to their own content. He's now a member of *USA Today*'s board of contributors, and he frequently contributes to CNN.com and the *New York Times*. He's easy to find, even if most health care companies pay him no mind. More and more, though, the opposite happens. Companies now on the prowl for brand influencers find that they often are far more subtle and a bit harder to find than Kevin is, yet they can exert just as much influence.

David Marshall was one of the most passionate customers for Dell's global consumer business. Known online as "gbakmars," David is a high school math and science teacher in Michigan. He has served as a missionary to China and Nepal, he's fluent in Chinese, and he's just an all-around good guy. As I started talking with him,

I realized my interaction with David and other top influencers wasn't just about responding to a complaint or sending out some product information. This was about passion and building a relationship for the long haul. The protocol and the rules that governed my relationship with mainstream journalists didn't exist here. The only rule was this: Build a normal relationship, just as you've done for years in all your communities.

It really hit me when David agreed to fly to Round Rock, spend a day with us, and share all his thoughts on Dell. By then, he already had contributed thousands of posts to Dell forums and advocated on behalf of customers who wanted us to be more responsive. But when he visited, I found myself spending as much time learning about David as he did about me. As we strolled into Rudy's Country Store and Bar-B-Q in Round Rock, our conversation turned to our children, living abroad, and our hobbies. We couldn't care less about laptops at that moment—just two new friends out for some good Texas barbecue. Months later, I'd get e-mails from David on the weekend checking in to say hello. We still keep in touch today.

David is a great person who happens to be passionate about certain topics.

TRY IT, YOU'LL LIKE IT

For the skeptics, the importance of identifying David, Kevin, and other online influencers becomes blindingly obvious once you go through the process. I regularly talk to executives who doubt an online content generator can have much influence on their customers. I encourage them to identify a few of the easiest-to-find influencers and just observe how the brand message sways. I have yet to find a business or executive who hasn't had some sort of "Aha!" moment, an epiphany as they discover a sweeping base of influence they've overlooked. And once they see it, they act on it:

- A leading technology company analyzed which influencers were driving conversations across several product launches. Despite seeing hundreds of influencers who could have a potentially important impact on each launch, they determined that four people, all at different Web outlets, drove two-thirds of the online news flow. The company quickly reached out to them.

- A diagnostics company discovered that the top community forums in their market segment constantly linked to the views of one small forum run by one woman. She drove a disproportionate amount of thought leadership around the brand, but the company never would've realized her importance if it had looked solely at her forum's online traffic. The company now brings her in for regular briefings about its products and services.

At WCG, we regularly help companies analyze how influencers share news and how that can impact both the length and the intensity of every news cycle. And that's where the real fun starts. As companies gain a deeper understanding of how information about their brand flows, they can start to extend the news cycle or up the intensity at key moments. For example, as the buzz about a new-product launch begins to ebb, a company can pump fresh content into the pipeline—new blogs, vlogs, podcasts, or other content. If the information is meaningful, topical, and new, it will recharge the conversation. Influencers will continue the conversation because they have a passion for the topic, and they have new content to share.

Conversations end due to a lack of content, not a lack of passion. The passion exists every day of every week of every year.

Mistakes We Can Avoid Now . . .

Some of the greatest global brands have littered the past thirty years with some of the worst product launches. Imagine how many we could have avoided if we could have listened then with the precision we can today.

- *New Coke.* Coca-Cola might have learned early on that its customers simply wanted the classic formula.
- *Crystal Pepsi.* Other than some marketing trends experts, who actually said consumers wanted a clear soda?
- *McDonalds Arch Deluxe.* People said they didn't want to pay more for an only slightly different burger.

I don't mean to call out these brands. Virtually every company has made their own misstep. Remember Smith & Wesson mountain bikes? Life Savers soda? Clairol "Touch of Yogurt" shampoo? Imagine how much money companies could save by simply responding to what customers already say and do online. Consider the invaluable information your influencers—the people who know your customers as well as anyone—can share with you at virtually no cost.

YOUR PASSION IS NOT THEIR PASSION

Next time you talk with one of your customers, give them a little pop quiz on the metrics you obsess about. Ask them to guess your most recent operating margin, or whether your capital expenditures are trending up or down. I can all but guarantee they won't know the answer, and I can all but guarantee your questions will be nothing but a bother for them. Customers don't care about the same things you care about, and neither do influencers. They don't sit down to calculate brand value. They don't figure out how much earnings are worth minus operating costs, taxes, and charges for capital employed. Most of today's online influencers couldn't care less about your ROI or cash flow. That's your problem, not theirs. It has no impact on how they look at things today, and their world is all about today. They either like a brand or they don't. And, quite frankly, they could care less if the brand exists five years from now.

We need an evolved model to reflect the full value that customers place on a brand. So save your calculator batteries, put away your net present value statements, and start looking much more closely at the value that each brand is building around the world with over two billion people online. Every day, they cast their ballot on the brands that truly matter in their lives, voting through their conversations and actions.

I've always liked *BusinessWeek*'s top 100 global brand survey. *Business-Week* and Interbrand put together a remarkably insightful list every year, and they deserve every bit of the respect the survey receives. However, it needs to be modernized to reflect how online influence shapes brand reputation in today's Pre-Commerce marketplace. Online influencers have a major impact on the world's top brands today, and they don't care about the same things researchers spend time studying. The *BusinessWeek* methodology says a company "must derive at least a third of its earnings from outside its home country, be recognizable beyond its base of customers, and have publicly available marketing and financial data." This definition excludes Walmart, most telecom companies, and pretty much every private company doing business today. Influencers don't care about those distinctions, and customers certainly don't, either.

If you want a quick way to see who has influence today in technology, go to techmeme.com and look at its Leaderboard. Of a hundred top influencers, about seventy-five are bloggers.

CUT THROUGH THE CLUTTER

Back at Novartis in 2004, Thomas Ebeling wanted us to figure out which message would penetrate and reach the right customers. He wanted us to know which messages our brand influencers would really care about, but he also wanted to know why.

If we were sitting in the same conference room today, we'd have the same conversation in reverse. I would say, "I know the top thirty-five influencers in France for our brand, and I know these five care more passionately about this topic than the rest." Thomas would flash his half-grin, searing-stare combination and ask, "What message can we deliver that will ignite their passion, and why will the message you develop work best?"

Companies can identify their influencers and build relationships with them, but the message still matters, too. How many times have you seen a great TV commercial but couldn't remember the product a day or two later? How many times have you sat through a fifty-slide presentation, heard the conclusion, and wondered what the conclusion really was? Companies just don't deliver many great messages anymore. It's not due to the media clutter—that's just a lame excuse. It's benign neglect. Few companies understand what it takes to create a successful message, and fewer companies understand what it takes to create a successful message that resonates online. If you can't get the right message to your customers, you have no chance of swaying their purchases.

But there's hope. Amid all the clutter, someone keeps crafting successful messages. Someone says something about your brand that other people listen to, engage with, and act upon. That someone is one of your influencers, and she's delivering the most important brand messages your company can have. You don't have to come up with a brilliant home run advertising campaign every time you swing the marketing bat. If you build a relationship with your influencers and give them the information they need to keep delivering fresh, high-quality content, they'll spread the message.

Just don't get too comfortable. Influencers aren't in it to regurgitate your messages word-for-word and beat-for-beat. If they don't like what they hear, they'll say so—and they'll say it loudly.

EMBRACE YOUR CRITICS

You won't have much trouble finding your critics. You simply employ the same processes we discussed to identify your brand ambassadors. The hardest part is knowing when to reach out and when you're better off just listening. Lord knows it's not fun to pick up the phone and call one of your most vociferous critics, but sometimes those uncomfortable situations turn to gold. Jeff Jarvis, a noted critic and author of the BuzzMachine.com blog, ripped Dell over his experiences with a laptop he'd purchased. He went through a nightmare customer experience, and wrote about it. Was it typical of most customers' experiences at Dell? Absolutely not, but that didn't matter. One of our customers had a problem, we didn't resolve it properly, and suddenly he was leading an anti-Dell crusade that's spreading across the Web.

It took several months before we reached out to Jeff, but once we did he started to share that experience, too. Years later, he said we were one of the first companies to really get the social media phenomenon—to participate in a conversation with customers, knowing full well that the customers shared control of the message. Jeff's Dell Hell saga won't go down as the crowning achievement in Dell's history, but looking at it with the benefit of hindsight it might prove to be one of the company's most vital realizations. Though still out on the horizon at the time, we at least caught our first glimpse of the Pre-Commerce world's shores.

Over my past five years at Dell, the Blog Council, and now with WCG, I discovered that online critics generally fall into three main categories. Whether they want to indiscriminately rip your company or simply offer a little constructive criticism, they follow one of the same three patterns of behavior. I call them *zealots, advocates,* and *service providers.*

Zealots aren't influencers in the strictest sense of the word. They might have influence, but it typically extends only to like-minded individuals who already share their views. A zealot's mind is closed, and even the most empathetic company will get zero credit from them. They believe they know all of the answers, and if you're not smart enough to agree with them they'll dedicate their lives to convincing everyone you're wrong. Think of them like seeds in the desert. Your ideas will find no purchase with them, so don't waste your time trying.

A zealot can argue almost any point on any topic, including the environment, world hunger, the deficit, or abortion. The issue doesn't matter. What matters is that they convince you they're right and you're wrong. *The zealots represent a very small percentage of your negative share of voice—very small.*

Advocates hear the anguished cries of their constituencies at all hours of the day. They can't rest at night because they might run out of time to help their audience. They obsess over a solution for a problem and don't rest until they've delivered one. In many cases, such as breast cancer, advocates have direct experience with their cause of choice. And that experience gives them a seemingly magical X-ray vision that allows them to see through the obstacles in their way. They will smash through the walls of governments, companies, and their own community organizations to get what they need, because people will die or suffer if they don't. Beware those who stand in the way.

A few advocates enjoy the ego boost they get when people notice their work, but most don't chase fame or exposure unless it helps their cause. They hope to put themselves out of business. They wish they didn't have to be advocates.

Advocates with a strong story often become extremely important influencers for your brand, and that can cut both ways. Get in their way, and they'll cut you down with a zealot-like fervor. Help their cause, and you become a hero. If they have an unbelievable passion for one of your brand categories, perhaps even on your brand alone, get to know them very well. They are worth every minute of your time.

Service providers often think of themselves as zealots or advocates, and sometimes it's hard to tell them apart. They make a job out of sharing information, providing services, and generally making sure the community they represent is well-served.

They have the least exciting job and often get less exposure than the advocates and zealots, but the service providers arguably take the most pragmatic and effective path of the three groups. They run Web sites, blog, send mailings, and post on forums, all to make sure the people in their community know what is available and how to access it. Service providers have a certain sense of honor about providing information, solutions to problems, and, in some cases, entertainment. They know they make a difference everyday and they know that few will recognize it, but it keeps them going nonetheless.

The service providers are your company's secret weapons. They will share positive information about your brand just as quickly and effectively as they share negative information. Every great online community has a strong group of service providers. Companies that identify and reach out to them will be building one of the Pre-Commerce world's most effective marketing channels.

CHAPTER FIVE

THE SECRETS TO SUCCESSFUL PRE-COMMERCE MARKETING

*Great wisdom not applied to action and
behavior is meaningless data.*

—PETER DRUCKER

You spent a week studying and the last two nights cramming. You created all kinds of bizarre acronyms to help you remember a crucial set of facts. Tired and in a pinch at 3 A.M., you even used an old T-shirt as a coffee filter. Now here you sit, with your No. 2 pencil sharpened and your palms sweating, preparing to take the biggest test of your collegiate life. . . . And that's when the professor says he's putting the answer key on his desk. All you have to do is come on up, read it, and figure out every answer on the test. "It's completely cool," he says as the class waits for the punch line. "Go for it."

Why wouldn't you take advantage of that opportunity? Yeah, your "A" grade on the test doesn't mean as much when the guy who didn't study gets the same mark as you, but taking an unnecessary risk by going blind reeks of even greater idiocy. Yet that's what almost every company

121

on the planet does today. Customers have provided the answer key to what they want to buy from you, and it's sitting there, online, available to anyone who wants to take a look. All you have to do is listen, ask a few questions, and accept the reality of what your customers tell you.

Of course, only a small few companies have started listening to the Pre-Commerce answers, and even fewer bother to ask questions and learn more. Worse, I probably can count on two hands the number of companies who've accepted the fact that their customers know more about the Pre-Commerce marketplace than their in-house and agency creative teams. They might not put it in your terms or interpret it for you, but face it, your customers know more than you. They're smarter than your boss. Heck, they're smarter than your boss's boss, and they're offering you the answers. "It's completely cool," they're saying as you're hesitating. "Go for it."

As I mulled over the idea of writing a book, it struck me that companies don't take advantage of the customer answer key because they have no idea how to read it. Business leaders haven't yet figured out how to properly measure Pre-Commerce activity. The current methodologies might give you a feel for a few of your customers' online activities—unique visitors or search trends, for example—but they fall woefully short of analyzing customer behavior.

WCG developed the Four As model to build a full picture of customer behavior, not just a listing of random online activities. The functional Pre-Commerce model produces a rich understanding of consumer behavior. It gathers the information and insight—not just the data—to tell a story about what your customers are learning, where they learn, and what they really think about your brand.

Consider for a moment the power that the Four As deliver if properly done. Your marketing agency walks through the door and presents two marketing campaigns, each based on real customer insight delivered by your Awareness efforts. You launch the first idea and within forty-eight hours your Assessment efforts show the campaign isn't connecting with customers. You're getting no Action. So you swap to the second idea, and it connects. You see searches for your brand go through the roof, recommendations shoot up, the online community spreads the message, and people sign up for more information. You increase your media spend, and sales and share of conversation skyrocket. You step up your interaction with the Pre-Commerce community, and you discover a new Ambassador who's excited about your brand and wants to spread the word. Customers are happy. You're happy.

Of course, that's not what really happens today.

WELCOME TO THE REAL WORLD

Today, your agency team struts into your conference room carrying a snazzy presentation, a confident handshake, and complete assurance they're about to deliver the mother of all marketing campaigns. This is the Big Idea you've always been waiting for—they've convinced themselves of it, and now they'll set out to convince you.

You listen to their ideas, and it strikes you that one of their ideas actually sounds terrific. You ask the agency to deliver on only that one, because the others were rather poor, quite frankly. (This, of course, is one of the oldest tricks in the agency book.) You know it's an expensive campaign you'll have to justify for months, but what the heck. This campaign might win awards. It will prove how progressive and innovative your company is. And it's going to work.

Of course, as soon as you start thinking like that, the campaign *has* to work. You've locked yourself into a three-month paid media plan now. But hey, you're used to spending big money, and it's a terrific idea, remember? Everyone around you agrees. So you launch it . . .

And it doesn't quite work. With a bit of finesse, you can pump up the results with some more spending. But you know deep down inside that this wasn't the Big Idea you hoped it would be when you invested all that time and money into it. But you sure can't tell anyone that, at least not above a whisper. If you do, you'll never get funding for your next Big Idea.

The Pre-Commerce model doesn't care about the next hit marketing campaign. It steadily and constantly focuses only on customer behavior and what customers want and need. Your marketing becomes an ongoing daily effort, rather than a sporadic events-driven and high-stakes approach. As customer needs change—and they constantly change—your media plan has enough built-in flexibility to adapt. You have several ideas ready at anytime, and you're not wedded to anything that ties you down. The only big idea you support makes the best and most productive connections with your customers in real time.

And now you start gaining credibility around the office, because you can see a losing effort a mile away and call it out immediately. You don't hesitate to adjust, refocus, and absolutely nail customer outreach. You can have more fun than in the old days, when you had trouble sleeping in the weeks before you launched the big idea—and before you knew whether customers would really care.

Kathryn Metcalfe, vice president of communications for Pfizer's Consumer, Animal Health, and Vaccines groups, said it well: "We have a 'fail fast' approach to innovation," she said. "When we think of Centrum, for example, one of our largest consumer brands, we will pilot an idea in a country, test its success, get the metrics right, and then scale it if it works or stop it if doesn't. We learn as much from failure as we do from success and, quite frankly, it's more fun to work this way."

KEEPING SCORE

I never quit playing basketball until the streetlights came on. I didn't set myself a lot of hard and fast rules, but this one was inviolable. Some evenings you'd find me at the Slayton Field courts deep into summer dusk. If the streetlamps weren't aglow, I was out there lighting up the baskets. I always imagined, somewhere across town, my nemesis staying an extra 30 minutes to take a few more free throws or practice a new shot. The kid smirked at me as he kept refining his jump shot, practicing his post moves, and building an advantage. I hated that smirk, so I would stay an extra 30 minutes and barely make it home for dinner.

I grew older, and I don't play basketball like I used to, but I can still see that smirk. I see it on the face of every business competitor. I see them sitting at their desk a half hour longer, checking the figures one more time and brainstorming a few more minutes. He's out there, pondering how to reach customers in the social media age. She's out there finding a new way to track and participate in the conversations her customers are having about her brand. Your competitor is out there, getting ready to dive in and learn as much as possible about the Pre-Commerce marketplace. And if you're committed to building a competitive advantage in this new age of commerce, learning and understanding how the Four As apply to your business is nonnegotiable. Without this platform, your company will never fully understand and assess its online impact—and your competitors will.

But if the Four As are akin to the fundamentals needed by every basketball player—free throws, dribbling, and so forth—the tools and models you use to measure your impact are unique to each player. The kid on the other side of town might've been a point guard who practiced his crossover dribble. I was a forward, practicing my footwork for post moves and rebounding. The Four As lie at the foundation of the successful Pre-Commerce model, but each company has to customize a measurement model that fits its business and its industry. Each company has to identify the behaviors that reflect the best possible experience for its customers. And to do that, every business leader has to gain a basic understanding of the four drivers common across all the FourAs— search, peer influence, active sharing, and available content.

4 x 4

The same four criteria will drive results across all Four As. When you measure your performance across Awareness, Assessment, Action, and Ambassadors, pay special attention to each of these:

- *Search.* Your brand's position on search engines and within the customer-search journey
- *Peers.* How peers position your brand vis-à-vis your competitor
- *Active sharing.* How people share positive and negative information about your brand
- *Available content.* On average, how readily fresh content is available about your brand

Social media experts have flooded the market with practical advice—some of it very good—for reaching customers through online blogs, forums, reviews, and the like. But no executive wants to waste his or her time hacking through the weeds of social media minutiae. I don't blame them; they have a lot more than marketing to worry about. That said, any business leader worth his or her salt knows how vital it is to have at least a high-level understanding of the factors that drive customers' purchasing decisions.

That's especially true now, given the fundamental market shifts set off by the emergence of Pre-Commerce behavior. You don't have to know all the details about what drives customer behavior and your brand reputation—the marketing teams can handle that with help from those dozens of books. However, every business leader has to have an overarching sense of the ways search, peer influence, active sharing, and available content drive the Four As of the Pre-Commerce marketplace.

How well your company optimizes these drivers will play an increasingly important role in your brand's success.

SEARCH

There are about 34,000 searches on Google per second. Since we often don't know exactly what we want, it is common for customers to conduct about four search queries to locate information about a potential purchase. For each of those queries, the customer rarely selects something other than one of the first three search results. So that leaves twelve sites of critical importance to your customers' experience. The list shrinks to just eight if you consider the mobile experience. (The smaller screens on mobile devices simply display less information.) Mobile customers still conduct four searches, but they look only at the top two results.

Business leaders have to take extra care to focus efforts on the best-possible learning experience in a narrow sliver of search results. Your marketing teams have to identify the contact for each link and reach out to them, both to build a relationship and to help provide the content they crave. Your team has to know the number of search results for each query, and at least once every quarter they review that data to understand how trends and results vary over time. The links and results will change based on what customers search for, and you have to be ready to change as the customers' experience does.

Finally, every executive should know the top five search terms related to the company's brand. The Google AdWords keyword tool will do this for you quickly and easily, and the knowledge you gain is invaluable. Consider the TomTom GPS example from Chapter One. If I type "navigation devices" into Google Adwords, the top customer search query is "buy global positioning system." Generic enough, sure, but the No. 2 result is "Garmin GPS," one of TomTom's top competitors. TomTom has no choice but to understand the behavior of customers who query "buy global positioning system," especially since it generates sixty times the volume of "Garmin GPS." But TomTom also needs to understand how and why potential GPS customers often search for its competitor by name.

Having ascertained where and how people start the search process, your company needs to go a little deeper and learn how customers use search to assess your brand and learn more about your products. When it comes to your brand, do customers tend to read text, watch videos, or both? Most people learn through a combination of text and video, perhaps with a little audio tossed in on the side. Your teams can start to track how company events, such as product launches, change the ways customers consume content about your brand. They might use different search terms, look for video instead of text, or go to an entirely different set of Web sites. If you're lucky, the changes will sway customers toward sites on which you have a strong brand message. If you're not lucky, you have to assess why customer habits changed and how you can adapt your online marketing to keep up with the changes.

Of course, the whole point of all this is to deliver the message that spurs customers to action. Pretty much every company on the planet already keeps tabs on how customers react to their marketing, hoping to align the customer's action with the behavior that benefits their brand, whether an actual purchase or a recommendation. As marketing teams develop more sophisticated methods for tracking online search, they'll start to learn how certain search terms relate to a customer's ultimate decision-making behavior. The phrase "camera Nikon" might indicate a general search, for example, while "buy new camera Nikon" indicates an impending purchase. Granted, it's often difficult to match exact sales data with online behavior, because so many variables influence a customer's action. But drawing correlations between online search patterns and definitive action can give business leaders a much clearer picture of the factors at play in the Pre-Commerce marketplace.

Finally, don't forget your ambassadors. They're the most passionate and consistent brand advocates you have, and more often than not they'll skew search results. Because they talk about your brand, product set, or industry on a regular basis, they show up in that coveted Top 12. As a business leader, you should understand the experience your ambassadors create for your customers. They might have a bigger impact on the market than the folks in your glass offices do. Take the time to build a relationship with them, and make sure your teams get to know them, too.

PEER INFLUENCE

The number of ambassadors for your brand won't overwhelm you. If you tell me you have 10,000 ambassadors, I know you're full of manure. They have real names, and you should know them because even though their numbers won't overwhelm you, their influence on your customers will. In the Pre-Commerce marketplace, ambassadors share ownership of your brand and your marketing messages. Work for them in the same manner you work for your shareholders. They can have more influence on their peers than you can ever hope for.

Ambassadors will spearhead your message online, but don't overlook the broader sphere of peer influencers. With an attentive eye and a few online tools, your marketing teams can readily identify the impact peers have on one another. Some of it is obvious, but very few companies understand the indirect impact these influencers have on customers outside the immediate conversational sphere. Search engines respect conversations just as much as they respect official company announcements. You put out a press release and a blog post, each of which include the phrase "Acme Rocket Skates" three times. Meanwhile, on an independent forum, potential customers have mentioned the term "Acme Rocket Skates" thirty-six times over the same period of time. The search algorithm doesn't care who said it. Your potential customers have twelve times more impact on the search results than you do.

Companies need to measure, understand, and influence the number of online conversations people have about your brand over any particular period. And your teams need to know what percentage of those conversations occur in the most influential communities. With some simple research through basic social media monitoring and analysis tools, you might find that 1,200 conversations occurred about "Acme Rocket Skates" over the last thirty days, an increase of 200 over last month. But on closer inspection, you realize that the number of conversations plummeted on the five community forums with the most influence on purchasers of Acme Rocket Skates. An increase in conversations is a good thing, but the sharp decrease in the most influential conversations—the ones that generate the most sales—completely offsets the increase. You might need to feed Wile E. Coyote, your top brand ambassador, some fresh content about the Road Runner's weak spots.

Every business leader should take a few minutes each week to look at peer recommendations, peer "shares," and peer conversations. These insights will give you a quick and dirty look at how customers are receiving your messages, what they think about your products, and how customer perception and behavior is changing over time. Executives should start to gain a sense of the number of times someone recommends their brand or shares content related to their brand, and they should know how that has changed since the last time they checked. This simple metric will let you know whether influencers have swayed perception in your brand's favor, or whether you and your teams have some work to do.

ACTIVE SHARING

Just as some community forums have more impact on your customers' purchasing decisions, so also do your company's individual online influencers. In almost every case, these influencers actively share content about your brand through their blogs, forum posts, and all kinds of other social media sites. Your marketing teams need to identify these active peers, know which ones take a positive, negative, or neutral view of your brand, and track how their opinions change over time.

At the outset, your company should know how many active peers it has and what they're saying about your brand, because by sharing content they increase their impact on their direct audience as well as search-engine results. As you go forward, you want to measure the increase or decrease in the number of peers who distribute content by linking to a blog, re-Tweeting a post, or through fresh content they generate based on what they read into the ongoing conversation. Ultimately, your teams should start to use an algorithm, similar to WCG's BrandMeme, that will measure the actual influence each active peer has on your customers.

As you continue to measure the rate of active sharing about your brand, you'll see how often people take the content your company generates and spread the word. Every company wants to see influencers take its message and put it in their own words, but few understand how to craft a message that allows influencers to easily do that. Do you put out content in the right medium (e.g., text or video)? Do you provide content, such as a promotion, that spurs customers to learn more, perhaps even buy? Do you create an environment that encourages interaction and active sharing?

It's easy to ask those questions and then let your active sharing slip off, unanchored, into the blogosphere. As a company starts to integrate social media into every facet of its business, it can start to bring the virtual and real worlds together in a way that naturally promotes content generation and sharing. Hewlett-Packard has used social media to amplify and extend some of its real-life signature events into the Pre-Commerce environment. "As our audience registers to attend an event, it's a good moment to open a conversation with them," explained Scott Anderson, vice president of customer communications for HP's enterprise business. "During our events, we also promote virtual conversations within and across the entire event. Influential bloggers and tweeters get access to products and key HP employees. They typically blog, tweet, or podcast right from the show floor. This works so well because others in the audience respond, and it initiates some great conversations. Additionally, it amplifies our message far beyond the walls of whatever venue we are holding our event in."

HP uses flat-screen monitors to stream Twitter feeds associated with the events. It holds tweet-ups to bring together the online community and solidify those relationships with a handshake. The company can initiate conversations before the event begins—in one case, Anderson said, it allowed the social registrants to choose the entertainment for the closing party. And after everything ends, social media allow the conversation to continue.

To keep the conversation moving, HP has to work diligently to track the types of content most often shared by its brand ambassadors and other influencers. The companies that do this will gain a significant advantage over competitors who don't—assuming those teams put the insights they gather to good use. Knowing how many conversations your ambassadors initiated during the last campaign or at the last real-life event doesn't mean squat if you don't give them the right content to help them initiate the next one.

SHOWING CUSTOMERS HOW TO MAKE CHEERIOS

David Witt and his colleagues at General Mills run one of the best company-created blogging networks on the Web. The network, called MyBlogSpark, is an excellent example of what an open mind and a dash of creativity can build.

"When we created MyBlogSpark, one of our main tenets was to make it easy for these great consumer journalists (i.e., bloggers) to interact with us," Witt told me. "We have endeavored to stay true to that tenet, and the bloggers continually let us know that's one of the main things they love about the network. More than 90 percent of the members have found MyBlogSpark through word of mouth, and it continues to prove what we learned early on—consumers are not just willing, but very willing to interact with us."

General Mills didn't stop there. The company created a program called MyGetTogether, which made it easy for interested consumers to host in-home parties. It also started *Pssst . . .* , a network of more than 200,000 connected consumers who have opted in to a program that gives them access to behind-the-scenes views of General Mills operations, special offers, gifts, and news about the brands they follow. While only a fraction of *Psst . . .* members have blogs, they influence thousands of other consumers through their online and offline relationships.

Witt said he realized the power of these communities at one of the first events the company hosted for its MyBlogSpark bloggers. "I tried to speak individually with as many of the bloggers as possible," he said. "The theme was the same: 'Tell us more about General Mills. We want to hear more.' They asked to see firsthand how Cheerios were made and they offered to vet any of our marketing or new product ideas. It was clear that they wanted to be part of the process."

AVAILABLE CONTENT

How far content about your brand spreads will make or break your rankings on search engines. With each campaign, companies have to provide fresh, pertinent, and easily shared content to allow its ambassadors, influencers, and other customers to take part in the conversation. As a business leader, you have to understand the relationship between available content, your company's share of conversation on the most-influential social media sites, and how both of those impact your brand image and your sales.

A pharmaceutical company with a new diabetes medicine might focus on the top areas of online influence—the most trusted sites for information about the ailment. The firm checks YouTube video results and discovers 5,000 relevant videos about diabetes. Of those, only fifty videos discuss its newly released medicine, giving it a 1 percent *share of conversation*. The company looks a little deeper and finds that videos about the top five similar medicines have been viewed 50,000 times. Of those, its brand has only generated 5,000 views, giving it a 10 percent *share of voice* within its competitive set. Armed with this information, the marketing department realizes it has to make more content available to its influencers.

I can't stress enough the importance of providing fresh and useful content. The brilliant chaps from Monty Python featured a hilarious and useful sketch in their movie, *The Meaning of Life*. In the sketch, a plaid-coated waiter presents a middle-aged tourist couple with a menu of conversation topics. The couple peruses the menu and, upon the waiter's recommendation, chooses a discussion about the meaning of life. The waiter starts them out with some talking points, but of course the conversation goes awry—it is Monty Python, after all. After a brutally awkward attempt to discuss the meaning of life, the couple eventually selects another topic. Put on your plaid jacket, because you're the waiter in this scenario. If you don't provide the right content to the right audience at the right time, your customers will go talk about something else—probably your competitor's brands. (Either that, or they'll badmouth your jacket and stiff you on the tip.)

If you've focused your marketing teams on the Pre-Commerce environment, they'll know the questions customers are asking about your brand. They'll assess the traffic on your industry's top Q&A sites. They'll count the downloads related to the most-asked questions. And they'll calculate the share of answers you provide versus your competitors. It's not enough to have key questions answered on your Web site if it takes customers three extra clicks to get there. You have to build marketing teams who recognize a deficit of content and know how, when, and where to fill it—whether on Yahoo! Answers, Twitter, Facebook, or the other dozens of sites where customers go to find, assess, and buy your products. You want 100 percent of your online customers to have easy access to important answers and insights, not the mere 10 percent who visit your Web site.

You don't have to do this alone. Your ambassadors will be more than happy to help you, assuming you're willing to help them, too. By this point, you should know your ambassadors personally, and your teams should know their habits and preferences. When you need to push more content into the marketplace—whether to fill a gap or to turbocharge the ongoing conversations—your teams should know what content your ambassadors want to see. How do their most-shared items compare with your most-supplied items? What percentage of the content you supply do your ambassadors share, and how does that compare with overall shared content on the topic at hand?

You'll see a content gap, especially at the outset. Online content producers rarely see the content they really want and need to keep and build their audience. As a leader in your company, you have to make sure your teams can fill the gap and provide your ambassadors with the exact content, in the right medium, at the right time. They'll appreciate your effort, and they'll share your content.

ACTION DRIVERS: SHIFTING OUT OF NEUTRAL

I have frequent flyer accounts with ten major airlines, from American to Virgin and most of the major U.S. carriers in between. Each one reaches out to me with letters from leadership I never read, e-mail offers I never use, and new membership cards with special perks because I fly a lot. I'll admit I take full advantage of the perks, but I couldn't care less about most of the stuff they send me. I'm just another name in their databases, about as neutral as you can get. Yet with a little effort, any one of these airlines could stir up my passion.

Most businesses can reach their customers pretty easily—another database!—but few companies use the access customers grant them to build any sort of relationship. So a massive swath of customers goes neutral on the brand. They might get aggravated on occasion by yet another impersonal e-mail or enjoy a particular experience, but for the most part they pay the brand no mind.

Decent marketing departments love to measure positive, post-transaction responses. They pore over negative feedback in search of improvements. But few take the time to study the lack of response, and that's a dangerous oversight. *Neutrality translates to a lack of passion, and a lack of passion is deadly in the Pre-Commerce world.* In fact, it can be more toxic than a negative response, which at least gives you an opportunity to address the problem. Said another way, if you deal effectively with negative share of voice, your response can draw otherwise neutral customers in your direction.

Neutrality is, in many respects, the first step in the death of a brand. It doesn't prompt any action. Worse, it leaves your customers open to your competitors. Most companies have access to their customers, but few use that access to pull customers out of neutrality. That's why I fly ten airlines I don't really care about, instead of one or two I really love.

THE NEW BIG IDEA

Step back into the conference room where you launched your last Big Idea marketing campaign. Only this time, you know how the drivers of Awareness, Action, Assessment, and Ambassadors impact your brand image and your customers' experiences. You've studied the Pre-Commerce marketplace.

The agency crew comes in, led by the senior account leader in his Cole Haan shoes, platinum cufflinks, and that ever-hearty handshake. His team has the next award-winning campaign ready to aim and fire, with the copy and a few flashy sketches to show you just how brilliant an idea it really is. It's a can't-miss Big Idea, he assures you.

Only it does miss. And you know it misses because you discovered the real Big Idea in a Pre-Commerce marketplace—you listened to your customers, and they told you what they really want.

Companies no longer can get by with the old school approach. The usual method—agency develops brilliant copy, focus groups verify the brilliance with a few tweaks, company adds more brilliance, and customer is blown away by brilliance—simply doesn't fly anymore. It's not the end of internal innovation or fresh ideas; it's the grounding of all that creativity in direct, real-time input from customers. The marketing gurus seek to learn from brand ambassadors. Ad executives consult with their audience to strike the right tone, message, and copy. Product developers ask users what new bells and whistles will enrich their experience.

The whole marketing cycle exists inside a Pre-Commerce ecosystem that's shared by the company and the customer. The executive who best understands this symbiotic relationship wins, which explains why Sona Chawla can point to an impressive record of success. Chawla serves as senior vice president of e-commerce at Walgreens, a position she earned after years of working and researching online commerce and customer behavior, including leadership positions at Dell and Wells Fargo. In the early days of e-commerce, she told me, online tools enabled utility and efficiency. Companies took routine customer activities, reengineered the processes underlying them, and offered customers a more convenient way to do those tasks—for example, checking your account balance on the Web. As that happened, though, customers started to reshape their own behavior to take advantage of that convenience, and they started to demand more of it.

"We noticed that customers who used online options became better customers," Chawla said. "They had lower attrition, higher satisfaction, and bought more products from us. This effect did not just exist with our 'best' customers. We saw this change in all customer segments once they started using online, regardless of income, tenure, age, etc." As e-commerce experts noticed these new levels of engagement, Chawla said, they realized they could use online tools to strengthen customer relationships. So they started to push the envelope in search of ways to enrich that interaction even further.

Chawla and other Pre-Commerce leaders are jumping headlong into the new uses and new technologies that are changing customer behavior today. Interaction through mobile devices has exploded over the past three years, especially with the introduction of smart phone applications. Walgreen's, for example, offers a "drugstore in the palm of your hand" app that allows people to refill prescriptions on the go or print iPhone photos at its brick-and-mortar stores.

This layering of new customer behaviors over old is creating a rich, online-offline experience, Chawla said. In some industries, the real-life store will become little more than a showroom for online purchasing. "People want choice, control, and convenience, and they will access what they want, where they want, and when they want," she said. "The customer experience will continue to improve, and the lines between online and offline channels will blur, especially thanks to the growth in mobile."

To connect with the Pre-Commerce customer, business leaders have to look beyond the surface and see the Web as more than a transactional channel. As Chawla's insight shows, *basic customer activity doesn't provide any insight on its own. The insight comes from observing the real behavioral change.* Traffic and page views, for example, offer only an early-stage measurement of your new ad campaign's success, but it can just as easily mislead you if you don't understand the behavior driving those activities. A highly inefficient site might generate a lot of click-throughs, but only because customers can't find what they need at first glance.

Web site traffic measures *activity*. What the customer did before and after visiting your site starts to address *behavior*. The new school of marketing watches how search traffic changes in response to a marketing campaign. The smart business leader tracks how much content her potential customers are sharing, and she will push her teams to supply fresh content and keep the conversation alive. Today's marketing executive will abhor silence and understand that neutrality equals an opportunity to activate customers in new ways.

A NEW APPROACH, AND A NEW LEVEL OF BRAND LOYALTY

The difference between activity and behavior is subtle. The winning company will commit the time and effort to interact and relate with Pre-Commerce customers and get a truer understanding of their behavior. The company that merely responds to online activity might get it right every now and then, but they consistently expose themselves to the likelihood of failure. I've talked with dozens of companies about these subtleties, because the consequences of each are starkly different. The best way to coax your customers toward behavior that favors your company is to make it personal, to build a direct connection between them and your brand.

Ferg Devins did a brilliant job of building connections between beer drinkers and Molson Coors Canada, where he's the chief public affairs officer. The company had dipped into social media to supplement its community-service and philanthropy efforts, Devins said, but the work didn't really pay off until it found a human and conversational tone. "I often said, 'What is more social than beer?'" Devins said. "It was a natural for launching into social media." He and his teams focused on bringing a human face and voice to the Web. Despite 224 years of brewing, he said, many beer drinkers see Molson Coors Canada simply as a "big brewer" and question its commitment to crafting really good beers.

"There are a couple of instances where people have remarked in a snarky manner about our beer," Devins said. "When we pick up those conversations we tend to invite those individuals to our brewery. They meet with our brewers and have a tour of the art of brewing and packaging. I would say that 100 percent of the time the individual is left altered and left with a more positive impression of our beers and the art of our brew masters and employees."

But Devins and his colleagues also made sure to engage the core of their customer base. Two days after noticing a Twitter user searching for the company's Molson Canadian beer in Maryland, Devins' team responded with a list of U.S. retailers who carried the brand. And during the 2010 Winter Olympic Games in Vancouver, Molson Coors Canada unleashed its employees and sent them out as roving reporters. They reported the games and associated activities through their own eyes, and the company used those dispatches to build a daily feed from the Games. The project generated more than 38,000 views of videos on the company's community Web site.

"You can take an unusual step now and then," Devins said, "and you can create loyalty that you never would've dreamed possible years ago."

CHAPTER SIX

BUILDING AMBASSADORS FOR YOUR BRANDS

*It's not the size of the dog in the fight, it's
the size of the fight in the dog.*
—MARK TWAIN

When David Marshall flew to Round Rock to meet with Michael Dell and our fledgling social media team, we hoped we could transform his previous negative experience into a much more positive one. But we didn't understand in 2006 how much impact such a simple, straightforward gesture could have.

David, whom I introduced in Chapter Four, contributed thousands of posts each year to various technology-hardware forums. He was a real enthusiast for the Dell XPS 700, the company's top-of-the-line gaming desktop, but he started running into some recurring problems with his equipment. Thanks to his participation in several top PC forums, he realized other gamers were experiencing the same problems. He could have taken the easy road and called our tech support, explained his problem, and asked for a fix or a special deal. He probably would have gotten all that he asked for. Instead, he became the leading voice for all the like-minded customers who were suffering through the same issues.

When Lionel Menchaca and our social media team at Dell started a dialog with David, he wasn't too thrilled with us. Frankly, we deserved his wrath, and we knew it. But we made it clear we wanted to change. We'd gone too long overlooking the hundreds of online conversations David and other Dell customers engaged in every day. So our teams had started reaching out to a lot of customers through social media. It seemed like the right thing to do, and we were getting a great response, but I didn't fully understand the point until David drove it home for me. He wasn't just annoyed with his experience, nor was he an enthusiast only when we got things right. In a sense, he felt his daily online contributions were critical to the lives of his audience—and to Dell's success as well. We found, much to our surprise and delight, that he felt as committed to helping us as we were to improving our service.

I finally realized, fully, what an online brand ambassador was all about. Ambassadors are genuine, honest, and motivated by a desire to help their peers. They don't have fancy titles or giant media brands backing them, yet they have a tremendous influence on Pre-Commerce customers. They're not part of a marketing campaign. They don't deliver testimonials or accept speakers' fees. They are their own people, making strategic decisions every day outside the knowledge of the company whose brand they love or hate.

So he flew down to Dell headquarters and we ensured he had time to speak directly with Michael. We took him out for barbecue and got to know him as a real flesh-and-blood person. Sure, we had selfish motives. We wanted to learn from a leading voice in the technology community, one who could speak to thousands of people about how we could improve. But as we got to know David, we knew we had to open a two-way street. We had to contribute to his cause, too. He wanted to make a difference to his audience and keep them informed with quality content. That was his passion, and we needed to feed it.

Your online brand ambassadors write hundreds or thousands of blog and forum posts each year. They can reach millions of your current and potential customers with a single post. They talk about your brand almost every day, because it's a central part of their lives. Whether positive or negative, they're your ambassadors. You need to meet them, understand their passion, and figure out how you can become a relevant and helpful part of their work.

SOCIAL MEDIA MYTHS

Ambassadors exist in virtually every category for every brand, but you probably don't know them. Pretty much every semiconductor company on the planet has an ambassador at forums.overclockers.co.uk. If your company researches Parkinson's disease, lizzy4451 knows you better than you think. The 70-Something Blog knows how to put you in touch with senior customers. But the fact remains: Few companies have any clue about their ambassadors because they don't hide in e-mail lists and databases. They live in the Pre-Commerce world, where they drive their own influence. They might like you, they might not, but they passionately discuss your brand with their peers, sharing ideas and knowledge or solving problems. They reach people you don't even contemplate with your traditional approach to marketing.

So like anything we don't know or can't see, we start creating myths in a vain attempt to explain the phenomena we see. With all its wild explanation and expectation, the Pre-Commerce world would make ancient Rome proud.

The most popular myth involves *viral video*, the brilliant marketing campaigns that spread far and wide across the Internet. The ad agencies love this one, and so do companies. Yet it starts with the unfounded command-and-control notion that "we" know what "you" like, and we'll give it to you.

You might recall the Chevy Tahoe SUV promotion in 2006 that offered people a chance to build their own commercials for the Web. Sounds like a great idea, but hundreds of videos emerged that lashed out at General Motors as an environmentally challenged company. GM has done a significantly better job of online marketing since then. It's a leading innovator in a lot of its social media efforts. But its failure with the Tahoe promotion taught everyone a lesson: You can't tell your customers how to share their experience with you. They don't respond on cue like trained circus performers. They respond to who they want, when they want, where they want.

I call the second myth *artificial turf,* because companies sometimes think they can just synthesize ambassadors from thin air. A few years ago, Edelman public relations came up with an idea to have "Jim and Laura" travel around the United States in a recreational vehicle named Wally 1. They slept in Walmart parking lots and blogged about all of the nice people they met along the way. But readers quickly saw through the campaign and blasted Walmart and Edelman for fabricating what they passed off as the everyman's experience. The campaign backfired so spectacularly, it spawned an entirely new term—flog, a fake blog. The Pre-Commerce world doesn't do fake.

I know the folks at Walmart and Edelman. They're great companies with smart people. Like General Motors, both of these companies have done some fantastic social media work since their early blunder. You will make mistakes. It happens. But if you make honest mistakes—and admit them when you do—you should have no problem rebounding from them. Just please, please, please don't be fake or intentionally misleading.

"You will get caught if you try anything sleazy," said Andy Sernovitz, head of SocialMedia.org. "You are being watched by millions of eyes that have the tools to out you if you try anything that even appears inappropriate. Your brand will be called out, you'll be humiliated, and the damage will be a measureable loss in sales. There is no more gray area. There is no more hiding behind corporate communications."

Business leaders still love the mythical *power of the database*. Companies often brag about how many people reside in their databases, as if the people inside them care. These faceless collections of information have their uses, admittedly, but none of your customers will brag to friends about their residence in your database. The last thing you'll ever hear at a cocktail party is, "You wouldn't believe it, but I was entered in two new databases today! I can't wait for the company to send me personal-looking e-mails that have nothing to do with my interests. I love deleting useless e-mail." Companies often associate database denizens with loyal customers, even though many, if not most, of them simply filled out a one-off registration to simply pick up a promotion you offered. Be careful you don't overestimate their allegiance to your brand.

If the myth of *general reach* were true, companies could tap every potential customer on the shoulder at a moment's notice. At one point or another, almost every business leader I've met has talked about how many people the company can reach—"ten million people by e-mail!" or "one million every month with our catalogs." At least 99 percent of your current and potential customers toss the catalogs and delete your e-mails before looking at either one. All you have to do is look at your personal e-mail account each day and you realize how many companies are "reaching" you with their deals and advertisements. How many of those do you actually read before hitting the delete button? Companies simply don't reach as many people as they like to think.

Finally, we have the grand myth of the *testimonial*. Now, don't get me wrong: If you can convince someone to provide a positive testimonial for your brand, well done. Maybe they didn't even need much convincing—all the better. Either way, none of it means anything if they don't influence anyone. Testimonials by people with low or no influence lead to, well, low or no chatter on your brand. Worse, more cynical customers might scoff at your brand for betting on a social media also-ran. Remember, the best testimonials are from real people who we can relate to, whether they are a celebrity or not.

MAKE IT PERSONAL

Each myth ultimately boils down to the same simple truth: You don't get to choose your ambassadors. You can't create them. The online communities of the world make that call, and you have to become smart enough to find them and become a relevant part of their world. It shouldn't take too long for an observant and thoughtful marketing team to discover their company's ambassadors. Once you look in the right places, they're all but impossible to miss.

The tough part is becoming a relevant part of their lives, because it requires a real interaction that seems anathema to most businesspeople. Too many business leaders still operate under the Godfather Principle: "It's business. It's not personal." But the Godfather Principle only works when the company (i.e., the family) can strong-arm its customers, its competitors, or both. That doesn't fly in the Pre-Commerce marketplace, where personal relationships, mutual respect, and the Golden Rule dictate success or failure.

Don't take my word for it. Here's how David Marshall described his trip to Dell in a comment he left on Jeff Jarvis' blog, Buzz Machine.com:[1]

> In September I emailed Michael Dell, briefly outlined my
> concerns, and offered to fly down to Round Rock and share my
> ideas on what Dell could do to take better care of its customers.
> Two days later Michael Dell's VP of communications emailed
> back and extended an invitation to come on down. Was I

surprised? Yes and no. A recent *Wall Street Journal* article on
Dell, that featured me in the opening paragraph, didn't hurt my
chances, but to make it to the top was encouraging to say the least.

Dell, to my surprise, took my visit seriously. They not only gave
me the red carpet tour, but they sat me down with vice presidents
and engineers; anyone and everyone that had the power to make
a difference. Why was I so confident that Dell was truly listening?
Because they wrote down my suggestions! Dell was interested in
what I had to say. They were interested in me. They really did
care about the concerns and feelings of their customers.

I met with Michael Dell for over a half an hour and this is what
I learned. He was a compassionate man, who genuinely wanted
HIS customers to experience the value that Dell representatives
are famous for speaking about. I had a burden and a message
that I had traveled with. I came to challenge Dell to do what few,
if any, American Corporations are willing to take a risk and do:
Admit failure, say 'I'm sorry' and make it right. I even used the
word challenge, which in hindsight was a bold thing to say to
the founder of one of the world's most successful corporations.
I challenged Michael Dell to turn this failure into success. When
that meeting ended, I knew I wanted to be that guy's friend!

About Lionel Menchaca, the company's chief blogger and Marshall's
official sponsor for the trip, Marshall wrote this:

> He allowed me to see the human side of Dell. He showed me
> compassion and care. He never bragged. He was never guilty
> of the kind of listening that nods and quickly moves to his next
> point about what he was doing. My concerns were real and
> Lionel never tried to explain them away with Dell philosophy.
> [. . .] He apologized for Dell's failure to meet customers with their
> concerns. He took criticism with every intention of becoming a
> better company. And most importantly he made me feel that Dell
> wasn't just using my advice to make Dell better, but to make it
> better for Dell's customers.

When my Dell colleagues and I started reaching out to the David Marshalls of the world, we started to realize that business in the Pre-Commerce world was, in fact, personal. Sometimes that means you can't win someone over. Some zealots will dislike your brand—and dislike it very loudly—and you won't win them over no matter how hard you try. Others care deeply about a topic that involves your company, even if they're ambivalent about your specific products and services. You can work with them to solve a problem or work for the greater good, whatever that might be. Still other people have a real passion about your products. They want to see you succeed, and they're willing to help your teams find that path to success. Learn from them. Take advantage of the opportunity to improve by listening to your customers. Invite the David Marshalls into your halls, then sharpen your pencils and start taking notes.

GET TO KNOW YOUR AMBASSADORS

The Pre-Commerce marketplace lives on the Internet and flows through all kinds of high-tech gadgets. But behind each ambassador's screen name is a real person. At some point, you have to set all the technology aside and get to know them. Start by collecting this information for each of your ambassadors:

- First and last name—You have to know exactly who they are.
- Their network—Describe how they have influence (e.g., leader of a top forum, or one of the top fifty drivers of share of conversation for your company).
- Location—Where do they live? Try to meet them during your business trips.

- Topic of expertise—Influencers are passionate about topics, not just brands. What are they most passionate about?
- How to reach them online—Who is their best friend at your company?
- Last time we talked—How frequently do your teams speak with this person?
- Content shared—An updated synopsis of the content your company provides them.
- Requests from customers—What do your customers want and how often do you bother to ask them?

If you can build a list of fifty people with whom you have a strong personal relationship and regular interaction, you're way ahead of the game. If you have hundreds or thousands on your first try, you're not defining ambassadors narrowly enough. If you have less than ten, you're like most of the world's top brands.

CUSTOMER INNOVATION

Brands attract ambassadors for a variety of reasons. Some companies have a corporate philosophy that customers rally around—think of Tom's Shoes and its joint mission to sell shoes and put them on the feet of kids in need. Other companies, such as Apple, build innovative new products that generate a ton of demand and spawn dozens of followers who want to break down the hardware design, the software, and the other product attributes. Ambassadors also love companies who provide them with options. Whether building your own computer or getting the right cup of coffee, if you have a choice you'll find an expert to offer some advice. Finally, good service never goes out of style, and if service is a key part of the experience, you'll find plenty of people ready to help you improve.

It's simple, really. People care passionately about the things that impact their lives—whether it's their country, a disease afflicting a family member, or the product that somehow enhances their lives. Every brand has a unique mix of factors that attracts customers, and companies can take advantage of those bonds to learn directly from customers and use that knowledge to improve their products and services.

Nokia is one of the most-respected brands in the world, and it pays the same high level of respect to its customers. The Finnish mobile phone titan created betalabs.nokia.com, a Web site that solicits feedback about products still in development. The company created the Web site, it says, "to share some of the exciting new things that we at Nokia have been working on and to gather feedback about how they work in real-life situations and how they can be improved." Essentially, Nokia has told its customers: We need your help if we want to build the best products for you. The site includes products in the beta phase, so they're under active development and of reasonably good quality—but not yet ready for prime time. The company doesn't promise that any product or customer suggestion will make it to market, but it might "graduate."

Nokia doesn't invite everyone to join the beta site, or the flood of information would make the program unwieldy. It asks users whether they own a relatively new and advanced Nokia product, whether they can handle a few rough edges in exchange for access to cool stuff, and whether they like to share ideas to improve the gizmos they use. The company targets the influencers and ambassadors who passionately care about its cutting-edge technologies—and then it listens to what they have to say.

IDENTIFYING YOUR AMBASSADORS

Nokia uses a few simple questions to identify the right type of ambassador for its product-development site. It works well for their approach, but what works for Nokia might not work for your company. In fact, it probably wouldn't. Anyone who tells you they have a foolproof and universal method for identifying specific ambassadors is trying to sell you seaside property in Kansas.

Fortunately, the Pre-Commerce research conducted by your marketing teams will help narrow down the list of top suspects. In almost every case, your ambassadors are included among the top fifty influencers who drive share of conversation for your brand. They also typically reside among the top ten influencers for all the topics that involve your brand. For example, Sony's search for its ambassadors might start with the fifty people who have the most online influence on its customers. The company can then search the top ten commentators about televisions in general, and maybe the top one or two influencers on social media discussions about the 54–890 megahertz frequency band.

Intuit came up with an idea that, at the time, was a novel way to identify its real ambassadors. (Dozens of companies have copied the idea since.) The company created a community site for its TurboTax software that allowed customers to solve other customers' issues, all out in the open and available for anyone to read, learn from, or, if necessary, correct. Any time you can empower customers to help each other, as Intuit did with its TurboTax community, you activate at least one of the three things they like to do—share ideas, knowledge, and solutions.

Your ambassadors and influencers love to throw out new ideas, whether you solicit them or not. No matter where and when they speak their piece, what your ambassadors say matters to the people who follow their blogs, Twitter feeds, or forum posts. You can't expect to provide one platform or launch one outreach program and have all your ambassadors magically walk into the fold. Short-sighted viral campaigns go away after a few months. Great ambassador-outreach efforts last forever.

Maker's Mark came up with a brilliant program to involve current ambassadors and find new ones. The popular distillery, based in Loretto,

Kentucky, has done a brilliant job of building a recognizable brand. It sells its bourbon in unique square-ish bottles, the necks of which are dipped in red wax. Every time I see the wax tendrils dripping down the neck of those bottles, I immediately recognize it as Maker's Mark. But even the most recognizable brands have to find ways to attract new customers.

Maker's Mark realized it could never sell itself to new bourbon drinkers as well as its biggest fans could. So it came up with the Maker's Mark Ambassadors, a program that engages its most-ardent enthusiasts while leveraging their support to spread the word. Ambassadors receive special promotions and a greater level of access to the company, but they also can invite new people to join the club. It sounds simple, and it is. If you make whiskey, you know you have a relatively small set of customers who really care about the ins and outs of the distillation process. But you also know you have a much larger set of customers who care deeply about their favorite brands. Maker's Mark made a conscious decision to tap into those enthusiasts. It lets them find new customers, explain why its bourbon is so good, and invite them to join the club. The company just patiently waits for their collection of advocates to grow and grow.

MICKEY MANTLE AND THE NEW AMBASSADORS

When I think about how easily companies can locate and work with ambassadors in the Pre-Commerce environment, I remember how stressed I felt on that TWA flight from Newark to St. Louis. It was 1986, more than a decade before anyone had put the words "social" and "media" together in a pop culture phrase, and the marketing executives at CIBA-GEIGY (now Novartis) had sent me out to land a key ambassador for the upcoming launch of our new arthritis drug.

The glass offices made one point exquisitely clear: They expected us to make Voltaren the No. 1 nonsteroidal anti-inflammatory product in the United States—no exceptions. Our plain-spoken vice president of marketing, Mike Kishbauch, put his cards right on the table. We needed to come up with something big, he said. We had to find a popular, well-known person with whom our target customers could relate. We had to convince this celebrity to try our product as part of a clinical trial. And, if the drug eased his pain, we had to cast him as the everyman voice of arthritis and joint-pain sufferers.

The easy job landed in my lap. All I had to do was fly halfway across the country and get some time with Mickey Mantle. No pressure or anything—just land a meeting with one of the most popular athletes in professional baseball history, convince him to try a drug he's never heard of, and sign him up as the brand ambassador for it. So there I was on the TWA flight to St. Louis, resting my head against the window and coming to a stark realization: "If I don't have a successful trip, I'm screwed." I didn't even know if Mantle would speak with me, let alone agree to try a drug he's never heard of. But this had to work. I didn't have a Plan B.

I got little sleep that night. ("We don't have wake-up calls here," the manager of the $14 a night motel told me. "That's for the big hotels.") Tired and more than a little nervous, I hopped in my rental car and took off for the golf club in Joplin, Missouri, location of one of Mantle's homes. Barney Barnett agreed to meet me there, and sure enough, this big, strapping man approached me as soon as I walked in the door. Barnett was Mantle's sandlot baseball coach, and the two had remained friends throughout Mantle's extraordinary career. In today's age of hyperexposure, he would've been the wall between Mantle and me. Back then, he was the gate. Upon hearing about my family connections with professional baseball, he launched into stories about baseball and about "The Mick."

About twenty minutes into our conversation, Barnett abruptly stopped and asked, "Did you say you're from a farming company?" I corrected him, explaining that I worked for a *pharmaceutical* company.

A little cloud of confusion passed over his face, and a knot took hold in my stomach. But we went back to baseball for another thirty minutes, until Barnett stopped again to ask what I know about farming. "Pretty much nothing, Barney," I said, again a little tense. Our conversation went back and forth like this for three hours. Years later, I realized Barnett wasn't trying to feel me out. He'd done that the moment we shook hands. It turns out Mantle decided to go fishing until noon that day, and Barnett was simply playing the good host. Mantle, retired for eighteen years, liked to hang out at the club, fish, and play golf with the boys, and this day was no different. When he finally showed up around noon, the great slugger immediately treated me like a friend. I can only figure he got the nod from Barnett—and heck, if this twenty-four-year-old kid flew halfway across the country to meet me in my favorite place, well, he can't be all bad.

As soon as I started telling Mantle about Voltaren, he hiked up his pant legs and started wiggling his knees to show me how loose his joints had become. He was in a lot of pain, he said, and he would appreciate a medicine that would help. He even called his wife, Merlyn, and asked if she wanted to enter the clinical trial, too. Soon after, Whitey Ford, another former Yankee, called me to ask if he could enter the trial. A blind call on Mickey Mantle, and now he, his wife, and Whitey Ford were on board with the clinical trial. Call it luck. Call it good, old-fashioned relationship building. Whatever it was, I'd struck gold with one of the most popular athletes in the country.

When we launched Voltaren in 1987, we told the world that Mickey Mantle and Whitey Ford participated in the clinical trial, and with excellent results. It should've come as no surprise given how bad Mantle's knees were—by then, millions of people knew as much about his bad knees as his seven world championships. The word of mouth took over. People with arthritis flocked to their doctors to ask about Mickey Mantle's drug. Within a year, Voltaren was the No. 2 nonsteroidal anti-inflammatory drug on the market.

I'll never forget that meeting with Mickey Mantle, and I'll never forget the power of the bonds he had with our customers. People relate to other people like them, even if they're alike in only small ways. Mantle and Barnett identified with me for some reason, whether because of my baseball background, my support for the Yankees, or the fact that I'd flown out to Joplin to meet them face-to-face. But beyond that, Mantle could identify with our target customers—people with arthritis—and they could identify with him. They couldn't relate to thousands of fans cheering for every at-bat, but they could identify with Mantle's balky knees. Before Voltaren hit the market, thirteen other companies had launched similar drugs with smart campaigns, great messages, and lots of money. None of them did as well as Voltaren. None of the marketing campaigns did as well as the simple relationship between The Mick's sore knees and John Doe's own aching joints.

We entered the market with a simple message from someone who, despite being famous, still had that one-of-the-guys appeal. And given his well-known knee problems, anyone with serious joint pain could cast aside the veil of celebrity and associate with him as a peer. Mantle went from fishing to a clinical trial. And when the drug worked for him, he went out and started telling people his story. He connected, and people decided to learn more on their own. They took action.

I don't know if I should laugh or cry when I think about how stressful—and ultimately, rewarding—it was to visit Mickey Mantle and get him to sign on for Voltaren. Today, any company willing to put in the time, thought, and effort can find their online ambassadors in minutes. You don't need to court celebrities. You don't need a famous athlete to endorse your brand. You simply identify the online ambassadors who influence your current and potential customers. In the Pre-Commerce marketplace, these are your Mickey Mantles—and you don't even have to fly to Joplin to get to know them.

CHAPTER SEVEN

THE TECTONIC PLATES
OF THE PRE-COMMERCE
WORLD

There's a way to do it better—find it.
—THOMAS EDISON

In the short five-year span from 1993 to 1998, at least sixteen companies introduced what they hoped would become the world's
greatest search engine. You might remember some of the names: Alta
Vista, Lycos, Excite, and WebCrawler to name a few. Each one flashed
brightly across the Web-o-sphere before another brilliant algorithm or
business model came along to outshine it. But then two young gents
from Stanford University, Sergey Brin and Larry Page, developed a
game-changing search algorithm, wrapped a streamlined ad-revenue
model around it, and launched Google—now the world's most popular
search engine.

Around the same time those also-rans were fading into Internet
oblivion, a few wireless phone makers started searching for new ways
to commercialize an old technology platform. The technology allowed
users to send small bursts of data at very little cost. Nokia had tried
this short message service as a business-to-business service a few years

before, but it didn't truly take off until consumers got their hands on it in the early 2000s. Jack Dorsey, Biz Stone, and Evan Williams took it another step in 2007, when they introduced Twitter and took SMS to the Internet masses. In less than a decade, SMS has become the primary mode of communication for both younger generations and people in emerging countries.

Inevitably, other innovations will come along to challenge Twitter and Google. Companies already have introduced ever-more customized search engines, including Wolfram | Alpha and its computational knowledge engine that looks up formulas and helps users find data faster. Facebook, MySpace, and virtually every social network on the planet have incorporated SMS into their platforms.

Technology and its uses change constantly, but the underlying trends move more slowly. I call them the tectonic plates of the Pre-Commerce planet. Many executives feel overwhelmed when they try to parse through these technologies and trends, boggled by the myriad and constantly evolving ways people adopt and employ these new ideas. The small things change very rapidly, but the Web's dirty little secret is that each shiny new device or snazzy new application only changes the game incrementally. The technologies that truly shift the direction of the tectonic plates—a Google or Twitter, for example—come along but once every few years. Most executives simply waste their time if they try to keep track of all the incremental advancements that barrage us every week. Frankly, business leaders have more important things to do. But if you also ignore the shifting tectonic plates—if you turn a blind eye to the trends that truly transform the way customers interact—the foundation of your business will crack and crumble beneath your feet.

In the Pre-Commerce marketplace, the progressive business leaders who study the major trends, such as search and SMS, will begin to see the next trends faster than competitors hopping from one incremental technology to the next. They will push their employees to become students of history, so they can put today's innovation into perspective and have a cleaner view on the next incremental innovation. They will take an "AHA" approach to learning and analysis—analysis, history, and application—to your business. They will step back from the hype to understand what is really happening, learn how this technology or approach has evolved over time, and then figure out how it applies to improving their business.

To learn effectively, you need to understand the history of technology, how it has changed, and why your company should care. Leave the rest of the distracting and incremental advances to the specialists in your company—unless, of course, you really enjoy developing algorithms and analyzing code in your spare time.

SEARCH

Search might be the archetype for technologies that blind us with constant but incremental changes. Search experts around the world make it sound far more complicated than it should, and those same experts typically hide behind the complexity. It's how they make millions of dollars selling new technologies and consulting services. Don't lose the real point. Customers use search for a very simple reason—it helps them quickly and easily find the information they want. A company can contribute content that appears in customer searches, and it can advertise on search engines to attract customers and generate sales. This should remain at the core of your search education, and you'll see it play out in three main areas as you continue learning.

Simply put, search engines automatically look for links across the Internet in a constant rediscovery of new or updated Web sites. These so-called "spiders" find new stuff and create a master index of their discoveries. When you search for something, in essence you search against this index. (You might hear your people say "that was indexed in search.") The index makes it easier for search engines to find what you want, so you of course want to ensure your content is indexed.

Of course, the spiders find oodles of new content on a daily basis, and some of that information is more relevant to your search than other information. Relevancy gets a little more complicated, and it lies at the core of the differentiation from one search engine to the next. Search engines return results by relevancy, deciding which content comes closest to fulfilling the searcher's intent and listing it front and center. Each search company has a set of algorithms that determine this—Google's secret sauce, as it were. Generally speaking, the diversity of content you provide, including images, text, and video, will improve your search position. The algorithms will factor it as more relevant.

Because of the constantly updated conversations on social media channels, spiders keep scraping those conversations, and algorithms place a higher relevancy ranking on them. So if you mention your brand one time and a community forum mentions it another forty times, the community forum has forty times the impact of your single mention. If you only share text and avoid images, podcasts, vlogs, and the like, you decrease your chance for a higher ranking because you lack diversity in your content. The simplest study of search should make you think differently about press releases for the rest of your career.

Of course, the big catchphrase is "search engine optimization"—all the different ways to improve your ranking to be on the top of the search results. This is how you leverage your content to improve the likelihood that customers will find your link high up on the first page (separate from the paid advertising links). If you want to reach people via advertising, then we use search engine marketing, where "marketing" means "paying for ads."

It's easy to get lost in the weeds as you dive deeper into each facet of search, and plenty of people out there will try to complicate things, usually because they want to sell you something that will help ease all that complication. Make sure you remember the basics of search—contributing content for searches and advertising on search engines—and focus on a few basic questions:

- What are the top five questions being asked by your customers today via search?
- Are you teaching your employees who build content about search engines' desire for diversity?
- Do you know the exact words your customers use when they describe your products, and if you do, how do you integrate this into all external copy you produce?

As you start to answer these questions, you can embed this education into the DNA of your company. It will help build an ongoing advantage, one that's sustainable through all the incremental changes in search algorithms and business models.

SEARCH: THE HONEST BROKER AND DECISION ENGINE OF THE PRE-COMMERCE EXPERIENCE

Lukas Cudrigh, the senior director of digital solutions at Microsoft, always sees around the corner to determine how technology will change the ways we do business. He shared some thoughts on search.

Search is the primary tool for shopping online. More than half of all e-commerce transactions originate from search engines.

Search is the honest broker of e-commerce. Horizontal search engines such as Bing are different from e-commerce platforms due to their ability to compile a multitude of information sources into a single view of a product and serve as an honest broker of shopping information.

Bing is a decision engine. One of the key goals of a modern search engine is to understand user intent and respond accordingly with highly relevant search results. This happens by recording consumers' search histories and behavioral information over time, and then using that insight to provide suggestions based on what we know about them.

Companies have to integrate Web search with their own, onsite search capabilities. Once customers are "on-site," they expect a highly relevant search experience based on search history and other behavioral patterns.

Mimic the offline shopping experience. With Bing, for example, visual search galleries allow users to navigate and browse product categories like they might browse in a department store or at a specialty retailer. Once a product category or collection is selected, Bing users can then toggle between the traditional search result list view and a grid view that enables improved visual comparison of products within a search result set.

Show relevant products when browsing. With collections, we use sophisticated and user-centric algorithms to pull together items from across product categories and make them easy to browse by functional areas or seasonal shopping events. Bing uses collections to present relevant products within visually appealing layouts, such as product catalogs or slide shows.

SHORT MESSAGE SERVICE

D fucha lang of on9S short4m msgN. The future language of online is short-form messaging.

Your customers, especially your youngest ones, speak a new language. Short-form messaging—SMS, text messages, and so forth—have become the lingua franca of the up-and-coming consumer generations.

To them, e-mail is lame and a colossal waste of time. The content produced by most companies today revolves around newsletters, two-page white papers, thirty-minute videos, and hour-long town hall meetings. If you enjoy talking to yourself, you're on the right track. Companies that don't learn to speak in short-form will have an entire Pre-Commerce generation pass them by.

SMS language is just a term for the abbreviations and slang people use to communicate through fewer words and characters. It started with mobile phones, when longer text messages cost more than short ones. But the real driver of SMS language is its efficiency; given the small touchpads and keyboards on smart phones and other mobile devices, it's simply faster and easier to use a shorthand of sorts. Vowels go away. Convenient misspellings replace longer words. Symbols replace certain syllables. You might prefer the Queen's English, but then the queen isn't exactly hip with the younger audience most companies want to attract.

A successful Pre-Commerce company will start speaking SMS language with customers and using it in targeted pieces of advertising campaigns. It will make sure all its Web sites are mobile-ready. It will send product tips and promotions by text message or Twitter. Progressive business leaders will apply this language in every facet of their communication with customers under thirty years old—and eventually, perhaps, everyone.

As Pre-Commerce advances, customers will want more information faster, and they'll turn around and just as quickly share what their likes and dislikes are with peers. Some of this will happen in plain old English, but an increasing amount will go over the SMS transom. As we discussed in Chapters Two and Three, almost half of Twitter users introduced to a brand will search online for additional information. In other words, short messages can lead to much deeper engagements.[1] Don't cut out a significant portion of your customer base by speaking the wrong, long language.

MOBILE DEVICES

SMS logically takes us to the mobile phone, which really isn't just a phone anymore. The old cell-phone bricks people used to carry around have transformed into pocket-size devices with remarkable processing power—more in a single smart phone than in the NASA computers that guided Neil Armstrong to the moon. Mobile devices have become a central and indispensable business tool and an increasingly vital avenue for customer communication and commerce.

It's not just happening in developed markets and through all the coolest iPhone apps. Entire generations are bypassing landlines in emerging countries. The majority of the world now learns through wireless phones and other mobile devices. "Brazil, India, and China are strong adopters, especially as it relates to using mobile devices," said Manish Mehta, Dell's vice president of social media and community. "The tools and platforms will evolve, but the fundamental of engaging in conversations remains a global truth."

Mobile commerce is no longer just a concept. Farmers in Africa use their phones to determine the best market for their goods. Japanese consumers point their Bluetooth-enabled devices at the Coca-Cola dispenser to pay for a can of soda. In a world of roughly 6.7 billion people, telecom companies have sold more than five billion wireless subscriptions. And the potential usage patterns mushroom when you start adding in the popularity and capability of tablet PCs such as the iPad.

Since the 1970s, phone manufacturers reduced the weight of the phone, the reception, and the voice quality. But in the years since 2000, phone and PC makers have packed incredible amounts of processing and data capacity in those very same devices. While the innovation has rocketed, few companies have kept pace with the changes. Many companies have mobile-ready Web sites, but they haven't shifted their sales approach to reach people on the go. Only a handful of companies have started to fully research the ways mobility changes their customers' habits, language, and consumption patterns. Even fewer have adapted their marketing or created a mobile app to account for those changes. The Pre-Commerce world is always moving.

"I think it is less about a particular device and more about the ubiquity of technology—in our cars, in our homes, on the plane, wherever we are," added Mehta. "I think we will continue to see a range of devices and permutations of various devices. It's no surprise, but mobile and becoming untethered-yet-connected will become the norm. The convergence of location, content, context, and conversations will be even more critical."

COMMUNITY FORUMS

Community forums looked a little different in the early days of the Internet. Everything came only in text—and in a lovely, monochromatic shade of green to boot. A crude search would deliver a list of "threads," each of which contained post after post in reply to the topic at hand (or, usually, on some digression off the original issue). They came posted on bulletin boards and e-mail lists from companies such as CompuServe and Prodigy. As old and quaint as it all sounds, they enabled millions of academicians, students, and geeks to share information and learn from one another. They gave birth to the whole idea of social media. Forums let us learn and share back then, and they allow us to do the same today, much more easily and to a much broader audience.

Customers flock to online forums for a simple reason: They like to interact with like-minded people. They typically go to sites that are dedicated to a specific topic, product, or theme. They don't mind letting in anyone, including corporate types, who can add value to the discussion. But because they jointly participate in such an open forum, they've become extremely adept at self-regulation and the communal enforcement of the social norms expected on the site.

The forum concept hasn't changed much from the first time someone discreetly told me to turn off my caps-lock key so it didn't look like I was shouting in neon green every time I posted something. The forum has stayed true to its inherent utility—enabling like-minded people to congregate, share information, and learn together.

Forums have become one of the most powerful motivators in the Pre-Commerce marketplace. No executive can track every word posted about his or her company on the Web's vast collection of forums. The key is to know which forums matter the most to your brand and to use them to help build an understanding of what your current and potential customers really care about. Forum conversations reflect real life. If your teams can identify the motivators and concerns customers share there, you don't need as much primary research to tell you what tens of thousands of customers are thinking.

BLOGS

The whole concept of blogs grew out of those early online forums. While forums allowed people to learn from one another, blogs went a step further and gave users an easy, flexible, and powerful platform to share more content with larger audiences. It remains one of the best examples of social media today, more than thirteen years after Jorn Barger initially coined the term *weblog*. Of course, we've had offline blogs for more than a century—we just called them personal diaries. With blogs, people could post their diaries for anyone to see. It was useful to share information with friends and family, and because many blogs were available to anyone online they helped create a broader public history.

Customers couldn't resist the ability to broadcast their thoughts, ideas, and beliefs. Every day, hundreds of blogs might mention your brand. In the Pre-Commerce world, you can't ignore those conversations, especially as the blogosphere joins mainstream media as a forum for breaking news and information. According to a 2010 survey conducted by the Pew Research Center's Internet and American Life Project and the Project for Excellence in Journalism, about 92 percent of Americans get their daily news from multiple platforms. Almost 60 percent get their daily news from a combination of online and offline sources, the survey found.[2] Increasingly, blogs are the source of that news, said Richard Jalichandra, CEO of Technorati, the top blog search engine. "It's about the speed at which stories break and then trend in the blogosphere," he said. "Bloggers are very influenced by mainstream media—and vice versa—but the blogosphere is the place where stories break and spread, and has been for close to a decade now. I don't see that changing anytime soon. Blogs as the primary source for other blogs will continue."

That works for corporate blogs, too, Jalichandra said. A blog provides a forum through which an organization can present its view on products and issues. But when actively maintained with insightful, relevant, and informative content, the same organization's blog can supply fodder for other bloggers to spread, he said. "I've always believed that your brand should be out amongst the people, and the Internet made that easier right from the get-go," he said. "But I think most brands only get this if they're dragged kicking and screaming into the crowds."

The sheer number of blogs out there shouldn't surprise you anymore. If it does, let it go because it doesn't matter. What matters is the sheer power of persuasion any one of those bloggers can wield if they strike the right chord with the right audience. If you're relevant to them, you might have some influence on their next story. They might, in turn, influence the major journalists who cover your company. And collectively, they'll influence a significant portion of your current or future customer base, either for you or against you.

SPAM AND SECURITY

Technology innovation doesn't have an inherent morality. For every positive advance technology delivers, there's equal potential for the downside. Look no further than spam. Companies have contributed to Mount Spam for years. If a customer didn't directly request that you e-mail them regularly, or if they only signed up for e-mail to get something else you offered during a registration process, you've essentially spammed them. Of course, I view spam a little more harshly than most marketing professionals. As far as I'm concerned, spam includes any unwanted content a company shares with customers who didn't ask for it. At WCG, my colleagues and I did an analysis of twenty-two pharmaceutical-related brands, including more than 117,000 posts. By our definition, more than 90 percent of posts were spam.

Spam creates issues beyond clutter. It impacts bandwidth. It drives up the cost of reaching customers and spurring them to action. But it also creates a number of security risks—both for a brand and a company's infrastructure. When you think of spammers, include the Web's "pirates," who are trying to steal your intellectual capital. They regularly strike software developers and movie studios, but they just as easily can co-opt virtually any brand. It's all the same process. Companies that spam a lot are much more likely to have their brand co-opted by spammers and scammers who pretend they're from your company. A typical company should acquire subdomains for their brands at about one hundred of the top social media sites, such as YouTube, Flickr, and Slideshare.net. If you don't, spammers will swoop in, acquire subdomains that include your brand name, and pose as your company. And when they start spamming and scamming your customers, much of the blame will fall on you.

Business leaders also play a vital role in maintaining the open and secure environment in which Pre-Commerce thrives. Although most of the responsibility for protecting one's identity and sensitive information lies with each one of us as individuals, the most-progressive and most-trusted companies will address common security lapses and make it easier for their customers to avoid them. Consumers often provide too much personal information to scam e-mails and Web sites that conduct phishing schemes. Securing subdomains, as mentioned above, can help limit this sort of phishing. Customers also tend to choose weak passwords or use the same password for multiple sites. To combat those issues, companies such as Bank of America and PayPal use multifactor authentication, requiring extra security measures beyond a simple password. Those extra steps can make all the difference.

It's easy to ignore this side of the security issue and pass it off as the customer's responsibility. But the vibrancy of the Pre-Commerce world relies on an open, interactive, *and* secure environment. Helping facilitate all three criteria benefits companies as much as it does customers.

SECURE YOUR IDENTITY

Identity theft is one of the most threatening Web-security issues in the Pre-Commerce marketplace. Although companies have to take steps to help protect their customers—providing safe and encrypted transaction portals, for example—we all have to take

(*Continued*)

our own precautions as well. Paul Beverly, executive vice president of marketing and president of the North America business division at Gemalto, the world leader in digital security, offers these twelve steps to securing your online identity:

1. Educate yourself about how identity theft happens.
2. Protect your personal information. Shred financial documents and paperwork with personal information.
3. Don't keep passwords, birthdays, or other personal information in your wallet.
4. Keep a copy of your credit cards, driver's license, passport, and other personal cards you carry in your wallet in a safe place at home.
5. Avoid giving out your Social Security number.
6. Never give out personal information on the phone, through the mail, or over the Internet unless you are sure you are dealing with whom you think you are.
7. Be suspicious of links in e-mails you receive, as well as phone numbers given to you in letters or in phone calls made to you.
8. Always enter links (or use your own shortcuts) to banks, online retailers, brokers, or any other trusted sites.
9. Always check the address bar to confirm the address and check for a secure link.
10. Avoid unauthorized sharing of music, movies, TV shows, or other files online.
11. Never give out your personal security codes (PINs) or passwords to anyone.
12. Use a smart card digital security device for online payment or banking.

VIDEO

YouTube isn't just for video anymore. The public got its first glimpse of the video-sharing site in May 2005, and since then it has become the second-largest search engine on the planet. YouTube didn't set out to become a massive search engine, but its transformation into exactly that makes perfect sense. Our brains learn better when we can interact with text, video, and images concurrently. As I mentioned in Chapter Three, the study by Baylor College of Medicine professor Dr. Wei Ji Ma showed that visual information can improve the understanding of spoken words as much as six times.[3] This is how your customers want to learn.

We found that out with one simple video at Dell. Bob Blomquist, who led our electronic broadcast team, asked a colleague to shoot a basic video: "How to fix your printer." Bob didn't write a script or provide any major direction. He just asked for a brief explanation with a Dell printer as a prop. It took about ten minutes to shoot the video. It took fewer than ten days for it to become a hit, and we topped 100,000 views a short time later. It was exactly what customers wanted to see.

The printer video hit a chord with the way customers adopt new technologies. The desire to find an answer to a question really drives video consumption, and that's what Dell customers wanted when they clicked on Bob's short clip. And it's the same motivation—that search for quick, easily understandable answers—that helped make YouTube a power as an online search engine. We want our entertainment to be easily found, and we want video to serve our needs and answer our questions.

Business leaders would do well to keep the Dell example in mind the next time someone suggests spending a lot of money to create a highly polished video and a carefully crafted script. That type of corporate video fails just about every time. In fact, failure is so nearly assured you're better just donating the money to charity and saving the time it would take to do the video. At least you'll help more people that way.

Now, I don't mean to suggest that your video production should fly by the seat of its pants, *sans* any sort of strategy. A corporate video strategy is vital, and it should encompass much more than a calendar of content for a YouTube channel. The Web contains dozens of video sites that hold promise for your brand and your interaction with customers. VideoJug, ExpoTV, DailyMotion, and Tudou each have millions of users, and one might reach your target audience better than another.

Finally, remember that virtually all of these video sites have social media tools that allow users to interact. A fairly basic search can identify people outside the company who shoot and share the most influential videos about your brand. Get to know those people—they're as valuable as the influencers on blogs and other types of social media. Find out what questions customers are asking through YouTube's search engine or on other video-sharing sites. Learn the geographical location of the people who view your videos and those produced by key influencers.

Prime time has changed. Throughout the world, people consume the most online information from 9 P.M. to 1 A.M. local time. What special content can your company deliver for that time period? Customers increasingly turn to video to learn more about your brand. The company that delivers the topically relevant video at the right time will engage customers with a much richer interaction than competitors who rely on text alone.

WIKIS

Ward Cunningham needed to find a better way for software developers to communicate. So in 1994, he developed what he described as "the simplest online database that could possibly work." He called his creation the WikiWikiWeb, the name inspired by the Wiki Wiki Shuttle at the Honolulu International Airport. (*Wiki* means "fast" in Hawaiian.) He shared his creation on his company Web site, c2.com, and the wiki phenomenon just blew up from there. Almost immediately, users found the wiki was one of the best ways to crowdsource knowledge. Today, the most famous wiki, Wikipedia, features more than sixteen million articles contributed and edited by millions of users around the world.

Cunningham created a platform that made it simple to accomplish what people naturally seek to do with large collections of information—create links between the information we have so we can learn more effectively and generate more insight. Companies have used knowledge management, best practices, business process improvement, and dozens of other methods to improve the quality of work and the analysis of data. Executives, consultants, and analysts look for connections that help improve knowledge a step at a time, always building on the most recent insight.

Wikis weld a rocket engine on that process for many of the same fundamental reasons people love the Web. Customers want to share ideas, share product knowledge, and provide solutions. By engaging people in what they already want to do, wikis allow a company to create larger, collective pools of brainpower to build the knowledge and insights that used to come from a small group of experts. Some people prefer to share original content. Some share deeper knowledge about that content. Still others like to edit and improve on ideas incrementally. It's all the same behavioral system at work. If you want to expand and improve the level of collaboration about your brands, think wiki.

SLIDES

When I started out in business in 1985, we created acetates for our presentations. We'd whip together all these plastic sheets full of information and throw them on the overhead projector as we discussed our goals and achievements. We'd have a second or third set of copies in case we lost any key acetates, but mostly we'd put piles and piles of them on the shelves, never to use them again.

In 1987, around the same time I kept myself busy putting marker to acetate, Microsoft acquired a graphics company called Forethought. Forethought was the forebearer of PowerPoint. And although I lump myself firmly among those who complain about PowerPoint, we all have to admit it beats acetates. And frankly, starting with PowerPoint 97, it changed our business lives. If done with a little bit of care, providing a set of graphical slides that encapsulated our presentations made the sharing of information quicker and easier.

We could always e-mail our PowerPoint slides back and forth, but true sharing and collaboration came in October 2006 with the launch of Slideshare. YouTube had started just a year before, and the folks behind Slideshare figured they could do the same for static images that Google did for video. The idea was brilliant in its simplicity: Let people share slides for anyone to see. Companies can post a presentation for interested customers to read at their leisure. They can share nonconfidential ideas with partners and business-to-business customers, and do it in a language both sides understand. Your customers and partners care about open access to information. They want to learn more about the topics that impact their lives and their businesses. And Slideshare has more than 30 million unique visitors per month to prove it.

PODCASTS

Guglielmo Marconi sent his first radio transmissions in 1895, and people have loved radio communication ever since. We won't return to the Golden Age of Radio anymore than we'll return to the Golden Age of Television. But make no mistake, billions of people still listen to the radio, whether in the car or in a small rural village in the developing world. Regardless of all the new media in our lives—media that are starting to reach that village dweller, too—we still enjoy listening to music and the spoken word.

The emergence of the Web gave birth to a new tool to share and listen to audio. Podcasting, or playable on demand audio, rose to popularity around 2004 and remains a popular way to share content. Someone pre-records an audio file that interested consumers can download and listen to at their convenience. Some podcasts cost money, most are free, but all of them have flexibility to thank for their appeal. People can listen or watch podcasts *whenever* they want, *wherever* they want.

Neville Hobson, my colleague at WCG in London, noticed the potential for podcasts almost from the technology's inception. In 2005, he launched a regular podcast with Shel Holtz, principal at Holtz Communication + Technology and a widely known expert on all things social media. They called their podcast "For Immediate Release: The Hobson and Holtz Report," and within months it was known to tens of thousands of subscribers as simply "FIR." Listeners responded and said they loved the content, Neville said, but that on its own didn't drive its growth and make it notable. "FIR is about community," he said. "While the two presenters are the foundation, it's a network of comment contributors and regular reporters in the U.S., U.K., and Singapore who have given the show a sense of genuine community. So today, the content of a typical FIR episode is made up of at least 33 percent listener contributions and reports, and those listener suggestions and recommendations drive much of the direction of the show."

Of course, Neville acknowledges that podcasting might have remained a niche pursuit for enthusiasts had Apple not seen its potential at an early stage. When the company released a new version of iTunes in 2005, it included podcasts in the iTunes Store. Within days, it had sold more than one million podcast subscriptions. The explosive growth of iPods and other digital music players gave podcasts a shot in the arm, of course, but so too did the ease with which people could create them, Neville said. It takes little more than a PC, a microphone, and some basic editing software—add a camera if you want to do video, as well—and users can inexpensively create polished content that would have required a recording studio or videographer in the past.

Many companies have developed sophisticated uses for the tool. It's a great way to reach a mobile sales force so they can learn on the road. Leaders can record a quick message to post on an internal blog. And marketing teams can interview both company and external thought leaders to share expertise with your employees or customers. Whatever knowledge or news you want to capture, podcasting provides a quick and easy platform for sharing it. If you record something interesting or useful, people will listen.

"In much less than a decade, it's become a medium of communication widely used by individuals and organizations of all types and sizes," Neville said. "Fortune 100 companies, nonprofits, governments, small- to medium-size businesses, the mainstream media—you name it, and today they're podcasting in one form or another."

FROM REGION TO REGION: THE DIFFERENT CULTURES OF SOCIAL MEDIA

We know many of the obvious differences between the United States and Europe, but the social media cultures vary as well. Yann Gourvennec, head of Internet and digital media at Orange Business Services, learned this years ago. In 1996, Gourvennec started a blog called Visionary Marketing, and ever since its founding he's had companies around the world beat a path to his door in search of his global experience and his social media perspective. He says U.S. companies need to gain a better feel for the different social media tendencies of Pre-Commerce in Europe.

- *On higher telecommuting rates*—"When telecommuting adoption rates for instance, range from 35 to 3 percent in Europe, such discrepancies are bound to mean something regarding the adoption of collaborative technologies and social media tools."
- *On the use of professional social networks*—"LinkedIn is the No. 1 professional network in the U.K., but Xing is prevalent in Germany and Austria and German-speaking Switzerland because it is favored by German-speaking professionals. Viadeo in France is three times more important than LinkedIn because it is French and was developed here. These differences are significant. Send a LinkedIn invitation to a German professional for him to join your network, and that German professional will send you back an invitation for you to join Xing, even though you may not even know what it is."
- *On Europeans' continuing reluctance to replace their home networks with others*—"In Germany, individuals tend to desert Facebook because of its lack of commitment on data privacy—a no-no in Germany, where people are very conscious of privacy. In France, young users tend to use Facebook, which has replaced blogs for most of them, but middle aged citizens continue to favor local social networks like Copains d'avant. The situation is contrasted and complex, it's far from being a bipolar Twitter/Facebook world."
- *The penetration of expert blogging has been somewhat better in France than the U.K., but it varies throughout Europe*—"Language issues are once again coming to the forefront: Should a person write in Dutch or English? If your prime audience is Dutch, I would tend to say Dutch, but those questions are still being debated amongst us at the moment."

SOCIAL MEDIA COMMUNITIES

I saved social media communities for last, because it proves the point I made at the outset. When you look at the plethora of social media tools, you find only a few major trends—those tectonic plates. But for the most part, developers simply iterate and innovate based on what they already know. Don't get me wrong, they come up with some brilliant and cool ideas, but they're rooted in history. Facebook and other social media communities have their roots in those early online forums, but they come at it in a much more inviting way.

Forums reside at the center of online conversations. Social media communities, rather than living at the core, offer a wide-open, all-inviting place that proactively works to build a larger and broader audience. If forums thrive on individual topics, social media communities thrive on the widest possible connections they can employ while still attracting new users. A successful forum might feed off discussions of WiFi standards, drawing a small but ardent crowd. A social media community casts a large net in hopes of collecting larger and larger numbers of friends, family members, and associates. And while forums generally let the audience evolve organically, social media communities try to encourage proactive "friending" and other ways to build communities.

These communities vary, but at their core they follow this same pattern. People build them based on what they perceive to be the most ubiquitous needs for like-minded people to congregate. Bigadda has done a wonderful job of this in India, where it's one of the faster growing sites for youth. The site claims to reach widely into Tier III cities, collecting users in Guwahati and Surat in addition to Delhi and Mumbai. Bigadda can do this because it plays to the commonalities of Indian youth wherever they live. From a business perspective, this type of penetration into the smaller cities of emerging markets, particularly India and China, will prove critical—not to mention potentially lucrative—in the years ahead.

SOCIAL DIVERSITY

Social media communities come in all shapes and sizes. While the core motivation behind social media sites is tied to a common thread, the sites display a diverse set of quirks and attributes. Companies that accept and understand the differences can tailor their content and their messaging to better reach their customers.

- On Biip.no, Norway's third-largest community site after Facebook and Nettby.no, people identify themselves by nicknames instead of their given name.
- CafeMom has become one of the most widely visited sites for mothers in the United States.
- Orkut used to rank among Iran's top social community sites until the government started censoring the site. Users quickly migrated to Cloob.com.
- Some of the most progressive online communities reside in South Korea. For example, CyWorld encourages online friendships through a small home page, and it generates revenue by selling users virtual goods, such as background music and pixilated furniture.
- Many social communities spread well beyond their geographical borders. Orkut is operated by Google Brazil and is the largest social networking site in that country. CyWorld is gaining popularity in China and Vietnam.
- Twitter has gone global, and Japan is one of its top markets.
- Upstarts will continue to emerge. Because China censors most Western sites, including Facebook and Twitter, locally created

(Continued)

communities such as Kaixin001 are increasing their reach and value.
- Mixi, a Japanese community focused on entertainment, requires a Japanese mobile phone to participate.
- Muslim users have gravitated toward several social media sites, including Muxlim.com, which was created as a community that adheres to Islamic principles regarding adult material and other offensive content.

Most people think of Facebook or MySpace when they consider social media communities. And why not—Facebook now has more than 600 million users worldwide. But communities can bond around different issues and serve different purposes. Foursquare integrates a user's physical location with the online community to accomplish interesting new things. At the moment, its main operation targets coupons to communities in certain locations, but some intriguing new possibilities could arise when combining physical and virtual communities. Craigslist has taken a more straightforward tack, building community around what used to be the newspaper's classified ads and allowing people to buy, trade, sell, or share almost anything. Similar sites have come together throughout the world, including Grono.net in Poland. More are bound to emerge.

THE LIQUID NETWORK

Customers move like water when they go online. They flow to the content that matters to them. If a company doesn't provide the right content or interrupts the style of a particular community—if it runs too many intrusive ads, for example—the community simply will flow elsewhere. A company might be able to capture some customers like a dam on a river, but no company can dam the ocean.

I call this concept the "liquid network." Like water, the liquid network is constantly moving, and when a lot of it moves in the same direction it can wield tremendous force. The liquid network can disappear, evaporate away in the blink of an eye, and then reappear like rain in an online community that's thousands of virtual miles away. We're all part of a liquid network, whether we realize it or not. We change based on our personal desires, the influence of our peers, and new technologies. In fact, we can change far faster than most companies expect, and only those executives, employees, and companies who actively and thoughtfully participate in the liquid network can begin to understand the subtle changes at work.

Every company is immersed in the liquid network, but very few have learned how to go with the flow.

CHAPTER EIGHT

HOW IDEA GENERATION WORKS

Mindless habitual behavior is the enemy of innovation.
—ROSABETH MOSS KANTER,
HARVARD BUSINESS SCHOOL

My colleagues and I sat in a small Manhattan research facility, splitting our time and attention between food trays, e-mail, and the focus group on the other side of the one-way mirror. Occasionally, we would sit up and take note of an especially interesting comment or suggestion, then go back to checking our calendars or picking through the *crudités*. I'd like to think I was riveted by what each of these potential customers had to say, but I'd suffered through more than fifty focus groups by then and I'd come to realize how ineffective this process could be.

Here we sat, listening to a lightly prepared researcher interview another group of ten potential customers, hoping the group would deliver a few nuggets of insight to improve our next product. The subjects attended for all the right reasons; they wanted to help further our research and help others who faced similar issues. So they would jockey to share their points, all of which they considered gospel. We'd go do this in two more cities, and our market research firm would take another three weeks assembling a special report about what we'd learned. Eventually, we'd reconvene in a cramped conference room—packed with people who'd skimmed through the executive summary merely to confirm their agreement or disagreement with its premise—and we'd make our grand final decisions.

The thirty consumers who joined our focus groups got a few dollars, a free meal, and the gratification that comes with helping a cause they support. The company, well, we didn't get much of anything.

For the business leaders who've started to consider the Pre-Commerce marketplace, those results won't suffice anymore. Their teams will do focus groups, but they'll supplement that research with direct feedback from thousands, even millions, of customers who share ideas through social media channels. Michael Dell and Marc Benioff, the salesforce.com CEO, wondered what would happen if they solicited ideas from customers twenty-four hours a day, seven days a week. They wondered what would happen if customers could see all those ideas, vote on them, and add their own suggestions to make a good idea a great one. But it couldn't stop there. Dell and Benioff had to make sure those ideas got back to the teams who could act on those suggestions, and they encouraged the employees to join the conversation, ask questions, and clarify ideas.

We could ask thirty people for ideas in a scripted environment, or we could conduct the world's largest focus group, keep it going nonstop, and let it feed off itself. At Dell, this became IdeaStorm.com, a site where visitors could share ideas, comment on them, and throw support behind the ones they like.

DIGGING BELOW THE SURFACE OF THE MIND

The more I thought about the limitation of focus groups, the more I realized that most of our traditional research tools test short-term memory only. Most phone polls solicit opinions in so obvious and direct a manner, they instantly trigger our conscience. We automatically start performing our answers.

George A. Miller, professor emeritus at Princeton University, published a seminal paper on human memory in 1956 while still at Harvard University's psychology department.[1] In his paper, Miller argued that people hold about seven items in their short-term memory at any given time. The number would vary slightly depending on the person, he said, but a reading of anyone's short-term memory would reveal a rather limited set of items. Simply put, we can't quickly recall as much as we think we can. So if we ask people to tell us what's on their mind, we're bound to get a limited response.

Properly employed, idea generation through social media can push people beyond the limitations of short- or long-term memory. By asking customers for ideas, then providing them and their peers a platform to iterate and update those suggestions, we start to engage a deeper, collective memory bank. If the original idea generators can iterate their idea based on what the crowd suggests, they start tapping deeper into their experiences and their long-term memory. Once the subconscious mind kicks in, we start to tap an entirely new set of memories and ideas. (Of course, when others pick up the idea and provide their input, they bring an entirely new set of memories, too.)

When our teams at Dell came up with great new ideas, I liked to ask who came up with the "big idea." I could never get a definitive answer, but not because all my colleagues were so humble. Great teams rarely can credit any single individual, because they work through an inherently iterative process. A final product rarely comes from one mind. It's a collective effort.

The power of collective idea generation seems so obvious once you understand how the human brain and memory works. Innovation occurs when we engage both the conscious and unconscious mind in the creative process. When we do that, we generate cool and useful ideas, but even that combination doesn't guarantee a successful product. Linus Pauling, one of only two people to win Nobel Prizes in different categories, said, "The way to get good ideas is to get lots of ideas and throw the bad ones away." That's a little easier said than done, of course. We don't like sifting through lots of ideas. We like neat solutions. We like the simple multiple choice: A, B, or C. We want to see concepts on a board, fall in love with one, and go with it.

The best innovators will walk away from their old habits, models, and comfort zones and start looking for more ideas. Smart business leaders will bring in the online community to supplement their company's internal idea generation. They'll be more like Linus Pauling, constantly looking for good ideas and discarding the bad ones, a perpetual search for the next groundbreaking innovation.

WHAT WORKS FOR YOU, WORKS FOR ME

Ideas can help shape your culture. They can improve your decision-making process. They give you insight into your customers' purchasing decisions, and they help you improve your new products and services to match customer demands. They give you a better understanding of employee morale, opinions, and attitudes. They even give you a glimpse of what your competitors are doing.

As Ellen Rich prepared to launch EmployeeStorm, Dell's idea-generation site for employees, she turned to my colleague Caroline Dietz. Caroline managed the launch of IdeaStorm, and she knew how quickly things could change when our company leadership started soliciting ideas from the masses. Little did Caroline, Ellen, or any of the rest of us realize how quickly EmployeeStorm would change Dell's corporate culture. We all held onto our own little myths about the things employees really wanted, but none of us expected a better employee discount on Dell equipment to take the day. Most employees had convinced themselves they'd never get a deeper discount. One executive didn't mince words; he told me point-blank that it wouldn't happen in a million years. Turns out, a million years is shorter than either one of us thought.

A few months after Ellen and her colleagues launched Employee Storm, a request for a better employee discount was the No. 1 idea. The executive team agreed to increase the discount in the United States and reevaluate the discount for employees in the rest of the world. The collective power of our employees' ideas—and the peer support for those ideas—started to twist Dell's culture faster than we ever could do it through committee or internal lobbying up the regular food chain. When we empowered employees to speak for themselves, they moved the battleship far faster than anyone could have prior to EmployeeStorm. They changed culture along the edges. Within two years, Dell had implemented about 150 of its employees' ideas.

RUNNING ON ALL CYLINDERS

The old adage says "No one ever got fired for buying IBM." I have to figure that's not technically true, but the saying works because IBM consistently delivers market-leading innovation at some of the highest levels of computing technology. It's also one of the early pioneers in using social media to engage all its employees in a singular effort to foster new ideas. In 2001, CEO Sam Palmisano launched the first IBM Innovation Jam, believing the company's employees, each smart in his or her own right, could figure out a faster way to move products from idea to market if they worked collectively.

It was no easy feat. IBM is famous for its distributed network of talent, with employees working in offices, homes, and neighborhood coffee shops around the world. I briefly met one of those employees while hiking the French Alps with my friend, Eric Gillain. Eric knew an IBMer who owned and worked from a chalet overlooking Mont Blanc, not far from where we were hiking. "He oversees a team that's split between India and California," Eric told me, "and his chalet is in the middle." (Talk about location, location, location . . .)

Because of its employees' wide distribution across the globe, IBM created a series of online bulletin boards, forums, and Web sites around the Innovation Jam concept. They made it easy for employees to share ideas, ask questions, and collaborate over a set period. The initial collaboration, the so-called WorldJam in 2001, generated 52,000 posts, an incredible number for a first-time project that no one had encountered before. By the time the 2006 Innovation Jam ended, IBM drew participation from more than 150,000 people from 104 countries and 67 companies. It used the ideas spawned by the Jam to launch 10 new IBM businesses with a total of $100 million in seed funding.[2]

TEN IDEAS ABOUT IDEAS

IBM generated a lot of brilliant ideas over the years with its Innovation Jams, but it gained a lot more than some new product ideas. The jams provided valuable insight about its own employees and operations and the community idea-generation process in general. We found many of these same insights at Dell with IdeaStorm and EmployeeStorm. Here's a quick top ten to consider:

1. Very few ideas are truly original. You've heard a permutation of almost everything before, so look for the incremental innovation.

2. You already will be acting on many of the ideas you receive. Consider it positive reinforcement, and look for slight tweaks that might add value.

3. Participants' ideas will help guide decisions you have to make about product features and any trade-offs you might have to make. Listen to their feedback and make hard choices based on what customers want.

4. People get a sense of empowerment when you allow them to participate and recognize their contribution. Introduce yourself, thank them, and make yourself a relevant peer.

5. Ideas rarely improve with respectful dialogue over time. Idea generation is much less refined, and even rough and tumble at times. Roll with it. Out in the community, it's usually better to be street smart than book smart.

6. Most contributors take more interest in their ideas than contributing to a peer's suggestion. Recognize it for what it is: passion. At least they care.

7. You don't guide the conversation. The community guides the conversation.

8. You need a great moderator to organize, categorize, and make sense of the incoming insights. Pick a star and treat him or her like gold.

9. The real action occurs after the idea is received. How you harvest and act on ideas is key to success. You rarely receive enough information to act immediately, so add your expertise and find ways to generate richer insight (e.g., beta forums).

10. Leaders who nurture ideas create opportunities. Don't let your customers' ideas die on the vine. Your boss might give you a second chance, but your customers won't.

Best Buy installed a process called TagTrade. The program gave senior leaders insight into the most important corporate initiatives, but it also gave the rank-and-file an opportunity to weigh in with their concerns and ideas. GE created a program called Imagination Market, which collects ideas for product and business innovation. Business leaders at the most progressive companies realize they have to engage all their customers and their employees to find, harvest, and produce groundbreaking new products. Innovation doesn't just occur in the lab, shape itself into a fascinating new prototype, and jump onto your desk beside a lovely little report encapsulating its market potential. Business leaders work for years to put themselves in a position of expertise, so they can digest both internal and external insights and use them to produce successful initiatives. The more those managers tap into the expertise of their employees, the faster they can produce those ideas. And the faster they produce those innovations, the more success they gain against their competitors. It really is that simple.

HITTING THE TRIFECTA

A couple years after we created the Communities and Conversations team at Dell, we took a step back to study our body of work. We wanted to identify the commonalities that exist between customers from China to Brazil to the United States. So we put our whole collection of social media sites under the microscope, and we came across some very illuminating insights. Right off the bat, we realized customers chose to participate in Dell-related conversations to help their peers, not the company. It makes perfect (and common) sense—people care more for their peers than a corporation, even one that tries to put a human face on its operations.

As we looked closer, though, we saw a pattern emerge across all our social media properties in all our countries. If you strip away the hype, we found, people of every nationality and culture went online to discuss our products for one or more of the same three reasons:

1. To provide ideas to help improve products and services
2. To share their product knowledge
3. To provide solutions to problems

What I found even more remarkable, though, was how each of these three motivating factors matched up with our various social media properties. Every social media tool facilitates at least one of the three, but very few can accommodate all three at the same time. Idea-generation platforms can. In the same thread on IdeaStorm, we found customers offering insight we could use to improve products, sharing their knowledge with the community, and providing solutions to peers who had problems to solve. Customers could hit the trifecta on IdeaStorm, and that's why the site was so effective.

BUILDING THE ROAD FROM IDEA TO PRODUCT

Tim Mattox, Dell's vice president of strategy, doesn't go for a lot of fanfare. He prefers a quiet, cerebral approach, which is only fitting since he's as knowledgeable as anyone I've met in high-tech. He earned a bachelor's and master's degree in electrical engineering at the Massachusetts Institute of Technology and later added an MBA from Stanford University. He's not ostentatious about it; he simply operates at a higher level than most of us, which is why he spent years working directly with Michael Dell on the most important strategic issues and opportunities for the company.

Shortly after we launched IdeaStorm, Tim asked Caroline Dietz and me to meet with him and his team. He really liked what he saw happening on our idea-generation site, and he wanted to make sure all those great suggestions didn't get lost in the wash. He wanted to create a bona fide process to govern how we would identify the best ideas, how we would pass them along to the right teams inside the company, and how we would hold those teams accountable for acting on those ideas. We had no guide book and no best practices or benchmarks to use. We had to create an entirely new process. And given the wave of suggestions coming into IdeaStorm, we had to do it on the fly.

We learned a lot by trial and error over the subsequent year. Fortunately, we realized early on that we had to focus on more than just idea generation. We had to make sure we organized and nurtured good ideas throughout the product lifecycle—from the customer's idea all the way through our development, marketing, and sales teams. We first had to figure out a method to efficiently slot incoming ideas into the proper category. When we saw passion building in a certain area, we would set up a new category to make it easier for IdeaStorm visitors to find related ideas. When we saw discussions building, we would allocate more time for someone to moderate and encourage the conversation. It took some hard work, but given how much discussion it generated it was relatively easy to accomplish.

With a system in place to bring order to the discussion online, we had to figure out how to properly move those ideas into the company's ongoing operations. How would we get the right idea to the right people inside the company? This proved to be a greater dilemma. For months, we struggled to build the right series of virtual exit ramps that would channel idea traffic off the online superhighway and onto the avenues that ran through our development teams. Everyone bristled when we tried to force a ramp into their neighborhood. But a funny thing happened—while we tried to build a ramp here, another team would start building their own ramp somewhere else. As they got more and more exposure to the knowledge available to them, they started building networks on their own.

I can't begin to tell you how cool it was to watch that happen at Dell. Teams of developers—people paid to come up with brilliant ideas, and proud of the ideas they came up with—were pulling in ideas from John Doe and the rest of his Pre-Commerce friends. We were becoming a truly social company right before our eyes. We only had to encourage this organically sprouting process and add a little rigor here and there to support it.

Dell takes a customer-focused approach to everything, but now customers could come to us as much as we went to them. So by August 2008, when Dell geared up for the major launch of its next generation Latitude business laptops, our teams had pulled in and incorporated dozens of customer-generated ideas. At our launch event in San Francisco, Jeff Clarke, now the vice chairman at Dell, singled out the impact IdeaStorm had on the development of the new Latitude notebooks. More than a dozen features on the new laptops came directly from IdeaStorm suggestions, including backlit keyboards, a 13.3-inch model, and, on the suggestion of regular visitor "jervis961," a focus by our design teams to put some "attitude into the Latitude."

The ideas kept flowing in, and our teams continued to add incremental improvements over the following year. Dell's vice chairman thanked customers for their ideas during a highly publicized global launch, and customers responded in real-time with more ideas for the next product. It was a thing of beauty.

CONNECTING BUSINESS TO BUSINESS

Idea generation doesn't stop with the high-profile initiatives at a central headquarters level. In fact, it works at its most efficient levels when gathering insights from targeted or distributed groups of people who offer great value to your organization. An idea-generation site set up for a particular business unit, for example, might generate more specific ideas that would get lost in the clutter of the wider organization.

Consider what your teams could accomplish if you opened up a free-flowing channel for ideas between your company and your top business-to-business customers and your partners. How much additional insight could you gather if your account leader could open up a discussion between your teams who serve Client X, and Client X reciprocated by enabling its people to participate? From a technology standpoint, it's fairly easy to build a secure, common platform of blogs, forums, wikis, and other social media tools. You can repurpose it over and over again to open channels between all your big partners. Your account leader would oversee the new channel and encourage employees on both sides to share content and ideas.

The approach to business-to-business interaction is much the same as interaction with consumers, said Becky Brown, director of social media strategy at Intel Corp., the world's largest semiconductor company. In a B2B setting, companies still need to listen, analyze what they hear, create relevant content, engage with stakeholders, and measure outcomes, Brown said, but the way they engage and the content they create will vary widely from a consumer scenario. "A business technology manager might be more interested in communities and discussions around hot topics to their business, while consumers are looking at ways to enrich and improve their life," she said. "Facebook tends to be more effective reaching consumers, while LinkedIn is more effective in reaching business decision makers."

MAKING SENSE OF ALL THAT DATA

Whether dealing with consumers, partners, or business-to-business-customers, interactions in the Pre-Commerce marketplace inevitably churn up massive amounts of feedback. Making sense of all that data is next to impossible without the proper tools and a thoughtful process for turning data into insight. Intel has invested in the necessary tools and analytics, said Becky Brown, director of social media strategy. The company then uses a five-step process to transform that data into meaningful customer interactions and, ultimately, sales.

1. *Listen* to your customers. What are they saying about you, about your brand? Where are they having these conversations? Who are your key influencers?
2. *Analyze* what you've learned. Develop your marketing objectives and strategies by identifying who you want to engage with and how you will measure your effectiveness.
3. *Create* the content. Make it engaging, relevant, interesting, inspirational, sharable, and snackable, and use it to build communities.
4. *Engage.* Find the right places for your conversations based on what you've learned through the listening process and based on your objectives. Go *to* your audience; don't assume they will come to you.
5. *Measure* what matters. Measuring for the sake of measuring is pointless. Use different tools to measure what's relevant to your business and your various goals.

Some of the world's most successful companies rely on the sharing of information with suppliers. Walmart launched its Retail Link system in the early 1990s, long before anyone had heard of social media. The system automates interactions with vendors, including the sharing of information on sales trends and inventory levels. Almost a decade later, Retail Link has gone through plenty of changes, and Walmart regularly consults with vendors to improve it. It's still the gold standard in the retail industry. But even Walmart stops short of a full social media platform for its business-to-business relationships.

In fact, very few Fortune 1000 companies are doing this in any appreciable way. Eventually, more companies will realize that the same power of ideas in the marketplace can generate lucrative investment between them and their suppliers and other business partners. It strikes me as a no-brainer idea, especially because it could shoot return on investment through the roof.

I've talked with many Fortune 500 companies about this idea, and they all say the same thing: "That makes complete sense. We should do that." I couldn't agree more.

SMART CROWDS

Once you install an idea-generation platform and build a process that properly channels the ideas you receive, you'll start to see all kinds of ways to refine the program. One of the tried, true, and tested ways to improve company intelligence employs market-prediction software to enable small, select groups of experts to vote on a specific idea. A group of, perhaps, 100 to 300 experts weigh in on the best price for a new product or a new feature that would drives sales among a targeted section of your customer base. When you add social media tools to the mix, you can let this "smart crowd" vote and provide new ideas—and almost without fail, they'll prove smarter than your smaller teams, no matter how much you pay them.

Of course, you have to gather the right experts to create an effective "smart crowd." If you ask your neighbor to estimate the price of crude oil six months out, they probably won't have any better guess than I would. But if you ask two hundred geologists and engineers within the energy industry, you'll get the most reliable estimate available.

The more knowledgeable people you can find to weigh in on your top questions, the more insight you'll get. Your high-paid geniuses can't deliver the same level of precision, and you're getting all that insight for free. Even your smartest people have only one brain. Between all your employees, customers, partners, and enthusiasts, you have thousands of brains at your disposal. Bring them together.

LIMIT THE LEGAL MUMBO JUMBO

We can't have a comprehensive discussion of idea generation without considering intellectual property issues. If your lawyers are worth the first cent you're paying them, they'll bring up the topic. It's a worthwhile discussion to have, but don't let it kill your social media plans or too tightly restrict your ability to solicit advice from your customer community. There's a balance to find.

- The dirty little secret is that 99.9 percent of participants on your idea-generation site want to help you improve your products. It helps them, and it helps their peers. They're not in it to strike it rich. Those who want to strike it rich probably won't share their ideas publicly anyway.
- Include a clear terms of use policy that users must agree on before they participate. This should cover most issues that could arise. Starbucks, for example, lays out its terms of use clearly and up front: "The *submission of your Idea to Starbucks is entirely voluntary, non-confidential, gratuitous and non-committal.* . . . You grant to Starbucks and its designees a perpetual, irrevocable, non-exclusive fully-paid up and royalty-free license to use any ideas, expression of ideas, or other materials you submit (collectively, "Idea") to Starbucks and Mystarbucksidea.com without restrictions of any kind and without any payment or other consideration of any kind, or permission or notification, to you or any third party."

No one's thrilled about the legalese (except all those highly paid attorneys), but you can protect your company simply, quickly, and up front. From there, go empower your customers to help their peers. If they win, you win.

STREAMLINE AND ENGAGE

We talked in Chapter Six about the ways Intuit uses social media to identify and engage ambassadors for its TurboTax products. But the company takes its own medicine, too. Using idea-generation sites, it created a series of brainstorming sessions—the Problem Jam, Solution Jam, and Code Jam—that allows employees to help work on a wide range of customer-facing and internal issues. Each collaboration runs about six to eight weeks, during which time employees work with one another or with customers to develop new ideas. If it's a problem jam, employees will identify a specific issue and solve it. If it's a solution jam, they'll collaborate with customers to think of ideas to improve current products or develop new ones. And if it's a code jam, developers will work together to build, test, and iterate a new product or service.

Intuit, Starbucks, and Dell have come up with some powerful ways to engage a wider audience while simultaneously streamlining the process. Let's face it, bringing in millions of customers to advise product development would get out of hand really quickly if these two didn't develop hand-in-hand. The development of idea-generation tools and processes remains in its infancy. Companies have just started to figure out how to get ideas from customers and empower them in a manner efficient for all the parties concerned. But the possibilities lead down some very interesting paths.

- What if your company could receive and act on ideas received in the native languages of all the countries in which it operates?
- What if you could speak directly with a person who offers an idea, and do it with a Skype account and one click of the mouse?
- What if you could outsource the earliest phases of product innovation to your customers—and do it free of charge?

Lego came up with one of the more fascinating uses of idea-generation tools. It integrated its idea-generation sites with its main Lego community site in a way that brings together all its innovators, designers, creators, and customers. That's a lot of people. I mean, really, who doesn't like Legos? The company's online community, called Lego Click, tries to get "light bulb moments" related to toys and the way kids use them.

I love Lego's grand approach to developing new ideas. Participants can contribute ideas on Twitter, Flickr, or YouTube simply by adding the hash tag #legoclick. The company made it very easy to participate, and thousands of customers have done so. Now, Lego doesn't allow users to rank and rate ideas, something I see as a shortcoming. Still, it's one of the few companies to take a full-scale plunge into social media as a tool for generating ideas. If nothing else, the leaders at Lego see their customers as an extension of their R&D department, and they realize those thousands of additional viewpoints will help expand their vision.

NARROWING YOUR FOCUS

An idea community inevitably attracts a company's most passionate customers, but it also draws thousands of their closest friends. At some point along the development cycle, typically late in the process, your developers will need more sophisticated feedback. Only a handful of the five thousand people who voted for a cool new feature actually know how to make it work. It's not hard to figure out who's part of that handful—their comments offer richer insight, and they often end up guiding the conversation. As you identify them, you can begin to create smaller idea-generation forums to tackle problems at a higher level. I call these smaller communities *beta forums,* sites where influencers with more expertise can share feedback about your latest release, help iron out any bugs, and suggest ideas for the next product.

Nokia does this very nicely with its Beta Labs. As I mentioned in Chapter Six, Nokia uses the Beta Labs program to identify some of its top ambassadors and put them to work on products in the development pipeline. The program has no formal process for membership—smart, because most passionate geeks hate even a whiff of process—but it does have a few basic rules to make sure conversation stays focused on the task at hand. Users get rated on their participation, earning as many points for collaboration as they do for original contribution. Nokia still enjoys the benefit of crowdsourcing ideas, while customers get to try out some cutting-edge products, lend a hand in their development, and earn some community recognition for their contributions. The company's superstars help harvest ideas faster than they could do within the company's walls alone.

Beta forums work especially well for companies whose products change rapidly and require a higher degree of technical expertise. To date, they've gained the most popularity among high-tech companies, which must work continuously to upgrade current products even as they search for the next great gizmo. A *beta site* resides somewhere in the middle ground between a wide open idea-generation site and a beta forum. It's most effective when you're willing to adapt a product, but only along the edges. You might want to find unexpected bugs or improve its usability by giving a wider base of fans a sneak peek at the latest thing.

Some of the biggest beta sites include names you know (Google always has betas), as well as SlideShare, Technorati, Livemocha, Remember The Milk, and other lesser-known sites. These programs engage enthusiasts during the mundane downtime between product launches—periods when many customers get bored and move on to other things. Beta sites are as much about building traffic and awareness as anything else, but they also deliver some exceptional product insights.

The best way to get a feel for these beta sites is to try one. Pick a product or company you actually care about, and if you're anything like me you'll get a kick out of weighing in with your ideas. The company will appreciate it, and if it knows how to properly incorporate the feedback it receives, you and your fellow customers will get a better product to use.

OPEN, CLEAN, AND FLEXIBLE

As with any social media tool, idea-generation sites only work for you when they also work for the community you hope to attract. It helps to remember the 1/9/90 rule of community participation—an idea-generation site should accommodate everyone, whether they contribute, share, or simply consume the content available there. Make sure you create a clean design and concept that doesn't trip users with useless programming or content clutter. Cluttered design and cluttered minds do the same thing: create unnecessary obstacles between ideas and the community. Assign a great moderator who can manage the site, encourage participation, and unobtrusively guide discussions. If you believe this can serve as an extension of your R&D, then find a good person to staff it, for heaven's sake.

Internally, you should take time to introduce the ideas you receive to your network of managers, the people who ultimately will act on these suggestions. It helps to place more emphasis on education at the beginning. Try ramming it down your managers' throats, and they'll see it as yet another task. If you create an environment that values all good ideas, regardless of their origin, your employees will act on ideas out of passion, not responsibility. Of course, that doesn't mean you shouldn't build accountability into the process. Take the time to understand the full lifecycle of ideas, from community to development. Integrate that into your company, along with responsibility for reporting progress along the way. The goal isn't to act on every idea, but you should expect brief reports on your team's decision to shut down or move ahead on the ideas the community provides.

As you get more comfortable with community idea generation, start to identify your key ambassadors and experts. Find the ideas for which you can leverage the wisdom of your more technically sophisticated enthusiasts. Focus these smaller beta forums to make sure they're precise enough to deliver actual business and product advantages.

In all facets of the idea-generation process, be willing to experiment over and over again, but do so with a little structure in place. Put a deadline on the community's sharing of ideas—no use asking for advice on products you're phasing out. Place a similar deadline on action within your walls. Don't let a good idea linger until it fades into oblivion, and don't try to keep a mediocre idea on life support. See what gets innovation going and keep trying.

Finally, be willing to admit that sometimes your customers know more than you do. It's impossible for any company, no matter how large its payroll, to understand every facet of the customer experience. Let you customers help you learn more. They'll appreciate it, and they'll reward you for it. Besides, it's actually a lot of fun.

CHAPTER NINE

CUSTOMER SUPPORT

The New Revenue Stream

*Statistics suggest that when customers complain,
business owners and managers ought to get excited
about it. The complaining customer represents a
huge opportunity for more business.*

—ZIG ZIGLAR, AUTHOR AND
MOTIVATIONAL SPEAKER

From his first appearance in the late 1960s, the Maytag repair-man personified the best in customer support. A lonely man, he sat around with his sorry-looking basset hound and waited for some-one, *anyone*, to give him a call. Alas, the call would never come, because Maytag's equipment never needed a repairman. The campaign worked so well, the company charged a premium for its brand and the Maytag repairman remains an icon for customers of a certain age.

Most of us grew up among the generation of business leaders who feel the fewer customer-support calls they receive, the better. It means customers are happy with their purchases, smiling all day long and look-ing forward to their next opportunity to buy our products. As a com-pany, you could define how customers contacted you. You provided a specific telephone number during a set time on certain days—24/7, this was not—and if someone was available they'd help out a customer.

Companies held control over the customer interactions; customers were fortunate to get a word in edgewise.

The rise of social media and the advent of Pre-Commerce shifted the tide. And as Warren Buffet likes to say, when the tide goes out you learn who's been swimming naked. To be frank, the traditional customer support model is missing a few garments. Yet the bulk of the Fortune 1000 companies continue to hang on to a traditional model of customer support. They wait for the phone to ring, at which time their corps of support reps answer the phone and unenthusiastically work their way through the script. Their bosses time each call to ensure the fastest (i.e., least costly) resolution possible. The company puts a premium on handling the problem and getting the customer off the phone.

It's a dinosaur model, and it's on its way to extinction. The dinosaur model lived on powerless consumers, and Pre-Commerce has taken away its sustenance. Ten years from now, the traditional model won't exist, at least not in regularly successful companies. I'd like to think it will disappear long before another decade passes, but an entire industry has arisen around call centers and customer care as we always knew it. Companies and consultants have generated mountains of research and molded it into a set of highly scripted interactions, whether on the phone or online. They have monetized the whole procedure based on specific actions with specific customers. Like most ingrained models, its experts live to improve it incrementally. The customer-support industry has built up a powerful inertia; companies won't overcome that anytime soon.

Your customers, though, are abandoning it in droves. As Pre-Commerce spreads, more and more customers will realize they can rely on peers for help. They'll discover a powerful megaphone for spreading the word when you don't fix their problems. In some cases, they'll cut you out of the loop entirely—unless you light the fuse, plug your ears, and blow up the traditional model. The companies that let the dinosaurs die and seek to engage customers on their terms will start to realize the Maytag repairman approach hid an awful lot of customer-support blemishes. But they also will discover something remarkable: In the Pre-Commerce marketplace, customer support can provide a new revenue stream. What once was considered nothing but a drain on corporate resources—and was continually optimized primarily to reduce costs—now can generate new sales and income.

It doesn't happen overnight. A company can't just reach out to an unhappy blogger and expect that person to instantly pledge undying loyalty to its brand. As with any revenue stream, companies must create a hardwired process. It takes three steps: (1) a plan to reach the majority of your customers online, (2) the establishment of a rigorous supply chain of customer experience, and (3) the integration of customer support and e-commerce. The result is a new Pre-Commerce model for customer care that reaches more customers, continuously strives to improve their experience with your brand, and begins to increase revenue flow. Done right, you'll turn a drain on your resources into a new stream of sales.

SEVEN MYTHS OF CUSTOMER SERVICE

1. *Language*—Speaking the same language doesn't go far enough. Customers connect with support agents who understand their background and culture.
2. *Scripts*—Most companies want to control each step of the process, but doing so strips away the insight and innovation your staff and your customers can bring to bear on a problem.

(Continued)

3. *We can't control the wait*—It takes time to work through the phone queue, but companies can save time by pointing customers to Web sites and forums that provide answers. Give customers other options while they're on hold, and let them decide if they want to wait or solve the problem on their own.

4. *Everyone is equal*—Let's face it: Some customers bring you more revenue and profit. It's why business class flyers get the comfy seats and the special service. As much as it rubs other customers the wrong way, companies need to know their "business class" customers and make their lives easier.

5. *Customers need all of the details*—Some customers want to understand every facet of the problem, but most just want their product to work. Cut out the jargon, and get the customer up and running.

6. *Customers care only about their issue*—Few customers will call you to suggest a solution to a problem, but they'll flock to forums and other social media outlets to do exactly that. Companies can get incredible insight from customers if they open up a channel to receive it. Doing so cuts down on support issues, but it also drives brand loyalty and sales.

7. *Customers don't mind calling again if they have another problem*—No one wants to sit in a phone queue, no matter how great your hold music might be. Give them options to avoid calling you in the future.

REACHING YOUR CUSTOMERS ONLINE

Most companies talk to a very small portion of their customer base. Most top executives talk to an even smaller slice. How much time in your most recent quarter did you spend in conversation with your loyal customers? And how much time did you spend talking to people who weren't happy with your products?

Imagine the hypothetical case of Dinosaur Widgets, which sells widgets to five million customers each year. Dinosaur makes a solid widget, and 20 percent of its sales go to repeat customers. So over a five-year span, the company's customer base encompasses over 20 million people. Now, Dinosaur makes a high-quality widget, but even the best widgets break down. The company gets one million calls each year, and it has staffed up with a large team of excellent customer-support professionals. They handle about 2,700 inquiries per day, and they have an excellent record of resolving problems quickly and properly. Dinosaur's internal surveys show that nine out of ten customers are happy with the support they receive, and its executives boast of the brand's high customer loyalty scores.

By traditional measures, Dinosaur Widgets has done quite well. They regularly transform potential problems into retained loyalty. The problem is that they do this with just 5 percent of their customer base each year. The hypothetical holds true in reality. No executive really wants to admit it, of course, but most companies spend their entire customer-support budget to reach only a sliver of their customer base. The overwhelming majority of customers won't contact you at any point during the product's life cycle. Many are perfectly satisfied with your quality product, but more than enough experience a problem or two. More and more, they're turning to social media to find solutions, asking for advice on forums, looking for ideas at Yahoo! Answers, or simply asking their peers for advice. If they get a solution to their problem, their appreciation goes to the online participants who helped them. Unless a company participates in these forums, they have no chance of actively retaining customer loyalty.

More than 77 percent of the U.S. population, almost 240 million residents, had regular Internet access in June 2010, according to

Internet World Stats.[1] The online penetration runs the same or higher in many of the world's top markets, including the U.K., Germany, Japan, and South Korea. In the emerging markets that haven't reached those penetration levels, the rate of online penetration is exploding. We're now over two billion Web-connected people on the planet, and it's not too big a stretch to imagine three billion in the not-too-distant future. It's time to stop thinking in terms of "online" and "offline." Your customers are online, and there they can control their own brand experience without your input. They're developing their own customer-support communities. As I write this, Yahoo! Answers alone lists more than 210,000 questions about laptop computers. Participants have posted about 200,000 answers about flowers and another 300,000 about recipes. They have questions and problems, but your version of the Maytag repairman is still lonely, sitting there with his hound dog.

To reach its Pre-Commerce customers, a company has to know exactly where its customers go to solve their problems. And it has to commit itself to meeting all of its customers on their home turf.

TEAR DOWN THE SILOS

Many companies align customer support within their business units. The group that builds Gizmos provides customer support for Gizmos. The team that builds Gadgets provides customer support for Gadgets. And so on throughout the company. The result is an unwieldy labyrinth of customer support, with the answers locked up in silos at every turn of the maze. Each department has carte blanche to figure out how they will handle customer relations, and the customer-support teams are supposed to handle the major "problems."

Customers don't think that way. It's not how they see your
brand. They see their purchase, and they see your company. That's
as far as it goes. If they reach out to your teams for help, they have
either a positive or negative response. Each time you interact with
them, you have an opportunity to build brand loyalty or reinforce
their belief that they're just another unit of sale. Customers can tell
from a mile away how a company views their patronage. How
many will return if you send them off into the labyrinth?

THE CUSTOMER-EXPERIENCE SUPPLY CHAIN

In the traditional marketing world, real customer interaction began at the
point of purchase. A customer might have asked about your brand, and
they might have gone from store to store to gather some expert advice.
But aside from your advertising output, you had no communication
with them. You could run focus groups and research surveys, but you
rarely interacted with customers as they formed an opinion about
your brand and readied for a purchase. For all intents and purposes, your
customer-experience supply chain began with the purchase.

Pre-Commerce has changed all that. Social media and other Web
avenues have given companies a powerful new influence on customer
experience—one that begins long before the purchase. In this changing
environment, it's imperative that companies reassess their entire supply
chain of customer experience. Business leaders need to outline every
point at which their teams and their brand can touch customers. It
starts with the customer's first search for product information and ends
only with a repeat purchase. (Said another way, it begins anew with the
repeat purchase.)

When I first sat down at Dell to contemplate this, I was overwhelmed by the sheer volume of interactions we had with customers. Dell always focused on direct relationships with its customers, but now I was faced with tens of thousands of different interaction points across the entire social media landscape. In most cases, we'd have dozens of interactions with a single potential customer, whether through search, YouTube, Twitter, or dozens of other influential sites. I realized, much to my chagrin, that we rarely owned the first impression of the Dell brand. That could come from almost anywhere.

We had to map out each potential place where a customer could learn about our products, visualizing the online ecosystem as a sort of map on the wall of my cubicle. The map couldn't help us reach every single point of first impression. After all, each company has its own set of what former U.S. Secretary of Defense Donald Rumsfeld called the "unknown unknowns"—the things you don't realize you don't know. You simply can't expect your customer-experience map to include each point of interaction, any more than you can expect to find a hundred-person village on a map of the world. Rather, the map can help you organize the ways you reach out to major points of first impression. For example, offline and online sales teams within most companies will speak with each other, but they rarely coordinate their story. Customers who research a product online usually hear a different story when they call or walk into a store. In some cases, the promotions you run online don't jibe with the promotions you offer in store.

The Pre-Commerce marketplace's key interaction points come well before the sale. In fact, these pre-sale experiences drive Pre-Commerce customers. To succeed in this new environment, business leaders must extend their customer-experience supply chain to include these interactions. Your supply chain has to include the independent ratings and review sites that influence potential customers. It has to encompass relationships with influential bloggers and forum participants. It has to include a deeper understanding of the ways customers search for your brands and your competitors' products.

TOUCH POINTS FOR ONLINE SEARCH

Some fairly simple research can reveal the words customers use when researching your products online, and how those searches change when they move from initial curiosity to decision-making mode to the actual purchase. Using those terms, your teams can scrape these conversations so your top online support reps can speak directly with potential customers and help them make their decision.

Worldwide, people searched for the term "laptops" five million times a month as I researched this book. Within those results, I discovered that "cheap" was a rising term in those searches—"cheap Toshiba laptops" showed up about one million times and "cheap Acer laptops" showed up about 830,000 times. You can track the trend for "cheap" in the ways people searched for laptops. Similarly, a search for "recipes" delivered 20 million hits, while a look at related terms revealed the regular use of "easy" in conjunction with recipe.

When viewed as a whole, search can send a clear message about customer demands.

Because pre-sales interaction is a relatively new phenomenon, companies will need to commit the most resources to mapping out this phase of the overall customer experience. However, it falls to business leaders to make sure their teams also learn how the sales process itself changes in a Pre-Commerce marketplace. More and more customers will arrive at a company's e-commerce site with their decisions already made. Still, companies inevitably will bombard them with deals and promotions in a vain hope that it might sway a customer away from a competitor. It's the online equivalent of walking into a retail store knowing what you need, and then having a relentless salesman try to convince you that you really want another product. That doesn't mean promotions should go out the window, but the design of your e-commerce site should accommodate the fact that the customer has made his or her decision. Just make it easy and enjoyable for them to make the purchase. For example, focus your promotions on other accessories that complement the product experience. Also remember that customers sometimes visit your site to just learn. Know the ratio of learning visits to transactions and ask yourself if your site is meeting the real needs of your visitors.

At every phase, companies have to make sure the customer-experience supply chain looks forward to the next step. Once you make the sale, for example, your warranty and marketing groups will jump into the fray. Today, most companies send e-mails to the customer, proposing an extended warranty or upgraded service package. The marketers toss out more e-mails to suggest other products and send dead-tree catalogs. Few customers want any of these things, so engage them in ways that matter to them. Invite them to participate in a company-sponsored or quality independent forum or community of like-minded customers. They might participate, they might not, but either way they'll appreciate it much more than your corporate spam.

Customers who do participate in these sorts of communities also can turn to them if they have a problem with their products. More and more Pre-Commerce customers will turn to their peers to address a problem before they reach out to your customer-support teams. If you've guided them to a high-quality online community at the point of sale, you've taken the first customer-support step already. And if you're vigilant and maintain an active presence in these and other social media communities, you can find aggravated customers earlier and provide them the help they need. Nothing engenders more loyalty than a problem that's solved thoroughly *and* unexpectedly.

Few otherwise exceptional companies have bothered to stop and map out the customer-experience supply chain, so they're blind to the interconnections between each phase—from pre-sale, through the sale, the support, and to the return purchase. They wait for customers to approach them for information (ain't happenin'). They hope their e-mail barrage strikes a chord (ain't happenin'). And they hope no news really is good news, suggesting a decent chance that a repeat purchase might be on the way (sorry, but that ain't happenin' either). The company that maps out their customer-experience supply chain can add value at each step. They can identify a customer's online behavior and build appropriate bridges from one stage of the customer-experience to the next. They can eliminate wasted efforts and enact a program that will engender brand loyalty in the Pre-Commerce marketplace.

INTEGRATE CUSTOMER SUPPORT AND E-COMMERCE

The customer-experience map will help you visualize and understand your customer interactions, but it doesn't mean much if you, as an executive, don't integrate that insight into your actual business processes. This supply chain should take every bit of real, focused work as your traditional value chains. And as you build the processes that will integrate your online outreach with your e-commerce activities, you'll start to discover the greatest Pre-Commerce opportunities. You'll start to find that rich interactions exist along all the points of the customer-experience cycle that will drive sales in and of themselves.

I work with several Fortune 500 companies, several of which have at least five thousand customer support representatives. They handle calls and inquiries of all types, but they rarely interact with the

Pre-Commerce customer. I've encouraged several of these clients to select the fifty support reps who can best articulate the company's solutions to an online audience to build a dedicated Pre-Commerce team that can maximize the sharing of intellectual capital. They can reach out to customers at any point along the customer-experience cycle, a push that can lead directly to revenue. In the pre-sales stage, a diligent representative can sway a customer to the right product. At the point of sale, your teams can suggest additional products or services that will upgrade the customer's experience. And in the post-sales, customer-service phase, a Pre-Commerce team can continue to engender the brand loyalty that drives repeat sales.

When integrated with your commercial processes, the ongoing customer support supplied by your Pre-Commerce teams will lead directly to revenue. Most companies I consult with are skeptical, but I've seen it work every single time that a company does it.

Your Pre-Commerce support team members should be intimately familiar with Yahoo! Answers, Mahalo, Aardvark, and other sites customers go to for product and troubleshooting advice. The team should include people fluent in the languages that cover the bulk of your customers (remember, ten languages reach 90 percent of the people online). They should display a keen understanding of how to increase your company's reach through online search. They should "speak" in plain language, and they should interact with customers in as transparent a manner as possible without overstepping legal boundaries or company policy. In essence, they should be able to describe your products as if talking to their grandmother, neighbor, or second cousin.

You'll let these fifty agents identify themselves online—in fact, you'll demand they do so. You'll let them become personalities in their own right, real-life characters with whom customers can build a real connection. You'll train them and then trust them, so you can set them loose to make decisions on their own. And you'll give them the time and flexibility to learn as they go, to understand and gather customer-provided information that can improve your next product or service.

You empower your Pre-Commerce team to provide special promotions that spur sales. You let them surprise online friends with special coupons available only through your team. Every time your team sends a link to new information, you let them drop in a special deal to draw customers through to the information you want them to have on hand. You'll make it easy for customers to pass along all this information, because they'll be able to recommend these same deals to other customers. And pretty soon, the other 4,950 agents are going to want in. This is more fun than talking reactively to upset customers, and it's more rewarding because it rings the cash register bell. So now you expand your training program to reinvent how you do customer support.

But you don't stop with the internal teams. You build a syndication network that distributes your content across the areas of online influence. You share every key Q&A so it reaches forty times more people than come to your Web site. You let the world know what you know, but you also find and share what other people know about your brand, too. So you start to identify the top forums, blogs, and other sites on which your product line is discussed, and you and your teams join the conversations on those sites. You recognize your smartest customers and online influencers, and you start featuring them on your site and through your content-syndication network. Great ideas might come from anywhere, so you fully embrace the intelligence of the customer community. After all, they know how people use your products better than anyone. So you build a "best of the Web" site that features your customers' best solutions and your top Q&As.

What you won't do is hit your customers over the head with unsolicited information and spam. You won't complicate things by trying to present your brand as something it's not. You won't look at customers only as potential transactions. You won't put your support teams out of a job, because by reaching twenty times more people online than through a phone queue you'll want to have the smartest people you can find for your customer support. They will be your heroes in the Pre-Commerce marketplace.

The Pre-Commerce model for customer support shouldn't sound like anything especially radical. It centers on principles of great customer service that companies always espoused but rarely lived up to. It exposes the lip service companies always paid to genuine customer service. We say the customer is always right, but we furnish our support teams with a script and force agents to stay on a prescribed path no matter what the customer says. By default, we tell the customers we're right, and all will be fine in their world if they listen to us. We survey a small fraction of our customer base and extrapolate all we need to know about the rest. By default, we tell the remainder that we don't really care what they think—unless they reach out to talk to us (and do we really listen even then?). We have a lot of bad habits we try to cover up with rhetoric. It's what happens in a dying model; our own words enable us. We become our own worst enemy.

THE PRE-COMMERCE QUIZ

As business leaders build out their Pre-Commerce customer-support teams, it's important to make sure the answers to these questions don't waver. Answer them at the outset, and let them guide you as you develop your Pre-Commerce strategy:

1. How do I make sure I'm building customer loyalty with my strategy?
2. How much does it cost to add new customers and how do I gain access to them?

3. How do my costs change as I integrate a Pre-Commerce model to reach more customers?
4. What can I do to further empower my customer support team so they can solve problems and sell solutions?
5. How do I include customers and online influencers in my Pre-Commerce efforts? How often are my products recommended online and by whom?

The last question forces executives to rethink how they appraise customer experience. Customer satisfaction and net promoter scores no longer provide the full picture. They never really did, but they worked well for the 1990s. Today, your customers will flock to Google, YouTube, and Bing. They interact with peers to share information and opinions about your brand. They share answers online, whether yours or their own. They gravitate toward influencers who provide useful content and reliable answers.

Old diagnostic models only get you halfway to those revenues. Only your actual share of conversation and your customers' actions define how far you've moved the needle. Companies that understand Pre-Commerce will generate real and significant revenue with their online activities.

EVERY COMPLAINT IS AN OPPORTUNITY

It was one of those impossibly hot and humid days in South Florida, the kind of day that makes your temples sweat just thinking about it. I walked twenty yards from my car to the air-conditioned lobby of the doctor's office and felt like I needed a towel. I didn't need the heat;

I already felt enough tension that day to make me sweat. I was a newly minted sales rep for CIBA-GEIGY, and one of my first stops took me to this family practice in Englewood, Florida. I walked in, introduced myself, and, after an escort to a room where I would wait for the two doctors who ran the practice, tried to cool myself down. I was new to this whole thing, but at least I had a good product to pitch—a drug that could dissolve gallstones and put off invasive surgery. I felt I had a winner, and all I had to do was let physicians know about it.

It wasn't long before I was sweating again. The two doctors who ran the practice walked in, heard I worked for CIBA-GEIGY, and started dressing me down. They didn't like the past sales rep, and they were determined to take it out on me. The last rep, they said, let them down, never followed up on their requests, and they'd be damned before they'd prescribe another drug from my company. I couldn't believe how much vitriol they spewed. Heck, we'd never even met before.

A year later, they were one of my top customers. I don't know if it was a desire to please them or prove I could do better than my predecessor—probably a little of both—but I forced myself to listen to their complaints. It wasn't pleasant, but I learned what they needed from me and from the company. They complained, and through their complaints they provided answers I could use to meet their needs, exceed their expectations, and turn a bad situation into an opportunity for my company. They actually liked the product a lot, but they had to get certain questions answered and learn more before they could proceed. My predecessor never made the time to provide answers. He made promises he never kept. And he inadvertently taught me an invaluable life lesson: Every problem is an opportunity in disguise.

Years later at Dell, as we did our first analysis of the online world, we found we had a 48 percent negative share of online conversation in the United States alone. In other words, almost half of all the online discussions about the Dell brand weren't exactly stellar. But when we dug deeper, I started to realize I was back in the doctor's office in South Florida. The conversations were filled with passion and directed by people who wanted to like us but felt that we had let them down, sometimes more than once. They were letting us have it, and we deserved every bit of it. Now we just had to start acting on the feedback they'd given us.

It's like our parents yelling at us or our teachers getting frustrated and pushing back when we didn't try hard enough. It was our coach getting on our nerves to provoke a reaction and a stronger work rate. No one gets more frustrated with you than the people who really care about you. They get annoyed or mad precisely because they care and know we can do better. For the most part, customers aren't any different, and my Dell colleagues and I were really hearing it. Driven by Michael Dell and Kevin Rollins, we adopted a Pre-Commerce mindset and within two years had reduced our negative share of conversation to less than 25 percent—not great, but a lot better than where we'd started.

The biggest improvements came from people acting on common sense. Brad Laurich is a big dude, about six foot three, and he always looked especially imposing in his tiny cubicle. But Brad always had a smile on his face and always took time to consider what we could do better. His customer care background made him particularly good at answering questions customers posed on our Web sites. One day, I noticed that Brad had started to answer a few questions about Dell products on Yahoo! Answers. I got up, walked the four cubicles over to his desk, and asked him why he started doing it. He gave me a sort of surprised look and said it just made sense. Why not share the same answers he gave customers on Dell Web sites with a broader audience, so more people could learn from us?

It was such a no-brainer, I didn't even stop to think about the potential outcomes. I asked him to start answering questions on a methodical basis and track how customers reacted. Within a year, Brad had answered more than 300 questions and had a 92 percent efficiency rating, meaning the community put a very high value on his contributions. He had more than 500 fans who subscribed to his Q&As, so they could receive any updates he provided and pass them along to friends. He also landed a free spot in Yahoo! Answers' ad on the side of the technology section. Even better for Dell, Brad's answers impacted search results and reached entirely new audiences because they were syndicated through search engines. We'd stumbled, entirely by accident, on the ideal example of Pre-Commerce customer care—support delivered on an ongoing basis, not just when customers pick up the phone.

FINDING THE HIDDEN CUSTOMER

Not long after Brad gave Dell a presence on external Q&A sites, Sean McDonald stopped by my desk to suggest an idea for our own online properties. Sean ran our community forums with Natalie Davis, and the two of them had come up with a new idea that would give customers the option to solve their own problems. Sean and Natalie called it "Accepted Solutions," a new feature that allowed customers to post a problem on our Dell forums and let another customer solve the problem. Our teams would verify the helpful customer's advice, and if it worked we would publicly label it as an "Accepted Solution." The community would get the credit, and customers seeking help would have a go-to solution at their fingertips.

I loved the idea. We added it to our list of what I called science projects, because we had a hypothesis that sounded fantastic, but we had no real clue if it would work or how. We always made sure we let our science projects have a chance to percolate, so we started the Accepted Solutions experiment and pledged to give it enough time to definitely work or fail.

We built this new functionality with the help of Lithium, our community partner at the time. Eight short months later, we'd received more than 15,000 accepted solutions from the community. Even better, we had an average of 350 views per solution, a number that continued to grow from month to month. All told, our forum communities viewed their peers' accepted solutions more than five million times in eight months. Even if only 20 percent of those interactions actually helped our customers, our community produced one million customer-support interactions we never could have supplied on our own.

Of course, this piqued our curiosity. We wondered how this might impact our traditional call-center volume. But when we checked, there was no real change. The people who went to our forums in search of solutions never planned to call us. Our customer support was reaching an entirely new set of customers, a group we never really knew how to reach before. Companies that rely on traditional customer support don't know how to reach these folks. In fact, most of those companies don't even realize these customers are looking for help. Meanwhile, competitors who understand the Pre-Commerce marketplace are finding those customers, helping them, and stealing away their loyalty.

Dell certainly isn't the only personal-computer company patrolling social media for ways to help its customers. Hewlett-Packard created a forum called the I.T. Resource Center, through which the online community and HP's own support specialists take feedback and answer customers' questions. It's the combination of HP engineers and tech-savvy customers that makes the forum especially effective, said Scott Anderson, vice president of customer communications for the company's enterprise business. "The connectivity among the entire community is what it's all about," he said. "Our bloggers also get a lot of support questions. Incoming questions are a great way not only to address issues but also to hear feedback and learn what our customers think about our products and services. Since the day we decided to embrace incoming comments some number of years ago, we have welcomed and addressed feedback whether good or bad. Our mission is to understand, respond, and learn from what we hear."

Few companies have made customer support a central piece of their social media strategy as have HP and Dell. And no company ties fantastic customer service directly to sales as well as Zappos. The online shoe retailer, now a division of Amazon.com, is fanatical about doing right by the customer. They bend over backward to meet their consumers where and how those customers want to interact. And Zappos employees make sure that customer service is part of the customer experience—from pre-sale research all the way to the end of the product's life cycle. The company's tagline pretty much says it all: "Powered by Customer Service."

Even from the outside, you can see the Zappos mindset starting to soak into other parts of Amazon's business. The companies are establishing themselves as leaders in the Pre-Commerce marketplace, but they don't have any special sauce or trade secret. You and your teams can replicate what Zappos and Amazon are doing every day. But it takes the leadership of executives who are willing to put their money where their mouths are—to get everyone in the company focused on providing truly great customer service at every touch-point in the customer-experience supply chain.

CHAPTER TEN

POLITICS AND BUSINESS
Reshaping Our Beliefs

*If liberty and equality, as is thought by some, are chiefly
to be found in democracy, they will be best attained when
all persons alike share in government to the utmost.*
—ARISTOTLE

Years from now, we'll look back on the 2008 presidential campaign
as the opening salvo for Pre-Commerce politics. Hoping to engage
constituents on a more personalized and grassroots level, opposing
Senators Barack Obama and John McCain each beefed up their campaign staffs with social media gurus, blitzing the Web in an effort to
drum up donations, support, and political momentum.

McCain's campaign generated tons of content, using especially
short videos its supporters could share with friends and undecided
voters. Yet by all accounts, McCain's social media efforts failed to create the truly interactive and cohesive community that Obama enjoyed.
That community, energized by a feeling that it had at least some
small impact on Obama's agenda, swept the Illinois Democrat into the
White House.

In the end, Obama's staff became the first in U.S. presidential history to make social media a fundamental part of its political outreach.
The effort generated almost 500 million blog mentions, about 845,000

MySpace friends, and nearly 120,000 Twitter followers by Election Day, according to Sean Donahue, senior vice president at The Herald Group, a Washington D.C.–based public affairs, communications, and advocacy consulting firm. (Sean and I previously worked together on the social media team at Dell.) The campaign created its own social network, called My.BarackObama.com, where hundreds of thousands of supporters could interact with one another, donate money, or help spread the word on Obama's initiatives. And by allowing users to personalize the site and its content for their interests, they could build their own communities in support of the larger campaign infrastructure. The political campaign had gone social.

"For the first time in history, people who had absolutely nothing to do with the physical day-to-day operations of the campaign—whether in an office or out in the field—felt as if they were helping lead it," Donahue says. "While voters were encouraged to share and syndicate ideas, social media during the 2008 campaign was less about policy and more about belonging to and advancing a historic movement."

Sean has been on the forefront of politics and social media change. He first quenched his political thirst at twelve years old, as the youngest visiting member of the White House Press Corps. He was the senior White House correspondent for WBZ-Radio's "Kid Company." At an age I was shooting hoops and taking batting practice, Sean was interviewing President Bill Clinton, Sen. Edward Kennedy, and Sen. Bob Dole. He later served as an on-air analyst for CNN's Financial Network during the 1996 presidential primaries and, while still in college, was a member of the White House advance staff for President Clinton. He cut his social media teeth at Dell, leading the company's online environmental community at ReGeneration.org.

While the Obama campaign hinted that true interaction between civic leaders and the public they serve might be on the rise, Donahue says, his presidency has resulted in the same overly cautious skepticism

of social media. If the Obama campaign redefined how political organizations interact with voters, we have yet to see a White House that
fully embraces the power of social media. The reason?

"One word: control," Donahue explains. "Since the presidential
election of 1828, American politics has consisted of highly orchestrated
activities and events. While citizens have always been encouraged to
play a role in elections and the broader policymaking process, until
recently very few options for real-time communication existed."

With the rise of social media and the emergence of a Pre-Commerce
society, we now have dozens of platforms for real-time communication.
*Yet we also have a growing expectation that our civic and business leaders will use
them to facilitate a true interaction between themselves, their staffs, and us, the voting
and purchasing public.* Unfortunately, the momentum from Obama's campaign didn't carry over to his White House administration. Politicians
and executives will site privacy or trade secrets as an excuse for not
fully embracing social media. But it really boils down to this: Few business or civic leaders have come to grips with the fact that customers
and constituents have a newfound control over brands, messages, and
agendas—and they're ready to wield it.

NEEDS, PRINCIPLES, AND FILTERS

Try as it might, business will never separate itself from government, and
this fact won't change in the Pre-Commerce world. What will change
are the ways governments and businesses interact with one another,
their customers, and their constituents. In a world where troves of
information lie at our fingertips and ubiquitous social media outlets
offer a powerful public forum, the commonalities between government
leaders and corporate brands grow ever tighter. At a fundamental level,
political issues and commercial products become one and the same.

As customers and constituents, we fire our political beliefs in the same kiln we use to decide which product to buy.

Looking at it this way, we can start to get a clearer understanding of how our customers' and constituents' core needs and principles impact their decisions. On a fundamental level, let's start with Maslow's famous hierarchy of needs. In his seminal 1943 essay "A Theory of Human Motivation," Abraham Maslow laid out a framework of human needs that drive our actions, influence our beliefs, and shape our development.[1] Maslow's model resonates because it offers a glimpse into how we become who we are, and how that creates a foundation for the core principles we use to filter information about issues and products.

- *Physiological needs*—We have certain basic needs that can't be compromised. What companies are supplying those needs (or denying them), and what are government leaders doing to ensure our needs are met?
- *Safety*—We naturally want to avoid physical and emotional harm. Who will keep us safe, and whose oversight—whether intentional or not—puts us or our loved ones at risk?
- *Love and Belonging*—We want to be part of a community, and those affiliations help shape our identity. Who will work for our community's best interests?
- *Esteem*—We want to participate and be recognized for it. Do our political or business leaders give us an opportunity to participate in the public debate or provide input for product improvements?
- *Self-actualization*—We constantly search for ways we can improve our lives and the lives of our loved ones. Who or what will help us do this?

We might make a fortune, have a wonderful family life, and travel the world, but at the end of the day we never get away from these basic needs. We're pretty simple in that sense, and successful business and political leaders cannot overlook these basics. The best leaders, however, also understand that these basic needs establish the foundation for a breathtaking amount of human variation and complexity. There are almost seven billion people on the planet, and each individual has constructed an elaborate set of core, personal beliefs and principles that guide his or her life. Individuals use this framework of principles to filter all the external stimuli they take in—the information, the relationships, and the experiences they encounter every second of every day. And they filter all those experiences so they can identify how each one satisfies or threatens their basic needs.

I don't tell you this to impart any great wisdom, because this is just common sense. I tell you this because the way your customers or constituents filter their experiences has a direct impact on what they decide to buy and how they decide to vote. And I tell you this because the advent of the Pre-Commerce ecosystem has had a dramatic impact on how people filter the information they receive.

A couple decades ago, our experiences revolved around a relatively small set of people, places, and things. Today, the Web and social media deliver an explosion of people, places, and things most people could not have experienced in the past. We now have access to more information than we can process in a lifetime. We have access to easy-to-use but extremely powerful forums through which we can interconnect with billions of people around the world. Today we have to filter an ever-growing tidal wave of information and experience. So although our core principles might not change, the way we filter all those experiences does.

IN CRISIS, CONFUSION

The 2010 BP oil spill in the Gulf of Mexico provides an excellent example of how our filtering of experiences has changed in the

Pre-Commerce environment. BP didn't need a public relations guru to tell them they had a disaster on their hands. They could see it immediately by the public reaction—not just through major media outlets but across social media platforms, where millions of people vented their outrage and debated the fallout.

In the midst of such crises, companies often get caught up in short-term thinking. Whether we admit it to ourselves or not, these catastrophes fade to the back of our minds with the passing of time. What lasts over the long term is the way these major experiences subtly change the way customers and constituents filter these events through their core sets of principles. One person's interpretation of the oil spill might be guided by the impact it has on the Gulf's ecosystem and its people. He filters the events of this catastrophe through this lens, supplements it with his interpretations of similar, previous events (e.g., the Exxon Valdez spill), and decides that punitive action against the company is fully justified. The person across the table might view the oil spill as a series of extremely unfortunate technological and human failures. She might weigh the local environmental and economic impacts against the need to fulfill the country's necessary demand for energy. She might start to push for smarter, but not crippling, regulation of offshore drilling.

Same event, same set of facts available to both parties, but filtered in two entirely different ways, each one based on an existing set of personal principles. When it comes to major crises, whether commercial or political, the lasting impact has less to do with the obvious, in-the-moment phenomena and more to do with the way people weigh their observations against their beliefs. Yet companies, organizations, and leaders dump virtually all their time and energy into a crisis plan that mitigates short-term effects: "We did a great job of minimizing the negative fallout from the oil spill." They do very little to address the way each person's principles shape their reactions to the problem: "They want gas to fuel their cars, but they cringe when they see the impact our fossil fuel products have on the environment."

Leaders of any organization—whether a company, a government, or an NGO—have to understand how an issue touches on their constituents' core needs, and how their constituents process any threat to those needs through their deeply held set of core principles. You might survive a catastrophe in the short term, but if you don't understand the longer-term impact determined by your customers' or constituents' needs and principles, you're bound to lose their trust, their votes, or their business.

THE GOOD AND BAD OF REINFORCEMENT

One company screw-up rarely changes a customer's core beliefs or principles. Virtually every large company at some point makes a significant error that impacts customers. Most of them work hard to refocus and recover, and eventually they regain their customers' trust (if they lost it in the first place). But the companies that commit a series of significant mistakes and show no real evidence of improving their record will turn their customers against them. The BP rig explosion, which killed eleven workers, and the subsequent oil spill came just five years after a massive explosion at a Texas refinery killed fifteen workers there.

The human mind naturally ties together a series of interrelated events. Anything perceived as repetition reinforces prior experiences and beliefs. Combine that with all the information we absorb as we gather information and interact with peers online, and it becomes enough to influence how we filter an issue or brand through our principles. For BP, the spill in and of itself is

(*Continued*)

a short-term issue. They will work to clean it up and try to do everything by the book. But in the minds of customers, the voting public, and legislators, the spill ties into dozens of other environmental issues and catastrophes. The explosion on BP's offshore rig ties directly to its Texas City refinery explosion and concerns about workplace safety as a whole. This continuous reinforcement of issues touches on our core beliefs and principles, and that makes the issue much more dangerous for the long term. It sparks the ire of politicians and customers who demand retribution. It turns customers against your brand and sends them scrambling to competitors.

As any marketing pro can tell you, when you start to lose market share, it gets extremely expensive and tiring to win it back. But when you lose the principled support of lawmakers, customers, and partners, the difficulties increase exponentially. Flashy advertisements, confessional advertisements, and donations to charity don't fix that. In the Pre-Commerce world, people have search engines, blogs, video sites, Twitter, and forums to help them decide whether you're real or not. And what they find will impact the principles that guide their votes and their purchases.

SWAYING THE NEUTRALS

Rare is the bird that flies through legislative chambers without a partisan challenge. Pure politicking aside, that partisanship has its roots in the principles that guide our individual decision-making process. When the U.S. government passed the largest stimulus bill in the country's history, it strengthened more basic arguments for and against the proposal. For people whose principles aligned with Keynesian economics, the stimulus was an effective and necessary measure. Those whose principles aligned with free markets and *laissez faire* oversight of free markets interpreted it as a socialist power grab.

The partisans with strong principles related to economic policy already made up their minds, and they won't budge because the issue so strongly justifies their core beliefs. But a vast majority of the public took a more neutral stance on the issue. Most politicians understand the importance of wooing the independent voter, and they never really stop campaigning with them in mind. But few leaders have shown an ability to reach constituents in the Pre-Commerce world. Millions of independent thinkers are discussing issues on forums, blogs, and social networking sites. They crave an open and honest dialog, because they care deeply about their own wellbeing, as well as that of their family and community. People want to feel as though they've made an informed decision. Yet despite the forum social media provides, not a single politician has stepped up to conduct an ongoing, continuous conversation with constituents. Given a powerful new channel to reach independent voters, politicians have ignored it in favor of the same propaganda through the same tired avenues.

As for companies, even fewer spend time to even recognize the massive population of potential customers who, for now, don't care one way or another about their brands. These folks show up as neutral sentiment scores and typically comprise more than 60 percent of a company's overall potential customer base. Companies consistently overlook the neutrals, and in the past it didn't really hurt them. But the expansion of the Pre-Commerce marketplace brings an entirely new set of influences that are swaying more and more neutrals. Are they moving toward you, or has one of their peers convinced them that your competitor has the better solution for their needs?

Keep in mind, though, you haven't lost all your ability to influence potential customers. As we discussed in Chapter Nine, every single one of your actions plays out in the customer-experience supply chain.

Your long-term brand reputation depends on how customers view your products and services and how you handle your business in the public eye. And because each interaction along the customer-experience supply chain builds on the last, each one quietly confirms or changes the ways customers filter experiences with your brand. They'll do this whether you actively interact with them or not.

Few business leaders commit the foresight and social media resources to play a role in those interactions, despite plenty of evidence that shows the positive impact companies can still have on a customer's decision-making process. A business leader who handles a recall quickly and judiciously will stand out in the mind of customers (think Tylenol, for example). But leaders just as easily lose that goodwill if they don't also commit to providing the best customer-experience in more mundane times. A politician might garner a lot of voter support with the right stance on a hot-button issue, but a consistent pattern of votes that conflicts with his constituents' beliefs will kill his chances come Election Day.

FROM MAD COW TO MARTHA STEWART

I've worked on a rather eclectic mix of major issues throughout my career. I worked on behalf of the British government to help explain Mad Cow disease. I handled communications for an anthrax-exposure case in Manhattan. I helped craft the strategy around one of the largest battery recalls in the PC industry's history. I even dealt with the fallout of the Martha Stewart insider trading case through my work with ImClone on their top new drug.

I haven't seen it all, but I've seen a lot of it—from labor issues in Europe to intellectual property issues in India. And in every case, without exception, the company or government that focused on the long-term impact from the outset found the greatest success. The British government immediately understood the importance of stressing the dangers and the limits of Mad Cow disease. They didn't underplay its threat, yet they calmly explained that it didn't pose a risk to everyone who lived or visited the U.K. And sure enough, cooler heads prevailed with time. Before we issued a large battery recall at Dell, we knew every company who sourced batteries from the same manufacturer would have to issue a recall at some point, too. We went first anyway—in part because it was the right thing to do, but also because we knew customers would appreciate our proactive approach to product quality and safety.

It never feels good when you're in the middle of the hurricane. Armchair experts send slings and arrows flying from all sides. The risk-averse business leaders see too much risk with every move and question even the most obvious of decisions. We get caught up in all the mayhem and forget the foundation upon which each customer forms their beliefs. We forget the basic needs everyone inherently drives to satisfy. No matter what sort of organization you lead, when the dust settles your ability (or inability) to help satisfy your public's needs will shape your reputation.

THE OPPORTUNITY PART OF THE PROBLEM

I can't sugarcoat it for you: The Pre-Commerce environment gives you a lot of chances to make a mistake. But it also gives you an incredible opportunity to change public opinion about your brand or your agenda—both in the short and in the long term. Properly used, social media and its ability to foster real interactions between you and your customers or constituents can have a radical impact on your brand value. Not only can you and your influencers sway negative or neutral perceptions, but you can also start to subtly influence the principles through which people filter their experiences.

While this can deliver some incredible long-term value for your company or campaign, it requires an active involvement from you, your teams, and your influencers. You first have to identify both the rare and chronic problems your organization faces so you can prepare for them. Gather your teams and compile all the known issues your brand can encounter, and use that thorough list to build a radar screen that can identify potential bogeys as they appear. Start to track each of those issues proactively, using an online monitoring system, and make it part of someone's job to stay on top of this. (Dozens of Web companies have developed online monitoring that helps spot the smoke before it becomes a fire.)

As you track these issues, create a graph that charts the status of the issues, perhaps marking them in green, yellow, and red, depending on their severity. Collect links and data to support your rating of each problem, so you're making good estimates based on data and not just guessing. And share all this information with an organization-wide, multifunction group, so you can use their collective brainpower to connect dots you don't see on your own. If you do it right, you'll have one person focused on this as part of their job. Beyond that, it should take no more than twenty of your smartest people about thirty minutes a week to review the latest issues.

When you start to incorporate a system like this, a funny thing starts to happen. Your teams start to recognize potential landmines long before they reach the public consciousness. They can see whether a problem is universal or specific to one customer or small group of constituents. They can address a customer's problem proactively, delivering a better experience and hopefully building greater brand loyalty. Your people can engage directly with unsatisfied stakeholders and provide them with a solution, a bit of encouragement, or an alternative point of view. At the very least, if your initial efforts fail you can prepare a response in case the issue hits the mainstream press. If you still wait for an issue to reach the attention of the mainstream media, you're old school—and you're too late. You're taking the slowest and least helpful approach to problem mitigation.

During my last year at Dell, the company's "hot issues" team identified and proactively handled eighty-one of eighty-six issues before they went public. By moving quickly, we could fix those problems asap with much less effort and fewer resources. But we also found we'd gained new allies. We started to notice the problems, but we also started to see who wielded real influence on other customers, whether positive or negative. We could start to manage the share of conversation and, to some extent, influence the influencers on issues important to Dell. By working with both positive and negative influencers, we could shape the conversation before the manure hit the fan. We could show people we cared, every day, about the same issues they did. And when all hell broke loose, as it inevitably does, we discovered we had a whole corps of Pre-Commerce allies ready to defend us—or at least set the record straight.

I wish I could say you'll stop getting into trouble when you develop a social media strategy and engage your Pre-Commerce customers. As it turns out, it will only help you spot more trouble. But you'll find it before it gets out of hand and drains your resources. You'll work proactively, and customers will start to realize that you care about their experience with your products, your support, and your overall brand. And in the long term, you'll start to ingratiate your brand with the principles they use to filter their experiences and come to their decisions.

Ask yourself if you really know what issues are brewing for your brand right now. Do you know?

DEFINING YOUR REPUTATION

In February 2010, U.S. legislators took Toyota to the woodshed. The giant automobile company had conducted three separate recalls over the previous three months, including one recall of its prized Prius and Lexus hybrid vehicles. Drivers claimed problems with the accelerator or the braking system led to serious accidents, and Congress was eager to get to the bottom of the issue. The hearings raised some questions about the cause and the full extent of the problems, but Toyota pledged to address the issue and fix the vehicles.

Intuitively, most of us believe Toyota engineers have the expertise to correct the problem. And we rationally accept that regulations and government agencies, such as the Consumer Product Safety Commission (CPSC), prevent most potentially hazardous products from ever reaching the marketplace. But as Maslow showed us, safety is one of our most primary needs, so as customers we become skeptics of Toyota's engineers and the CPSC inspectors. We are conditioned by our basic needs to care about product safety, and when a problem with a product touches on this most fundamental of needs, as Toyota's safety issues did, a lot of customers will get very skeptical.

Their skepticism won't fade away with a clever ad campaign. Rebuilding the customer's confidence—and restoring your brand's reputation—takes interaction between your customers, their peers, and your employees. Toyota representatives can explain the problems with their cars and describe the procedures the company took to address it, and that helps. But customers also consult with other Toyota owners and independent automobile experts who have studied the problem, driven the repaired or new models, and can attest to their safety. "They go online and read what their peers have said about the problems, a persistent ability customers didn't have in the past," said Sandra Macleod, CEO of ECHO Research, which provides reputational advice and research to Fortune 1000 companies around the world. "There is a permanence to many items on the Web that did not characterize paper media," Sandra told me. "The rate of decay of a criticism of a corporation is slow or nonexistent, because it can sit on servers or search engines for months or years, which argues for crisis avoidance and reputational protection like never before."

It won't happen, but Toyota's recalls and PR nightmare should convince every company to move beyond traditional methods of identifying and dealing with problems and to integrate an effective and well-reasoned Pre-Commerce strategy. I realize it's easy and often misleading to play Monday Morning Quarterback, but it's possible that a robust social media tracking program would have allowed Toyota to flip the tables. Perhaps the company's Pre-Commerce team would have noticed individual complaints about its accelerators and braking systems and could have identified the larger problem. In theory, they could have moved proactively to address the initial complaints and perhaps positioned a voluntary recall as a preventative measure.

It's not always easy or possible to do this, and I have no interest in parsing through Toyota's responses. But what's clear is that a smart Pre-Commerce strategy puts you ahead of the game, not behind the 8-ball. Even if you can't act immediately, your Pre-Commerce teams give you options. For example, if you notice a component of your product is starting to fail, you can work with the supplier for days or even weeks before the issue becomes a problem. And when people start talking about it, you have a solution ready to roll out immediately. Your customers are grateful for your quick response.

Simply put, a Pre-Commerce strategy can help you offset, perhaps even completely reverse, a damaging blow to your brand reputation. You can take control of issues, their media coverage, and the factors that shape the whole discussion. But to date, few of the Fortune 1000 companies have crafted a thorough social media strategy. And almost

Figure 10.1 Most Influential Senators on Twitter*

	Name	Twitter Handle	Influencer Number	Name	Twitter Handle	Influencer Number
All Senators	Claire McCaskill	clairecmc	100	Daniel Inouye	Daniel_Inouye	10.29133069
	John Cornyn	JohnCornyn	61.17572714	Jeanne Shaheen	JeanneShaheen	9.778761686
	Orrin Hatch	OrrinHatch	55.11588724	Blanche Lincoln	blanchelincoln	9.7202961188
	Mark Warner	MarkWarner	53.01208813	Ben Cardin	SenatorCardin	9.004591348
	Tom Coburn	TomCoburn	48.40517817	Bob Corker	SenBobCorker	8.37533142
	David Vitter	DavidVitter	45.5699652	Tom Harkin	SenatorHarkin	8.828807944
	Arlen Specter	SenArlenSpecter	44.70476678	Kay Hagan	kayhagan	8.362371209
	Chris Dodd	SenChrisDodd	41.80311042	Tom Udall	SenatorTomUdall	6.409682902
	Russ Feingold	russfeingold	40.58287216	Johnny Isakson	TeamIsakson	5.915906017
	Joe Lieberman	JoeLieberman	36.64518439	Frank R. Lautenberg	FrankLautenberg	5.514915719
	Harry Reid	SenatorReid	33.86751526	Debbie Stabenow	StabenowPress	5.49613052
	John Thune	johnthune	30.31238238	Olympia Snowe	SenatorSnowe	4.644550915
	Bill Nelson	SenBillNelson	29.07250024	Evan Bayh	SenEvanBayh	4.493280709
	Bernie Sanders	senatorsanders	29.03680471	Charles Schumer	SenSchumer	4.473524869
	John Kerry	JohnKerry	29.01670408	Saxby Chambliss	saxby08	4.342740734
	Lisa Murkowski	lisamurkowski	25.67603178	Scott Brown	SenScottBrown	3.451428637
	Mark Udall	MarkUdall	24.17388496	Kay Bailey Hutchison	kaybaileyhutch	3.381710597
	Robert Menendez	SenatorMenendez	22.5235205	Mark Begich	SenatorBegich	3.043332894
	Jeff Sessions	SenatorSessions	18.829780083	Roland Burris	rolandwburris	2.649383237
	Sam Brownback	SenSamBrownback	17.480440668	John Ensign	SenEnsign	2.601594511
	Sherrod Brown	SenSherrodBrown	17.14545132	Barbara Mikulski	SenatorBarb	2.575996895
	Richard Burr	burrforsenate	16.92312505	Robert Bennett	senbennett	2.552434293
	Susan Collins	senatorcollins	16.36917038	Michael Bennet	mbennet	1.697628561
	George LeMieux	George_LeMieux	16.35767159	Byron Dorgan	ByronDorgan	1.225284551
	Jeff Merkley	SenJeffMerkley	15.66509075	Patrick Leahy	SenPatrickLeahy	1.152163457
	Roger Wicker	RogerWicker	15.320339906	Ron Wyden	SenatorRonWyden	0.679814674
	Ben Nelson	SenBenNelson	13.6188894	Daniel Akaka	danakaka	0.350836156
	Richard Shelby	RichardShelby	13.24649837	Maria Cantwell	US_Sen_Cantwell	0.253987725
	Lindsey Graham	GrahamBlog	13.127263658	Ted Kaufman	SenTedKaufmanDE	0.164130999
	Dick Lugar	senatorlugar	11.38944356	Michael Johanns	SenMojo	0.129397461

*John McCain eliminated from list of all senators

······· Contents are proprietary and confidential.

none of our civic leaders have, either, a fact that stumps Sean Donahue. President Obama pioneered the use of social media during the 2008 campaign, Donahue says, but he has done little to replicate that success. According to a 2010 report by the Congressional Research Service, only 205 representatives and senators (38 percent) were registered with Twitter (see Figure 10.1).[2] Facebook was a bit more popular, with more than 300 members of Congress officially signed up. But even that number is disappointing when you consider that Facebook has more than 600 million members, a citizenry that would make it the world's third-largest country.

LEADERSHIP

In choosing to largely avoid social media, leaders in the public and private spheres have given away a powerful opportunity to influence constituents and customers. They've deferred the chance to sway an increasingly large segment of the population. They've decided to ignore the Pre-Commerce world.

Let's face it: Today's public leaders are a brand unto themselves, and a brand that requires years of careful sculpting and polishing. The stands they take on each issue are the political equivalent of the company's products. They have to deal with many of the same issues faced by business leaders. They have staff focused on bolstering their brand image and developing the quality products their constituents demand. Yet their attention to their public image is exactly what stops them from embracing the Pre-Commerce constituent. As Austin journalist and author Bill Bishop noted in his book "The Big Sort," people tend to search for and engage with peers who share the same political mindset. They're branding their elected officials and other civic leaders, whether those officials participate in the conversation or not.

In the Pre-Commerce community, the town hall is as dated as the town crier. Conversations are unbounded now, and that makes a carefully scripted, soundbite-rich political existence rather uncomfortable. Kissing babies and shaking hands doesn't build a connection with voters anymore. People have so much more information about your political stance and history. They have so much more interaction and discussion about your ability to represent them. Companies have to learn to engage in true relationships with Pre-Commerce customers. Political leaders and staffers have to do the same. After all, if you think the public trust in companies has eroded, take a look at Congress's approval ratings.

In Texas, we have a good phrase to describe the usual political hack—"all hat and no cattle." Substance matters, and participating in honest and open conversations with constituents brings out substance. Future leaders will go online to address and discuss issues head-on. They'll make themselves and their staffs accessible for conversation through social media. They'll ask for ideas, and actually incorporate the good ones they receive. They will provide fuller transparency into how they arrive at their decisions. They'll make themselves and their staff available to constituents whenever and wherever those voters want to meet.

Just as every experience a customer has influences her perception of a brand, every interaction and decision a public leader makes will influence a constituent's vote. For better or worse, the online experience will reinforce voters' perceptions of civic leaders and their stance on the issues of the day. People will be less swayed by short-term bursts of advertising and more influenced by how a politician has handled themselves for the length of their term. Online conversations with like-minded peers will carry more weight than any stump speech or direct mailing. The voters are back in charge.

Social Media for Public Officials

In an August 23, 2010, article in the Huffington Post,[3] Sean Donahue offered civic leaders three simple ways social media can help them build stronger, more interactive and substantial ties with their constituents. Business leaders could heed him as well.

- Above all, empower through listening. While Senators and representatives cannot possibly be expected to spend a majority of their day monitoring Twitter feeds and Facebook profiles, it takes less than thirty seconds to pose a simple question or re-tweet an interesting constituent idea. Every local speech, town hall meeting, and campaign stop should include a follow-up question and answer session online. Think about it. From a policymaking standpoint, members of Congress will be sourcing ideas that directly resonate with their constituents. And from a PR and overall perception standpoint, they can credit the people they represent with guiding their thinking. Everybody wins.

- Second, allow for comments and sharing functionality on blogs (weighing in whenever possible). Mr. Obama took a significant step in 2009 by launching the first White House blog but to this day won't allow comments or conversation (which begs a legitimate question, is it still a blog?). True, some in Congress are light years ahead of their private-sector counterparts simply by hosting a blog or community forum on their official or campaign Web site, but many of these sites lack the most basic syndication functionality. As anyone who actively uses social networking sites can attest to, the ability to share

(Continued)

interesting posts, videos, and other digital content has come
to define the Web.

- Third, interact via mobile platforms. Just about every member
of Congress is either iPhone, BlackBerry, or Android-proficient
(or at least getting there). Without losing sight of the importance of privacy, wouldn't it be refreshing to see policymakers
sharing more stories from the road and, most important, pos-
ing related questions to spark discussion and debate? Or how
about hosting a vlog with a constituent who might have a
slightly different perspective on how to jumpstart the nation's
struggling economy?

SOCIAL MEDIA AT THE GRASS ROOTS

Doug McGinn is a communications and technology pioneer in the
public affairs world. An early practitioner in the use of Web-based
technologies for legislative, grassroots, and political campaigns, he was
at the forefront of efforts to mobilize digital-age voters. He developed
programs to bypass traditional media years before others in the political arena embraced new technologies and applications. He engaged
directly with those targeted constituencies that mattered most to his
clients and employers. Having worked the campaign and Congressional
circuit, including jobs with political luminaries such as William Bennett
and the late Jack Kemp, Doug joined with other forward-looking
public affairs professionals to establish The Herald Group in 2005.
Today, they are at the forefront of combining best-of-class, Web-driven
consumer and political style campaigns for issue management efforts for
leading corporations and associations.

"Online mediums give you direct lines of communication with targeted individuals. Don't waste them," Doug told me. "What is a priority for one individual is not the same for another. Rather than attempting to be all things to all people, focus on those issues important to a subset of your aggregate audience, then engage them individually and mobilize them into politically potent groups. That's a much more powerful and effective force."

More organizations have started to take this approach, but only in theory. The so-called "micro-targeting" programs popular today often prove ineffective, Doug said, because they don't embrace the other side of the communication held by the consumer or the voter. "Jack Kemp was fond of saying, 'People don't care what you know until they know you care,'" Doug said. "This holds uniquely true for the Web. The Web provides a medium to establish a dialogue that brings people into the process. It establishes an army that spawns 1,000 other conversations online and influences decision points offline. And it ultimately helps you meet your campaign objectives."

Government leaders around the world have started to realize the grassroots access social media can provide. Michigan state Rep. Justin Amash posts his votes on his Facebook page, along with an explanation of why he voted as he did. Proving you can teach an old dog new tricks, U.S. Sen. John McCain has almost two million followers on Twitter. Norway's minister of foreign affairs, Jonas Gahr Støre, regularly lays out his policy agenda on a blog.

The public is eager to participate. MoveOn.org, a popular political advocacy group among liberal voters, ranks among the 20,000 largest Web sites in the world. People love setting the record straight, as U.K. voters found on The Straight Choice, a site that revealed inaccuracies in election brochures and mailings. And, of course, we love poking fun at our elected officials. MyDavidCameron.com was a spoof of the election campaign posters distributed by conservatives in England. In Thailand

and Iran, government protestors used social media to coordinate activities and disseminate news about their revolution and the authorities' reactions to it.

People want to align themselves with companies, issues, and leaders who represent their core principles. And today, we're already seeing vivid examples of the ways social media can impact our customers' and constituents' most fundamental motivations, beliefs, and actions. That grassroots style of influence will only grow with the development of the Pre-Commerce marketplace—for politicians and their issues, as well as companies and their brands.

CHAPTER ELEVEN

CREATING YOUR INTELLECTUAL NETWORK

Common sense ain't common.
—WILL ROGERS

M y time at Dell gave me a front-row seat to the spectacle that is commercial technology spending. Each year, companies sink millions of dollars into their technology networks, upgrading servers, expanding storage, refreshing PC fleets, and connecting the myriad mobile devices workers carry these days. According to Gartner Inc., a leading technology research firm, global information technology spending topped $3.2 trillion in 2009, despite the worldwide economic slowdown.[1] Barring any unforeseen economic tremors, Gartner analysts expected that number to rise in 2011 and beyond. You'd have to search high and low to find a large enterprise that hasn't made technology an integral part of its operations.

But even as companies pump massive amounts of time and effort into keeping their employees connected, they spend virtually nothing on keeping their employees truly *interconnected*. The IT industry has created incredibly powerful channels through which workers can communicate and collaborate, and only the most foolish companies have ignored those possibilities. Yet only a few organizations have tapped into social media channels that take those communication and collaboration possibilities and pump them full of steroids. Few organizations have used social media to pool their employees' collective brainpower in an intellectual network. We spend millions of dollars to connect our computer systems. Why not invest our time in connecting the brainpower of our own employees via social media?

By now, this should be a no-brainer. As business leaders, we see every day how collaboration between multiple employees typically generates outcomes that an individual might never conceive. Most of us have read James Surowiecki's book, *The Wisdom of Crowds,* and realized when it came out in 2004 that harnessing the power of large groups of people could generate insights we could only guess at before. Today, we simply can go online to find example after example of people teaming up to accomplish extraordinary things. We can go to Wikipedia and find sixteen million encyclopedic entries compiled through the collaboration of millions of people who've never met. One of the most popular Q&A sites in the world is Yahoo! Answers, where the online community provides answers to questions in twelve languages. Digg.com lets people vote on the popularity and importance of news articles. When crowds of the right people weigh in on a topic, they typically deliver better outcomes than an individual. But even though every company has the crowd of right people within their walls—and has spent millions of dollars to connect through a sophisticated technology network—very few organizations provide a platform through which those employees can interconnect and pool their brainpower to process data and solve problems with comments, votes, and actions on social media platforms. To date, most business leaders have failed to capitalize on the full intelligence of their companies. They have yet to build a true intellectual network.

As an executive at one of the world's leading technology suppliers, I saw first-hand how organizations large and small would implement increasingly sophisticated and innovative computer networks. But I also had a chance to see the earliest sprouts of a new intellectual network, as Dell started putting social media to work internally. In 2006, then-CEO Kevin Rollins asked me to build an internal blog for employees. Rollins wanted to learn from our employees, and he hoped to build a forum where they could share their ideas and opinions in a more informal environment. Soon after we launched our external blog, Direct2Dell, we went live with One Dell Way, a play off our street address and the idea that we had a unique way to do business. We encouraged employees to share their stories and comment on the things they liked or didn't like about the company.

Internal blogs, forums, and other social media feedback channels have grown increasingly common around high-tech industries. It fits, given that many technology companies tend more toward innovative corporate cultures than a lot of other types of businesses. But even among technology companies with all their bean-bag chairs and ping-pong tables, the same challenges remain. No matter the industry or how progressive the company, business leaders have to learn how to relinquish some control to their employees, even as they install social media as a discipline across their operations.

THE EIGHTH DEADLY SIN

I tell a lot of people about the business leaders and mentors I admire. I've been lucky enough to work with a lot of brilliant executives over the years. I've run into my share of bad managers and colleagues, too, and in every case I can assert one of the seven deadly sins at the root of their poor performance and leadership. Take your pick—wrath, greed, sloth, pride, lust, envy, or gluttony—and if it's too easy to ascribe one of them to someone on your team, chances are the character trait is affecting their performance.

The emergence of the Pre-Commerce marketplace has introduced an eighth deadly sin: control. Whether on an individual or company-wide level, too much control will kill a company's attempts to unlock the potential of social media. The Internet is littered with examples of companies that tried to exercise too much control over a marketing campaign and only managed to make a bad situation worse. But too much control poses an equal danger within a company. Companies and executives who feel they must constantly control actions and, ultimately, results will fail to unlock the full power of their employees.

You can see it in your regular human resource surveys, which ask the same question over and over again whether it's relevant to your employees' concerns or not. Your mandatory Web-training module tells employees all the actions that will get them fired or humiliated, but it doesn't empower them to try something new. You block access to significant portions of the Internet, believing employees will waste time surfing the Web. Meanwhile, customers discuss your products on the blocked sites and your employees wink at one another as they pull out their smart phones and browse those sites anyway.

Your employees are no different from you. If you give your employees the freedom and the forum to share their ideas, they'll open up and tell you what they know and how they feel. Most of your rank-and-file employees care about your company, and they see what customers and pundits are saying about it online. Ask all of them for their views, and I guarantee you start to get insights your executive team never considered. If you constantly try to control what they watch out for and what they do, they become risk-averse and focus on accomplishing only what you want to hear. They realize you'll consider them more effective if they suppress their beliefs and focus only on accomplishing the task at hand (and getting that regular 3 percent raise).

Managers have to loosen their grip on their employees and their marketing messages. That's not easy to do when your legal teams cringe at every public statement that comes out of your company, said Ray Kerins, the Pfizer communications leader. "When it comes to social media," he said, "the communications and legal teams have to be one and the same. They need to be partners. Sitting on the sidelines is no longer an option. Consumers are much smarter than they've ever been, and if you don't give them information they need they'll get it somewhere else."

Every bit of your training and experience screams against giving your employees the freedom to publicly interact with customers. But as Kerins noted, customers expect it now. Besides, an incredible thing happens when you give all your employees the flexibility and the responsibility to interconnect with customers and with one another: They start to forge an online personality that's remarkably similar to that of your customers. Your employees will bring the value of their home experience to work. They will take the customer insight they glean from the Web and incorporate it throughout the company's social media ecosystem. *And ultimately, your employees will help align every piece of your company with your customers' expectations and their Pre-Commerce purchasing habits.*

SOCIAL MEDIA AS A DISCIPLINE

Of course, none of this happens if company leaders don't embed a social media discipline throughout their businesses—at every level and in every location. One training module won't deliver success. A mandatory training program filled with strong legalese won't make for a Pre-Commerce company. The company that shows an everyday commitment to the use of social media tools and techniques has to engrain a new discipline in all its employees. That takes time, day-to-day practice, and a willingness to constantly learn the Pre-Commerce marketplace anew.

The influence of social media and the power of crowdsourcing will start to appear in every corner of your company. The procurement team will use idea-management software to more accurately estimate the future prices of components. Marketing teams will have greater insight into how their customers behave and what their customers want. Customer support teams will learn from one another and from knowledgeable customers in real time, and they'll put those solutions to work immediately. Manufacturing teams will access the latest techniques for improving business processes straight from the Web. The sales force will have the richest and most recent competitive information at their fingertips at all times. And your monitoring systems will alert you to potential hot button issues before they explode into the public consciousness.

I've seen only a handful of companies consciously decide to prioritize social media integration throughout the business. Orange Business Services is one of them. Yann Gourvennec, head of the company's Internet and digital media practice, started by moving the company's entire marketing department into the Pre-Commerce world. Now he's building out from there, bringing in colleagues with whom the marketing people worked and moving social media into new business operations. "It changes the way we do business," he said. "Even in the largest organizations, where the business is mature and the processes are well-defined, social media is a game changer. Companies have to learn how to engage differently with current and prospective customers. Customers expect that, and they're only going to expect more of that as time goes by. This is not just a whim or a fad."

Gourvennec realized from the outset that he couldn't just tell people how to do it and expect the initiative to spread beyond a handful of people. If he wanted employees to embrace social media and make it a part of everyday business, he said, he had to let them learn by doing. He didn't forgo training, but he made sure he got people participating as much as possible as early as possible. It helped that he set expectations early. "Our top priority is for everyone to learn how one does business *with* social media," he said. "I always tell them up-front that they will never be bloggers, but that they will be *professionals using blogs.* Blogs will never be their main line of business, but it will become a major tool which they can use to enhance the way that they do business."

It helped that Gourvennec was working from a history of personal experience. He's run his own Web sites and blogs for years—learning by doing, just like his colleagues are doing now. That allowed him to test new opportunities before launching them in a corporate environment. It led him to a more pragmatic approach to working with social media and Web activities in general. "You have to have a pragmatic approach, look at innovation and ask yourself 'Why not?' rather than 'Why?'" he said. "My real Pre-Commerce moment was when one of my friends convinced me that I had to give up my old Web site and go for blogs way back in 2004. By forcing me to experiment he was instrumental in making me understand how to use these new tools."

Like Gourvennec and his colleagues at Orange, business leaders eventually will have no choice but to reshape their companies so they fully leverage the world's greatest operating system: the Web. But to do so, executives can't reflexively pigeonhole social media into one department. Unfortunately, though, that's exactly what most business leaders do with things they don't know well—give it to the people who display some sort of expertise and wait until they come back with some ideas. The executive who asks a leader in one department to pilot social media and then share the next practices with the company is building a model of success. The executive who asks a single department to "own" social media and then feels they have effectively handled the situation is in the process of creating a weakness. A subtle, but significant difference in approach.

RECRUITING THROUGH
SOCIAL MEDIA

Pharmaceutical companies wage a constant battle for talent, and they'll take advantage of any opportunity they can find to make sure the best potential employees don't slip through their grasp. So Herman DePrins and his colleagues at UCB, the Belgian biopharmaceutical company, set out to create a platform that would aid recruiting while also positioning the firm as an innovative, patient-centric organization. As chief information officer, he could bring together UCB's corporate communications and human resources teams to accomplish both goals.

The campaign had two phases. The first phase focused on the basics, getting the open positions published online and ensuring the listings got the proper attention from job seekers. "We chose a multichannel approach centered on a mini-Web site, www.itjobsatucb.com, which we linked to our recruiting system for online applications," DePrins said. "At a summer party we made videos about our team with some testimonials, and we put them on YouTube. Some of our people used LinkedIn to broadcast some of this, and we tweeted something every four hours about the effort. At the tail end of the exercise we issued a press release, positioning this as positive news for UCB as a whole."

Even before the press release, DePrins said, UCB had received a thousand résumés. Two weeks later, they had gotten more than 1,300. Encouraged by the success, he and his teams started the second phase a few months later. They created an event for internal and external technology managers, bringing them together to discuss social media and the ways it can help patients and businesses. The motivation behind the program was to show current and potential employees that UCB positioned information technology as a strategic component of its business.

"I've noticed the power of a multichannel social media approach when well planned," DePrins said. "I was surprised by the strength of the social network on the Internet. Our main recruiting site attracted 200,000 unique page views through this."

Pre-Commerce impacts every facet of your company, and to leave social media stuffed in one department leaves the rest of your operations without the resources they need to excel. This is why the commitment to social media has to start at the top, and leaders have to make a commitment to real discipline. When executives seek to instill a new discipline in a company, they insist on top-notch training programs and demand that all their employees use the new techniques and tools every day. A discipline is foundational. It doesn't go away. Effective leaders take it seriously, make sure their employees get it right, and never stop learning and improving.

If that's a little abstract, think of it in terms of the disciplines you've embedded in your company already. Goof up your financial reports, and the SEC is calling. Miss an analysis in marketing, and your revenue drops. Overlook a subtle change in customer preferences, and your competitors steal your market share. Every discipline critical to your company's success demands a high level of expertise, and the lack of that expertise can cripple you. Disciplines require in-depth study over time. It's why we have MBAs and CPAs. It's why we make sure our teams commit to continuing education.

Marc Monseau saw it shortly after launching JNJBTW, Johnson & Johnson's first business-oriented blog. The company already had dabbled in social media with a blog about the company's history, but this new blog would provide a fuller engagement with customers, a new level of interaction that raised a lot of legal and regulatory questions.

As J&J's director of corporate communications and social media, Monseau realized there was no way the company's diverse business units could replicate his social media efforts unless the company developed a formal, sanctioned pathway to guide them. But, he said, "We found that developing a set of policies was only the first step. There needed to be education to help people better understand the new rules of engagement and for our teams to determine how they would staff and structure the support of such projects. In some cases, this would require the development of new processes to review content or the establishment of teams that could be empowered to respond to the comments and posts made to our social media sites."

So with the support of the executive and legal teams, Monseau and his colleagues developed a disciplined framework that would include comprehensive training sessions. They also created an in-house blog to keep employees up-to-date and fully engaged with company policies, allowing anyone to raise questions and provide answers.

Ultimately, Johnson & Johnson put the same rigor and discipline into its social media efforts that most companies put into accounting and CRM. Building that internal structure is the only way companies can free their employees to fully engage with customers in the Pre-Commerce marketplace. The truth of that might be less visible to you, because it's not showing up in all the traditional places you track so diligently. But if one of your customers decides that your brand means a little bit less to them today than it did a month or year ago, your traditional research channels might never reveal the subtle change—or if they do, you won't see it for months. The same holds true for your employees, their morale, and their ability to share new ideas. A comprehensive, disciplined approach to social media will reveal so many more of these subtle changes, and you'll see it almost immediately.

JOHNSON & JOHNSON JOINS THE PRE-COMMERCE CONVERSATION

Marc Monseau almost cringed when he learned of it. On May 31, 2006, influential New York Times *columnist Thomas Friedman led his op-ed with this question: "Is there a company more dangerous to America's future than General Motors?" Friedman went on to argue that GM supported terrorism with its continued production of large sport utility vehicles. The United States was in a war on terrorism, he wrote, fighting against "an enemy who is fueled by our gasoline purchases." GM's promotion to credit customers when average gas prices in their state rose above $1.99 would only encourage greater consumption of gasoline, Friedman said.*

Monseau, the director of communications at another Fortune 50 company, Johnson & Johnson, immediately recognized the damage Friedman's argument could do to the GM brand. The folks at GM recognized it, too. Within a day, they'd prepared an op-ed of their own and sent it to the *Times,* only to learn that the newspaper would accept nothing more than a letter to the editor in response. So when the *Times* started editing GM's response, the automaker decided to post the entire exchange on its corporate blog and let people see the whole story for themselves.

"What I found particularly compelling about this example was how GM's blog post, which conveyed their side of the story, was picked up and spread through different communities and hit some of their key constituencies," Monseau told me recently. In communities where GM had plants, for example, local newspapers ran stories on the entire exchange between the company and the newspaper. The exchange and its subsequent dissemination started to sway popular opinion in GM's favor.

The incident brought Monseau to a Pre-Commerce epiphany. He and other business leaders at Johnson & Johnson had started to recognize that people increasingly turned to consumer-generated content for health-related matters. But Monseau also realized the company didn't have any way to directly interact with its online stakeholders. If GM could rely on social media to handle a potentially damaging situation, he asked, why couldn't J&J use the same platforms to reach its customers on an ongoing basis? Thanks to the leadership of Ray Jordan, the company's corporate vice president for public affairs and corporate communications, Monseau and his colleagues in the communications group started experimenting with social media channels. And after working closely with executive and legal teams to establish an acceptable set of policies for these external conversations, the company launched its first blog, Kilmer House, in July 2006. The blog focused on the history of the company and, because it didn't directly concern current products or issues, it gave Johnson & Johnson a relatively safe environment for its early interactions on the social Web.

"Recognizing that bloggers who were writing about the business of health care represented an increasingly influential group of stakeholders that we had little or no relationship with, I started exploring how we could better engage with them," Monseau said. "JNJBTW, which was launched in June 2007, was one way we found to engage with some of the key online stakeholders—and to respond to coverage of the company in the mainstream media in an unmediated forum."

In preparation for the launch of JNJBTW, Monseau and his colleagues reached out to influential bloggers through informal events and dinners. They started forming relationships with a range of online communities, forging new friendships with nurses, doctors, and patient groups—as well as many of its top online influencers, including Kevin Pho (KevinMD), Amy Tenderich (DiabetesMine), and Kim McAllister (Emergiblog). "It was only after we launched JNJBTW and started to post and engage with people

through comments that I gained meaningful insights into what
online engagement on behalf of a company would really be like,"
Monseau said. "Social media involves deeply personal communications, and it is only through experience that you can understand the
dynamics of what online relationship building involves."

FROM BEST PRACTICE
TO NEXT PRACTICE

My communities and conversations team had done an incredible job of
bringing Dell into the Pre-Commerce conversation, but at our weekly
meeting I knew I had to stress a challenging issue—our job would get
more difficult before it got any easier. Watching my crew walk in didn't
help ease my trepidation. Lionel Menchaca, our chief blogger, Bruce
Anderson, our lead for enterprise social media, Sean McDonald, my
top lieutenant, and Vida Killian, now at Starbucks in social media, were
deep into the day by the time the 9 A.M. meeting rolled around. They
typed away on their Blackberries, flipped open their PCs to finish up a
blog post, or gave me a "be there in a second" wave as they finished up
a phone call. No rest for the weary, they took nonstop e-mails, made
decisions on which customers to help first, put final edits on blog posts,
and scheduled time to shoot video for a vlog. And my message for the
day—making sure they knew it wouldn't get any easier—wasn't exactly
uplifting.

I didn't sugarcoat it: "We can't fall in love with our own headlines,"
I told the team. "We've only made it through the preface of a long book
about the ways social media is changing business. On top of everything
we're doing already, we need to become students of the change that's
occurring." Everyone agreed with me, but I'm not sure how well the
message resonated through the daily grind of what we already had to

do. The culture and operations of most companies stress the here and now. The disciplined student of Pre-Commerce doesn't always impact business in the short-term, but his or her work will prepare the company for success over the long haul. An unwavering commitment to the study of social media and how customers interact on the Web is an obsession for every successful online expert I know.

Corporations excel at identifying what to do, then locking in that exact set of behaviors. This culture of control lends itself to the Eighth Deadly Sin. When a business does manage to transform its practices, it typically does so by studying the past actions of competitors or other admired companies. It defines a best practice for its future and benchmarks itself against other companies. Then it locks, loads, and fires.

I promise you this: Your company will fall further behind each year if you conduct best practices and benchmark against your competition. You will lose market share, revenue, and your standing as a great purveyor of customer service. Best practices study the past to review methods and activities that achieve a certain outcome. They center on how you can be slightly more efficient than your competitors, saving more money or time through more efficient execution of similar processes. Benchmarking is the inbred cousin of best practices. Companies don't make a move into a new area until they can show a cost or quality improvement over the benchmarks set by competitors.

That all works well for most traditional business processes, but best-practice and benchmark reports immediately fade to obsolescence in the online ecosystem. The disruptive nature of social media is changing far faster than the companies it impacts, and you won't find enough companies to benchmark against because what worked for them yesterday almost certainly won't work for you today. *You will be successful in social media only if you build next practices, and next practices emerge only through ongoing study of the Pre-Commerce marketplace.* If the Web is your oyster, you'll find pearls of wisdom when you're faster than competitors at gathering and processing the insights your customers provide every moment online.

"It's highly important for today's global company to build the processes and systems—the discipline—to innovate, collaborate, learn, and scale as a team in close to real-time," said Kathryn Metcalfe, a pharmaceutical industry veteran from Pfizer. "To do this right, it means that you work together continually and don't wait for annual or quarterly meetings to share best practices. We focus on building next practices in real time. This is where competitive advantage is built."

You need all your employees on deck to pull this off, though. The company that stuffs social media away in one department works at a clear disadvantage to the competitor who instills a social discipline across every employee in every division. Your employees think much more than you realize. They have untapped ideas for a new conveyor belt, a more-responsive human resources team, and a bonus-payment structure that better rewards work that generates profits. If you install the social media tools and the discipline that encourages and captures those insights from all your employees, you can leave best practices in the past—you'll have moved on to next practices instead.

FINDING THE RIGHT PITCH

At some point, we're all guilty of intellectually agreeing with a concept but continuing with an opposing behavior anyway. It's hard work to put belief into practice. It takes weeks, months, even years of consistent work before we adapt our actions to match those we know to be right or most effective. The most effective executives have the discipline to stay focused on such adjustments, and they display the leadership skills that can spur the same commitment from their employees. In order to see and seize opportunities ahead of your competitors, you will need to commit yourself to learning and guiding your company as it builds a knowledge base around the Pre-Commerce marketplace.

Given the breadth of the Internet and the massive flood of customer information available through social media, it's easy to get overwhelmed. For business leaders who have more on their plates than reading blogs and tracking forums—that is, pretty much all of you—it helps to avoid the tsunami of data and focus instead on the important trends that become apparent. Collecting a lot of data doesn't produce any real insight, any more than randomly drilling hole after hole after hole will produce oil. The smart leader will study the broader landscape for good drilling locations and then study those more and more closely until he or she finds a handful of sites most likely to produce. Step back and look for the big picture your customers show you with their online interactions, identify the main drivers of the changes you see, and zero in on the factors that cause those changes. And like any decent wildcatter, the more you drill the better you'll get at it. When you focus on the factors that cause change, you'll start to identify trends more quickly—and you'll move more quickly to capitalize on them.

The drivers you isolate for study will vary from company to company, but every business leader should take a similar approach to learning. I call it PITCH. You can teach it in all kinds of ways; some people learn better from training modules, others might prefer hands-on training. But no matter how you teach it, business leaders need to make sure employees understand each PITCH principle: people, infrastructure, tools, communities, and habits. Just like a conductor uses his or her sense of pitch to create a beautiful orchestral performance, you can use PITCH to bring out the best in your employees—and your employees can use PITCH to fine-tune their own understanding of the Pre-Commerce marketplace.

People

We want to know how many people go online, where they go while they're there, and who they are. With an average of 500,000 new people jumping online every day for the first time in their lives, trends and behaviors will evolve. When people start doing similar things in large numbers, they influence how business is conducted, ranging from the impact of their buying habits to how they communicate to who has influence and more. They demand more bandwidth from their governments and they start changing the ways they learn, access content, and buy.

The best place to see this change occurring is to look at www .internetstats.com, which compiles country-by-country data on where people go online, the rate of growth, and local bandwidth. When you start playing with these basic, easily accessible numbers, you quickly understand why Russia and India will become dominate online markets in just a few years. You'll realize that South America's impact on e-commerce and Pre-Commerce is soaring faster than you probably expected.

If you can rattle off the top twenty countries in terms of broadband penetration, you've taken a good first step. If you know which countries will have the highest online growth in the next five years, you probably have a leg up on most of your rivals. If you know which countries will see their online participation double in the next four years, and you know the city or region in which those new Web denizens live, you've started to create a knowledge base few rivals can match.

As widely as people's beliefs and actions vary, we often behave more similarly than we'd like to admit. Companies that analyze the evolution from "first online experience" to "major online purchase" will find that people follow a similar path. Understanding the similarities will put you in tune with the Pre-Commerce customer base. Then it becomes a matter of singing a tune (i.e., product, service, delivery, etc.) your customers prefer.

Infrastructure

Remember the days of dial-up Internet access, when a Web site that featured a few photos took a full minute or two to load? It seems so basic, but the amount of bandwidth available to your customers will enhance or detract from their customer experience. It impacts the content they access, the devices they use, and the richness of their interactions with your company and their peers.

You and your teams should know the percentage of broadband use in the countries and cities you target, and you should begin to interpret the changes you see. If the online population climbs faster than broadband penetration, for example, customers can become increasingly frustrated as they try to access richer content geared for a more Web-advantaged region. Smart companies will know how easily customers in different regions can access and share content, and they'll adjust their content accordingly.

A truly progressive company might even search for ways to increase their customers' Internet speeds, because bandwidth and bucks are fully intertwined. When customers access more content, they build a larger personal knowledge base. With their heightened knowledge and greater access to fresh content, they'll participate in more online conversations and they'll want more stuff. If they want more stuff, they'll buy more. And if they increase their online participation, they're more likely to buy online or use the Web to inform their brick-and-mortar shopping habits.

But the impact spreads beyond the individual customer. As customers become more comfortable with e-commerce, they start participating in the Pre-Commerce conversations as well. They share more of their experiences with peers who crave their advice. Smart marketing teams will study the infrastructure of a country or city and identify ways they can present content to encourage participation, e-commerce, and, ultimately, Pre-Commerce interactions.

In such a nascent and rapidly evolving social media ecosystem, we really have just started to peck the surface of how customers adapt their Web usage to accommodate online interaction. But companies can take even this limited knowledge and put it to work immediately. If the online population in a country increases even as bandwidth and purchasing power lag, for example, you almost certainly will see a much higher ratio of mobile phone use. You can decrease your emphasis on e-commerce and speed up plans for a mobile-commerce, or m-commerce, platform. Many developing countries have leapfrogged landlines and gone directly to mobile phones and other wireless technologies. This jump to future technologies greatly increases the availability of content—and at a lower cost—but it also fundamentally changes the prevailing usage patterns. Your teams need to know how far these customers can go in terms of using their computing devices to do business, whether they buy goods or share content about your products with their peers.

Tools

We all love shiny new gizmos that look cool and let us do new things. Smart phones, iPads, tablet computers, and mini-notebooks open up intriguing new possibilities for marketing and e-commerce. They're fun to play with and great to have, but companies can get caught up in the hype and waver from a focus on the basics—that everyday grind of communication, work, and commerce those difference devices make possible. The iPhone created a tremendous opportunity for sharing content, but the good ol' boring laptop still allows greater original content creation.

Consider the leapfrogging, emerging country with its budding wireless infrastructure. As you study broadband and wireless access, you also can track the ratio between mobile phones and laptops within that country. Mobile phones are the "great appetizer"—once you have it, you can't wait to get to the entrée. The growth of laptop or tablet PC usage typically follows the growth of mobile phones as customers tap out the limits of their handheld devices and start to crave more power, a larger screen, and greater flexibility.

It's easy to think of "tools" in terms of hardware, but companies have to pay close attention to services and software as well. The explosion of mobile computing throughout the world has seeded the growth of the "cloud," in which customers can store data and from which they can access applications. As customers increase their use of cloud resources, they'll increase their ability to access, share, and act upon your marketing content. You'll start to notice regional differences in the applications customers use, and how they use them. Customers in some countries will adopt the applications developed elsewhere, and some will use home-grown programs. If you notice the latter, you'll want to know what they develop and why. The more innovation, the more you might need to localize your approach in the future.

100 FASTEST INTERNET CITIES

Akamai Technologies, a content-delivery provider for the world's top companies, releases a State of the Internet report each quarter. In the first quarter of 2010, the Cambridge, Massachusetts, company came across some interesting results.[2]

- Asia is home to fifty-nine of the top 100 fastest Internet cities, including Masan, South Korea, the world's fastest.
- Only twelve of the fastest Internet cities are in the United States, and all but five of those are in California.
- Umeå, Sweden, is the fastest city in Europe, ranked No. 18 overall.
- Europe is home to six of the top ten fastest Internet countries, but they're not who you might expect: Romania (4), Sweden (5), Latvia (6), Belgium (7), Portugal (9), and Bulgaria (10).

Community

No one belongs to a single static community. We bounce between dozens of constantly evolving communities at home, at work, and at play. I'm an avid participant in the community of New York Yankees' fans. While I certainly don't leave that community during the offseason, my interaction with other fans differs from our frenzy of activity during the playoffs. Your interaction with the neighbors on your left will differ from the neighbors on the right. It's common sense, yet most companies make the same classic mistake when surveying online communities. We study a community in our home country and ascribe the same traits to communities everywhere else. We look at how they act in one situation and assume they'll act in a similar manner a few months down the road.

Psychologists make a pretty nice career out of studying the ways we misread communities. Another common misstep mimics the "actor-observer bias" that Edward Jones and Richard Nisbett developed in the early 1970s.[3] Jones and Nisbett found that a student studying for an exam often had a different explanation for their work than an outside observer. The student would say they studied hard because they wanted a good grade. The observer typically attributed the study time to the student's strong work ethic. Marketers make a pretty nice career out of explaining the various attributes and behaviors displayed by communities of customers. But much like Jones and Nisbett found with their industrious students, the corporate marketing team's conclusions often clash with what the community relates about itself through social media. Companies waste far too much time and energy trying to put rigid definitions on communities that inevitably will evolve and redefine themselves. Their loyalty lies with the content in front of them at the time. They're not making a long-term commitment to your brand.

Now, don't get me wrong—I'm not about to suggest you curb the continual study of your customer communities. If you let the community define its own boundaries and motivations, you can learn to adapt to its constantly changing composition and viewpoint. Furthermore, you can refocus your energy to identify the more important trends and tendencies upon which your company can act. For example, a PC company that studies online communities in its various markets would discover that gaming drives a lot of the online discussion in Korea. In China, companies will find a growing number of conversations on Web forums, but the majority of discussion still goes through online bulletin boards. (Incidentally, I'm still amazed that so few multinational companies doing business in China bother to post in Chinese-language blogs or other social media sites. Companies can't stop talking about China's value outside of China, but few rarely take the next step and start talking within the country itself.)

PRE-COMMERCE WITH CHINESE CHARACTERISTICS

China is home to the world's largest online population, yet few multinationals have made anything more than a token effort to interact with this community on its terms. Only a handful of companies have Chinese-language blogs, despite identifying China as a market of vital importance.

- Entertainment is the top driver for online participation, with music, video, and online games among the top three entertainment applications.
- Chinese netizens tend to be more engaged in the creation and sharing of content than their counterparts in the United States.
- Bulletin boards, forums, and instant messaging are widely popular.

- Chinese users prefer different social media brands, sometimes favoring local sites, such as Kaixin001 over Facebook and Youku or Todou instead of YouTube.
- Business-related social networking sites, such as LinkedIn, aren't popular today.
- Like Web users in the United States, Chinese users suffer spammers and bogus campaigns.
- Chinese users trust their peers, but also tend to trust company employees more than their counterparts in the United States.
- When researching a pending purchase, Chinese users consult online communities for advice and are swayed by negative word of mouth.

In France, we see a very high consumption rate of video, led by videos at Dailymotion.com, one of the top fifty Web sites in the world with over 55 million unique visitors in August 2010. People in Brazil use Twitter on a regular basis, yet they prefer Orkut over Facebook when choosing a social network site. Indian bloggers love to participate on English-language blogs and forums based in the United States and the United Kingdom. The point is this: Customers will choose the communities in which they'll participate. You can't always explain why they gravitate to one channel or another, but you can identify the social media channels and the types of content that work for your target customers.

Habits

Social media channels provide a powerful channel for observing customer habits. Traditional marketing research about customer likes and dislikes pulls in a range of variables that can skew our conclusions. We might stumble over selection bias and inadvertently choose research subjects that readily confirm our predisposition. Subjects in research interviews or focus groups often put their game face on, knowing they're on the spot. We don't get an entirely untainted view of customer habits through social media—many people still put on a public face when they go virtual—but online conversations often provide a truer picture of the subconscious mind that governs customer habits.

The study of customer habits as related through social media remains in its infancy. We still have so much to learn about how customers engage, share, and interact online. But companies now have the opportunity to get closer and more personal with many more customers than they could through traditional marketing and research channels. They can compare what they learn online with other forms of marketing research. And if the two sides don't jibe, they can start to track down the differences instead of acting on faulty information.

Of course, some habits show themselves readily. With some basic research, we can say conclusively that Brazilians tend to stay online longer than people in other countries. Other habits require a lot more interpretation and work. What habits do Brazilians display that would help explain their longer online sessions? At WCG, we've found that consumers in India regularly participate in English-language forums, but reams of other data show they still prefer a more local experience whenever possible. We've learned that these conflicts don't disprove or discount our previous conclusions. Rather, they help guide our research, showing us places where we can dig a little deeper to understand customer habits on a whole new level. What looks like a challenge becomes an opportunity to understand customer behavior in new and richer ways.

You can supplement your understanding of customer and employee behavior by supplementing your traditional research, knowledge, and conclusions with a vast pool of information available through social media. Your customers supply it on a regular basis. Your employees will, too. After that, it's up to you as a business leader to take advantage of insights around you every day. The more curious you are, the more opportunities you'll find to improve your company and your leadership.

CHAPTER TWELVE

ANTIBODIES, ENABLERS, AND HEROES

We have met the enemy, and he is us.
—WALT KELLY, AMERICAN CARTOONIST
AND THE CREATOR OF *POGO*

I felt a shot of adrenaline as I walked into 777 Third Avenue that morning in June 1998. As I passed the Beverly Pepper sculpture in the plaza and glanced up at the gold "777" behind the reception desk, I couldn't help but feel some inspiration from Ed Meyer's success. It was here, at 777 Third, where Meyer built Grey Advertising into one of the world's iconic ad agencies. As of that morning, I shared the same address.

It was my first day as executive vice president for health care at Grey Advertising's communications firm, GCI. My boss, Bob Feldman, had decorated my thirty-eighth floor office with a plant and a good luck card—a nice welcoming touch. I felt at home, and I was raring to go. So when I joined my first staff meeting an hour later with Bob and his senior team, I was full of confidence. The team had much more agency experience than I did, since I'd worked for years on the client side of the business. And I was blown away by their plans for the coming weeks, from new products they were developing to how they expected to land a new Fortune 500 account.

I had no doubt I sat in good company, so I couldn't help myself when they asked me to share my expectations for GCI's brand spankin' new health care practice, which they hired me to develop. I looked around the room and said, "I'm going to build a top five global health care practice within five years." I had only one goal, I told them, and that was it. I could see more than a few people suppressing a snicker. They figured I was crazy, arrogant, or delusional. They gave me their full support, but they must have thought I'd never last. Less than three years later, the GCI health care practice was pulling in $25 million per year. We ranked among the top five health care communications agencies in the country, thanks to some fantastic work by my colleagues on the team.

When I think back on my tenure at GCI, I realize the inspiration I felt from Ed Meyer that morning set me up for my initial success. I went into the job with a confidence that allowed me to try new things and take some bold chances that worked beautifully for us. But years later, the same job taught me another invaluable lesson. Once we hit the top five, I stopped taking as many risks and tried harder to hold onto our success than build on it. I'd started to think too small. I'd become my own competitor.

The Pre-Commerce marketplace requires the same boldness and confidence I had when I started at GCI, because your biggest competitors will be sitting with you in your conference room. They'll try to prevent you from making change *inside* your own company. They'll throw up blockades, make excuses, and rationalize everything to maintain the status quo. They'll be relentless. They sit beside you in your conference room. When you look into the mirror, your competitor will be peering back at you.

We fear change, especially when it exposes us to something we don't know—and Pre-Commerce exposes the uninitiated in a very public way. But as Mark Twain said, "Courage is resistance to fear, mastery of fear—not absence of fear." If you learn to manage the antibodies, enablers, and heroes within your own walls, you'll have no problem challenging your external competitors in the Pre-Commerce marketplace.

ANTIBODIES

I've had a fortunate career filled with a lot of innovation. From launching an arthritis drug with Mickey Mantle to helping introduce Taxotere, one of the world's top cancer drugs. From building GCI's health care practice from scratch to starting the world's first global social media practice at Dell. And now I get to work with my brilliant colleagues at WCG on the leading edge of Pre-Commerce marketing and sales. At each stop along the way, I've seen how fear can cripple an organization. I've grappled with it myself—sometimes with success and sometimes not—but the experiences have taught me how to get over it and make a difference inside a company. First and foremost, it has taught me to overcome antibodies.

Within the human body, antibodies float around our bloodstreams and provide one of our immune system's key defenses against outside infection. They neutralize the little beasties that can kill us. By returning our body to a relatively healthy status quo, antibodies ensure our well-being. The corporate antibodies also work to preserve the status quo, but the status quo is toxic in a business ecosystem. People are so programmed to act like antibodies—to respond in certain, protective ways when we see foreign objects (read: new ideas). We treat new ideas like infections and try to protect the ecosystem as we know it. That's great when it protects the company from bad ideas, but overactive antibodies will attack bad ideas and good innovation indiscriminately. Executives must constantly work to reprogram their company's immune system.

Because we were moving into a brand new Pre-Commerce marketplace at Dell, we came up with a lot of new ideas—and attracted a lot of antibodies. They dressed well, smiled a lot, and had a reasonable degree of corporate power. Every time we prepared to launch a new idea, they would start circling, showing up at our planning meetings, or catching us in the hallway. They'd say the same things every time:

Looks like a great idea, but why don't we do that next quarter.
That seems expensive, are you sure we have enough budget? Why
    don't we wait?
We better benchmark our competitors first.
Have you talked to Joe's department yet?

My team and I started to see these exchanges for what they were: a natural reaction to a potentially disruptive idea. They would want to slow us down or stop us from innovating, unsure of the change at hand. We realized we could get annoyed with their reaction, or we could have a little fun with it. So in our meetings, we took to calling these people "antibodies." It stuck. In the middle of a meeting, someone would say, "I don't think we can . . ." and someone would interrupt with a resounding "Antibody!" It got to the point everyone would get a good laugh out of it, because we discovered we could laugh at ourselves for resisting change.

That rejection of fear in favor of humor unlocked a ridiculous amount of innovation.

Better yet, it fit well with Michael Dell's expectations for us. No one can root out an overactive antibody better than Michael. As we prepared to go online with our first corporate blog, Michael asked me when it would launch. I told him we were looking about three weeks out, because our IT staff didn't have it on their roadmap and needed time to get it up and running. Not good enough:

Michael:	"Do you have a credit card?"
Me:	"Uh, yeah."
Michael:	"Do you know how to use it?"
Me:	"Well, yeah, of course."
Michael:	"Great. Use it and get this blog up in the next two days."
Me:	"Consider it done."

It was vintage Michael. He could make you laugh at your own blind reliance on bureaucracy, and he did it in a way that made sure you wouldn't let anyone else block important innovation. So I called my colleagues in our IT department and let them know Michael had given them a choice: Launch the blog with me in the next two days or stick to their initial three-week deadline. Needless to say, they agreed a forty-eight-hour time line made a lot of sense. Humor in this case proved to be a remarkably effective antidote against antibodies, but sometimes it requires some stronger medicine. The hardest antibodies to cure aren't the ones who actively try to delay a project. The toughies are the ones who hang onto their past practices and slow the process through sheer inertia. You can have fun attacking the antibodies, but the stubborn ones require an element of toughness, too.

We'd crammed about a dozen people into a small conference room one morning to put the final touches on a new social media launch in the fall of 2006. I deliberately invited a larger, multifunction group to the meeting to make sure everyone was on board. So when I started going around the room asking for feedback, I was stunned with the reaction. Each person gave me another reason we couldn't get this done. I was bordering on livid, so I paused for a moment to gather my thoughts: "Thanks for all of your feedback," I said. "Now, going forward, I only want to hear from people who have ideas on how we can implement this idea. If you have something to add that will help, please speak.

If not, please don't." The room fell silent for what felt like a minute before someone chimed in with a good idea. And with that, we were off and running.

As an executive, you know you occasionally need to grab the organization by the lapels and shake it up a bit. Now and then, business leaders have to remind their teams that they can do amazing things if they put their heads together—and they can kill amazing ideas if they don't. The brain power we had sitting around that conference room table at Dell was staggering. We had some of the most brilliant minds in the PC industry in one room, but we almost wasted it by saying no. And that's what makes the most stubborn antibodies so dangerous: It takes only one person to come up with a reason it won't work; you need a team to develop and implement a groundbreaking new idea.

UNLOCKING YOUR PERSONAL INNOVATION

Case Study

Dr. James Milojkovic, better known as "Milo," travels the world teaching executives how to create high-performance cultures and ignite innovation. When we invited Milo to meet with our team at WCG and to help increase our capacity for breakthrough results, I discovered his cutting-edge methods aren't for the faint of heart. He demands that you take full accountability at all times, forcing you to address antibodies head-on and figure out how to solve problems with a long-term view. He doesn't accept stories, drama, excuses, or the list of other rationalizations we all use to avoid true breakthroughs. Milo knows that we fall back on excuses or stories to act as circuit breakers to deal with our own fear. You are 100 percent responsible for innovation and rapid results, he told us.

Milo uses a method he calls SWIFT® Innovation. The program forces teams to think strategically about the underlying network dynamics that facilitate the creative process and how new ideas and practices can transform a corporate culture. SWIFT® is based on the work of Milo's colleague, Dr. Richard Ogle, chief scientist at KnowledgePassion Inc., and it's grounded in the laws of network science illustrated in the case studies featured in Ogle's book, *Smart World: Breakthrough Creativity and the New Science of Ideas.* It should be part of your reading list in the future.

Milo and Ogle taught me that so-called best practices in innovation won't transfer across an organization unless leaders use, model, and promote an "Innovation Mindset." That mindset has to be designed and built for your particular organization and its people. In other words, you have to know your teams and then show them how to innovate through your own actions. I'll add one piece of advice from my own experience: Remember that you're building your innovation culture, so avoid all the pop psychology and tired organizational behavior theory. Figure out what works for you and apply the latest insights from neuroscience and network science.

Milo wouldn't let us off the hook with copouts, and as a business leader you shouldn't settle for the easy way out, either.

ENABLERS

We all have our vices. We all have our moments of brilliance. And we're all surrounded by people who, in ways subtle and obvious, enable our best and worst traits. If we're smart, of course, we try to gather people who bring out our best, and we try to limit our exposure to people who lead us astray. We do it in our personal lives, and as business leaders we do it in the workplace as well. But even a quick accounting of our friends and colleagues reveals the enabler's paradox: It's hard to separate the good from the bad, because the same person who encourages your best in one arena might be the devil on your shoulder in another.

As business leaders, we all work with a colleague who has all the details at his or her fingertips. We love these people, because they gather an exhaustive cache of pertinent information about the topic at hand and they use those details to make a well-reasoned decision. Yet we often end up tearing our hair out, because the same person never feels as though he or she has enough information to make a bold decision. The pressure to know everything can paralyze your teams. By definition, innovation involves the unknown—it's new, after all—so the get-all-the-details people can kill an idea before it has a chance to blossom.

Some bad enablers want to wait and see what your competitors do. They want to study best practices and get benchmarks for every new move. They make sure you're doing it better than your rivals. But when it comes to innovation, especially in the Pre-Commerce market-place, by the time your competitors move it's too late. Meanwhile, other colleagues boldly stride forward on a new project. They're more than happy to take the first step, only to stop and cower at the first hurdle they encounter. They don't realize that innovation and failure walk hand-in-hand, that one can inspire the other at any moment.

Bad enablers are easy to spot when you're looking in from the outside. It's harder to notice them when they're influencing your own actions. And when you're the bad enabler, well, only the best business leaders are introspective enough to find and fix their own flaws. I've worked with dozens of companies who want to encourage Pre-Commerce inno-vation in their company, yet they don't invite their social media teams to present ideas at staff meetings in every division of the company. I've seen some brilliant, forward-thinking executives rubber stamp the same traditional approach they've taken to marketing for years, then tell their staff to "add some social media stuff." They consider social media a random add-on that progressive companies do these days, not a funda-mentally different platform for every facet of their business.

The cold, hard reality is that bad enablers are everywhere, but that's exactly why the predominately good enablers we encounter have such a lasting impact on our lives. I can rattle off a baker's dozen in mere seconds: Joe Papa, Frank Fila, Sam Gibbons, Rob Cawthorn, Michel de Rosen, Jean-Jacques Bienaime, Joanna Horobin, Gary Shearman, Joe Scodari, Bob Feldman, Kevin Rollins, Michael Dell, and Jim Weiss. These colleagues share common traits that empower innovation among the people around them. They don't need to have every single fact before they make a decision. They rarely ask for a benchmark report before making their move. They prefer to support a reasonable first venture rather than wait for certainty—and they share the blame if the idea doesn't work.

Most important, none of them were ever satisfied with the status quo. Working beside them, you could feel their courage and their fearlessness. Innovation all the time was their creed, and my teams and I tried to live by that motto as much as we could.

Positive enablers know how to see around the corner, find the right people, provide the necessary support, and then let the team do what it does best. And in that sense, it's not hard to figure out if you're a positive enabler. If you are, your team knows they have to work hard and produce results. But they also understand that no leader—whether in business or life—reaches the pinnacle without a few mistakes along the way.

Go Bold or Go Home

Jeffrey Hayzlett dove into social media as chief marketing officer of Kodak, a company that's all about capturing personal experiences. To reenergize the business, he told me, the company had to engage its customers through social media. If Kodak wanted to help customers best capture their experiences, it had to provide the best customer experience. Hayzlett left Kodak in 2010 and now keeps himself hopping as one of the world's foremost marketing experts, a sought-after

Case Study

commentator, and the author of The Mirror Test. *He said business leaders have to take a bold approach to social media:*

I started twenty-five or thirty years ago. The basics of social media have been around forever in the form of networking and utilizing various social groups. That's existed since the dawn of man. Years ago, you would've known it as Kiwanis or Rotary, but now it's online, viral, and easier to participate. Any marketer or any business leader who values customers and their input will use it to their advantage.

It's usually a fear of what's new or unknown that leads people to build up walls against ideas that can transform, grow, and lead to success for companies. What worked in the past doesn't mean it will be the answer next year, next week, or even later the same day. At Kodak, I came in knowing that the people who put up those barriers would not fit our team. You have to surround yourself with people who want to take on the challenges and the change.

It's the companies that are not afraid of stumbling and those that adopt, adapt, and grow with energy and enthusiasm (especially with emerging technology) that become the leaders. The slow ones wait for everything to fall in place and work perfectly. With so many changes in social media, though, nothing will stay constant. In the end, the companies that wait for everything to be worked out will only be able to watch as their competition passes them by.

HEROES

Just hours before we launched our first corporate blog at Dell, we realized we'd made a tremendous gaffe.

With all the preparations completed and the blog ready to go live, I'd gone off to the beach at South Padre Island with my family. We'd moved to Austin from Switzerland just a few months earlier, and I'd been working seven days a week ever since. We were excited to have a chance to sit back and relax, which was exactly what I was doing that Sunday as I lazily walked along, the sand between my toes.

And then the phone rang. It was our chief blogger, Lionel Menchaca: "Bob, I don't know how to tell you this, but the name of our blog needs to change." The day before we would launch our first external blog, we realized our initial name, One2One, wouldn't work. If you did a search for the name it would lead you to some sites where, to put it mildly, clothing was optional. Not good, so we moved immediately to find a new name, take our hit for launching with the wrong name, and within a couple of days, had it rebranded as Direct2Dell.

We goofed. We didn't do our homework and ended up picking the wrong name. We were moving too fast to plan the blog and our content, and completely overlooked that rather important detail. I had to tell Michael we'd get some negative press before we'd even launched the blog—not exactly a fun update for me. In a company that suppresses innovation, we would have been nailed. We would have suffered through angry calls, furious e-mails, and threats to our jobs, but we got none of that. Our bosses made it clear something like this should never happen again—and we knew that—but they encouraged us to keep going and not slow down.

That move alone told me all I needed to know about Michael Dell and the kind of ship he runs. Innovation was always welcome, and if we did the best job possible an occasional honest mistake wouldn't derail our place at the company. We didn't have to get a hit every time, we just had to make sure we maintained the best batting average in the industry.

I didn't enjoy the next couple of days on the beach, but I immediately understood the concept of what a positive enabler really was, which had been a vague notion in my head. Positive enablers are the heroes of change in a company. They create an atmosphere of innovation and provide the support their teams need to get some real work done. The business leaders who put their faith and trust in their teams, giving them the leeway to take chances on innovation, will drive the successful Pre-Commerce companies. They unleash entire organizations and change how they do business.

I've had the good fortune to work with some outstanding business leaders, and I've addressed leadership classes dozens of times over the years. During each talk, I made sure everyone clearly understood two primary messages. First, I told the executives, you were hired to make the company better, so your teams expect you to challenge them, change them, and create some of the discomfort that accompanies growth. Your bosses and your reports want you to help them evolve, not reinforce the status quo. Second, I urged leaders to stop cowering from the possibility of getting fired. People who truly want to innovate and drive change realize the only way to do so is to stay true to their principles and remain focused on moving the organization forward. Pushing that change always creates friction—without exception. So the minute you start playing it safe, you become part of the machine. You become a negative enabler.

Case Study

THE MOTHER NATURE NETWORK

Joel Babbit and Chuck Leavell might pay attention to conventional wisdom, but they certainly know when to ignore it. If you would have asked if the environmental movement needed another educational Web site in 2008, most people would have said no. TreeHugger, Grist, and a host of other great environmental sites were pumping out a lot of great content. Joel and Chuck didn't see the mass of information that was there, they saw what was missing.

Chuck has a unique perspective on both culture and the environment. Since 1982, he's traveled the world as the keyboardist for

The Rolling Stones, and he also spent time with the Allman Brothers Band and Eric Clapton. He's played with some of the most influential rock 'n' rollers of our time. But he's also an avid environmentalist, author, and tree farmer. He maintains a direct working connection with nature, too, and the combination of activities give him a knack for culture and a nose for the issues that impact our environment.

Joel probably hasn't adhered to the status quo since the day he was born. His unorthodox approach to thinking through major business issues helped him mastermind some of the most creative advertising programs for the likes of Home Depot, Coca-Cola, and American Express. He's consulted on major corporate transformations, including KKR's acquisition of RJR Nabisco and AT&T's acquisition of BellSouth. And during the 1996 Olympic Games in Atlanta, Joel served as the city's chief marketing and communications officer.

By the time 2008 rolled around, Joel had built and sold a successful marketing services agency, but he stayed on after the acquisition. "I began to notice that many of our clients were spending an increasing amount of their marketing dollars on messages related to the environment—a subject which I knew very little about," Joel says. "I knew I had better get up to speed quickly, especially given the way the associated budgets were growing. So I started going to the Internet in search of guidance and information, only to find that the Web sites available were very technical and academic, narrow in their scope, and way over my head.

"I figured there must be millions of people like me—not experts, scientists, or activists, just mainstream businesspeople and consumers who wanted to know more about environmental issues. From a business perspective, it seemed like a great opportunity—a large and growing demand coupled with a very weak supply. I called Chuck, who I had met a few years earlier and who was the most passionate and educated environmentalist I knew. I asked him to look at this situation, and he came to the same conclusion. The next week, we raised close to $10 million in about twenty-four hours and I gave notice the next day."

In January 2009, the Mother Nature Network went live with a mission to provide the most comprehensive, accurate, and up-to-date environmental news and information available. And it would provide that information in a way that was engaging and easy to understand. Within eighteen months, MNN had the fifth-most visitors and page views out of the 7,100 environmental Web sites tracked by Alexa Information Services. It trailed only government sites, such as the U.S. Environmental Protection Agency. Almost two million people from 200 countries visit MNN each month, and traffic has increased every quarter since the site was launched.

MNN shows how visionary leaders like Chuck and Joel can ignore the conventional wisdom, look around the corner, develop an idea to drive their cause, and build the right organization to support their vision. Every business leader has similar opportunities awaiting them in the Pre-Commerce marketplace. Only a handful will go out and take advantage of them.

"The fact is that there are always a million reasons you can find to not start a business, and most people pay attention to them and stay where they are," Joel says. "But there are always a handful of people who put blinders on and move forward—win, lose or draw."

As a business leader, you've invested too much time in your education and your career to hold back any of your knowledge and experience. You have to maximize your ability to make a difference. Sometimes that means pushing the envelope, and sometimes that means pushing the envelope too far. When you're retired and sitting on the beach with a mai tai, you won't remember the milquetoast bosses or the number of times you squelched an idea. You'll remember the people who had an inspiring impact on your career. You'll remember the times you supported your people as they took a crazy idea, nurtured it, and enhanced your business with it.

The Pre-Commerce marketplace offers you a remarkable new greenfield for innovation. It's an ecosystem where mistakes signal an opportunity to build new relationships, not the death of a good idea. It's a community of people who reward the interesting, honest, and transparent companies but doubt the "perfect" ones. It's a market that doesn't accept the fearful but embraces the heroes that break out of the status quo.

The Pre-Commerce world loves a good hero.

GETTING STARTED

Vision without execution is hallucination.
—THOMAS EDISON

The flight attendant's voice crackles over the speakers, and as the plane heads into its final approach you dutifully close your laptop and put it away. But your mind keeps racing with ideas to embrace social media and move into the Pre-Commerce marketplace. You already have the name of your blog, a focus for your customer-support forum, and a pretty good idea of which employees will make great social media ambassadors for your company.

You feel pretty good, maybe even a little excited, as the plane sets down and starts to taxi toward the gate. You pull out your Blackberry to check on what you missed during the flight—and it happens. Reality sets in. Your calendar is blanketed with meetings the next day. Your boss wants her priority project done by the end of the week. And you have to leave early on Thursday to meet your kids' teachers at an open house. Before you know it, another Monday comes along and the file with your brilliant social media ideas gets buried in a folder of future projects that, deep down, you know you'll never get to.

The everyday pattern of business rolls along as it always did, but outside your walls the Pre-Commerce marketplace is revolutionizing the way customers interact with your brand. Every minute of every day, your customers go online to consult their peers, learn about your products, and make their purchasing decisions. It doesn't matter why you're not participating—whether you're ignoring Pre-Commerce or just not finding time to get your programs up and running—your customers are moving on without you. And they're not looking back. To create a Pre-Commerce company, you first have to instill a social discipline throughout your company. It's not about squeezing in time to create a Facebook page and calling it a day. *You have to make social media the priority project.* That's the first and most important step.

Once you've committed to becoming a Pre-Commerce company, you can start building the foundation for a vibrant social media platform. *It starts with listening.* You want to track down and discuss the latest insights, the emerging trends, and the moves your competitors make. A good listening platform, such as Radian6, can help aggregate the online chatter about your brand, and you can combine that with the insights your teams are gaining as they learn more about social media and how it impacts the company.

As you listen to your customers and employees, you'll begin to get a sense for the ideal share of conversation for your brand and topic. You will *define what constitutes online leadership* for your brand, and with that you can determine exactly how you can improve your share of the conversation to reach that threshold. As a business leader, demand complete transparency from your teams. Outlaw vague pie charts and require precise information about who has influence on your brand.

Identify your influencers by name. You can use available algorithms to narrow down precisely the top influencers for your brand. You can quantify and rank them with tools that aggregate and analyze their social media participation. And you can create a nice Top 25 list of influencers and ambassadors. But none of that helps you unless you can pick up the phone on a moment's notice, call the people on that list, and interact with them directly.

As you get to know them and their work, you'll realize they can't do it all on their own. Only a sliver of the Pre-Commerce populace generates original content. Join that small group. You have to *create informative and relevant content,* make it easy to share, and distribute it where and when your influencers and customers want to see it. Develop an editorial plan, analyze the gaps between online conversations and the content you supply, and then plug those holes. Identify the words and phrases your customers use to search for information about your product, and ensure all your content hits those searches.

As you create new material, make sure you *distribute that content when and where it will have an impact.* Syndicate your network by brand so you're represented across all the areas of online influence. If you share content across those top ten areas of online influence (Chapter Two), you'll reach twenty to forty times more people than you do through your Web site. Reconfigure your Web site to make it social media friendly. Load it with content your customers want to see, make it easy to share all of that information, and then reintroduce the site to the Pre-Commerce world.

As you get your internal social media platform running, start to look out across the Web and *mitigate the potential external threats* to your Pre-Commerce programs. Protect your brand against spam by locking in URLs and subdomains for the top twenty sites that could impinge on your company's social media efforts. Take control of your brand's online image by controlling how the brand name will be used throughout the top ten areas of online influence. For all its incredible upside, the Internet's openness also allows illegal and threatening activity; guard your company against it.

As you lock down the basic protections against spammers and other miscreants who'd misuse your brand name, you can turn your attention to issues management. Institute a portfolio of tracking and analysis tools that can *identify potential hot-button issues before they reach mainstream awareness.* If you still respond to a negative issue only when mainstream media calls your PR team, you're stuck in old-school mode. A Pre-Commerce company will see issues emerge well before journalists do 90 percent of the time. Build dark sites for top issues so you're ready if and when they become broadly known, and make sure that site will hit the top ten results for search queries about the topic at hand.

You have your defense set, so go on the offense. *Determine how you can help customers fulfill their desire to help their peers.* Customers want to share ideas that can improve products and services. They want to share their product knowledge to help inform their peers. And they want to provide solutions to problems their peers are having. The Pre-Commerce company focuses its content and distribution to help online influencers satisfy one or more of these desires. Remember that you want to reach 100 percent of your customers online, not just the 10 percent who might call each year. Get your team active on Yahoo! Answers and other forums, so they can add your company's expertise to the ongoing conversations about troubleshooting, product innovation, and upcoming purchases.

If you listen, your customers will give you some brilliant ideas. The same holds true inside your own walls. Create an internal social media platform and *encourage employees to share their intellectual capital.* Invite them to help build the next generation of products and services. Create educational and training programs that engage them and solicit their feedback on ways you can improve your operations. Make sure your legal, regulatory, and technology teams are your closest partners in your Pre-Commerce outreach. Their expertise will help you see around blind corners, so you can establish a technology roadmap and legal framework that's strong and flexible enough to build competitive advantage for your organization.

Finally, go back to where it all begins: Listen and learn. *Use the Four As to identify the projects that actually shape customer behavior.* Support and refine your successful social media efforts and quickly scrap the things that are just creating noise.

One last word of advice: Never think you have it all figured out. I wrote this book to introduce business leaders to the revolutionary changes Pre-Commerce is introducing to their markets. I wrote this book to help the same leaders understand and start building the social media foundation they'll need to reach the Pre-Commerce customer. I didn't write this book to give you all the answers—no one can do that. Nothing stands still in the Pre-Commerce marketplace, so business leaders constantly must learn it anew. Look around, listen to the community, and work collaboratively with your teams and your customers—and your own peers.

This book will do nothing for you if you don't take the next step and join the Pre-Commerce conversation. We've built a Web site, www .PreCommerce.com, where business leaders can share their insights and learn from one another. The site includes more perspectives from the people included in this book, as well as additional experts I highly regard. More important, the site provides an interactive forum where everyone can share what they're learning. As progressive business leaders, we can pool our insight to create a new Pre-Commerce discipline—one that works for our companies, our customers, and ourselves.

ENDNOTES

CHAPTER 1

1. Sucharita Mulpuru and Peter Hult, et al., "U.S. Online Retail Forecast, 2009 to 2014" (Forrester Research), March 5, 2010.
2. Ben Pring et al., "Forecast: Public Cloud Services, Worldwide and Regions, Industry Sectors, 2009–2014" (Gartner Group), June 2, 2010.

CHAPTER 2

1. Whitney Heckathorne, "Speak Now or Forever Hold Your Tweets" (Harris Interactive), June 3, 2010.
2. Nielsen Global Online Consumer Survey, "Global Advertising: Consumers Trust Real Friends and Virtual Strangers the Most" (The Nielsen Company), July 7, 2009.
3. "The Silent Click: Building Brands Online" (Online Publishers Association and comScore), June 2009.
4. Michael Kahn, "The Impact of Social Media" (Performics and ROI Research Inc.), November 6, 2009.
5. Chris Copeland, "The Influenced: Social Media, Search and the Interplay of Consideration and Consumption" (GroupM Search), October 2009.

CHAPTER 3

1. Press release, "ITU Sees 5 Billion Mobile Subscriptions Globally in 2010" (International Telecommunication Union), February 15, 2010.
2. Michael Kahn, "The Impact of Social Media" (Performics and ROI Research Inc.), November 6, 2009.
3. Wei Ji Ma et al., "Lip-Reading Aids Word Recognition Most in Moderate Noise: A Bayesian Explanation Using High-Dimensional Feature Space," *PLoS ONE* 4 (3): e4638, March 4, 2009, doi:10.1371/journal.pone.0004638.

CHAPTER 6

1. David Marshall, April 3, 2007 (9:05 P.M.), comment on Jeff Jarvis, "Drinks with Dell," *BuzzMachine*, April 3, 2007, http://www.buzzmachine.com/2007/04/03/drinks-with-dell

CHAPTER 7

1. Michael Kahn, "The Impact of Social Media" (Performics and ROI Research Inc.), November 6, 2009.
2. Kristen Purcell et al., "Understanding the Participatory News Consumer" (Pew Research Center and the Project for Excellence in Journalism), March 1, 2010.
3. Wei Ji Ma et al., "Lip-Reading Aids Word Recognition Most in Moderate Noise: A Bayesian Explanation Using High-Dimensional Feature Space," *PLoS ONE* 4(3): e4638, March 4, 2009, doi:10.1371/journal.pone.0004638.

CHAPTER 8

1. George Armitage Miller, "The Magical Number Seven, Plus or Minus Two: Some Limits on Our Capacity for Processing Information," *Psychological Review* 63 (1956).
2. "IBM Jam Events," IBM Corporation, accessed October 14, 2010, www.collaborationjam.com

CHAPTER 9

1. "Internet Usage and Population in North America," Internet World Stats, accessed October 14, 2010, www.internetworldstats.com/stats14.htm#north

CHAPTER 10

1. Abraham Maslow, "A Theory of Human Motivation," *Psychological Review* 50 (1943).
2. Matthew Eric Glassman, Jacob R. Straus, and Colleen J. Shogan, "Social Networking and Constituent Communications: Member Use of Twitter during a Two-Month Period in the 111th Congress" (Congressional Research Service), February 3, 2010.
3. Sean Donahue, "Washington's Great Digital Divide," *The Huffington Post*, posted August 23, 2010, accessed October 14, 2010, www.huffingtonpost.com/sean-donahue/washingtons-great-digital_b_690918.html

CHAPTER 11

1. Press release, "Gartner Says Worldwide IT Spending to Grow 4.6 Percent in 2010" (Gartner Group), January 21, 2010.
2. David Belson, Tom Leighton, and Brad Rinklin, "The State of the Internet, 1st Quarter, 2010 Report" (Akamai Technologies), July 2010.
3. Edward Jones and Richard Nisbett, "The Actor and the Observer: Divergent Perceptions of the Causes of Behavior," in *Attribution: Perceiving the Causes of Behavior*, ed. Jones and Nisbett et al. (New York: General Learning Press, 1971).

ACKNOWLEDGMENTS

When I was a child, I remember my grandfather speaking proudly about his brother, who made his living as an artist. What I learned is that he had helped "Tio," as we called him, live and dream the life of an artist. Years later, my mother, who had always been artistic, decided to start painting in mid-life, at around the same age as I am in writing this book. She took it seriously and within a few years, her works of art were being exhibited and bought in galleries in New Jersey and New York.

To create anything worthwhile, you have to dream and be willing to imagine you can create something that simply doesn't exist today. A book, in many respects, is simply another piece of art that happens to focus on words.

This is why I remember with fondness how my family has always celebrated letting your ideas be unleashed. I didn't fully appreciate it until I started to write a book myself, but that is the point. You have to be willing to let yourself go and put what you know on the sheet of paper or the canvas, and then let people judge your work.

So thank you Grandpa, Tio, and Mom.

My Dad is responsible for the willpower I have to write, despite working close to seven days a week. I was lucky to grow up with a role model who had a great work ethic, is as honest as the day is long, and who showed me that there is always enough time in the day to get done what you need to do and still enjoy life. He also instilled in me a life-long love for the New York Yankees, which, of course, I found a way to mention in this book.

My wife, Donna, deserves an entire book to thank her for all she has done for me professionally and personally. We've moved five times to places like Switzerland and

Florida and now Austin. She has tolerated my flying close to 250 thousand miles some years. And she has encouraged me to write a book for a while. I get to do some cool stuff because she is willing to help me make it happen. She's the definition of a true partner, friend, and wife.

All that said, the book would probably not have happened at this time if Jim Weiss, our CEO and my colleague and friend, had not convinced me to write it. Jim is passionate about how the communications industry is changing and what our role, as WCG, is in shaping how our clients think, work, and act. Jim is the ultimate "we can do it" leader and it's his coaching, counseling, and support that made the concept of Pre-Commerce go from vision to reality.

The book itself was fun to write, but as a first-time author, I have to say I was continually impressed and pleased that I asked Dan Zehr, a former reporter for the *Austin Statesman* and personal friend, to help me edit the book. Dan was able to finesse my writing throughout the process and, in doing so, has taught me more about how to write in the last year than I ever learned before. If you like the book, please remember that Dan's contribution was a very important one. I see future collaborations ahead for "Professor" Zehr and me.

I am very thankful for Katie Levine putting me in touch with Susan Williams, my executive editor at Jossey-Bass/Wiley. Susan provided me with the counsel I needed to get the concept together and to figure out what is involved in writing my first book. She is also pretty cool to work with and is someone I recommend to aspiring authors. I also want to thank Rob Brandt, Mark Karmendy, Erin Moy, and the team at Jossey-Bass/Wiley who make it all seem easier than it really is.

And last but not least, I want to give a shout out to my colleagues at WCG. They are the smartest team in the business and it is their thinking that helped me develop the concepts you read about in this book. I don't have space to list them all, but I'd like to at least mention Paul Dyer and Paulo Simas, who have fleshed out our 4As and Engagement models, among others, and who are a constant source of innovative ideas; and Paige Hutson, who has been leading the way in establishing Pre-Commerce as a key way of thinking in the marketplace, in support of this book.

In closing, I thank you, the reader, for taking time to learn about Pre-Commerce. I hope you find it enlightening and worthwhile.

ABOUT THE AUTHOR

Bob Pearson is chief technology and media officer at WCG, a global communications company. WCG's clients include Pfizer, General Mills, Intel, and Warner Brothers. Bob is past president of SocialMedia.org, and is vice chair of the State of Texas Emerging Technology Fund. He also serves on the Procter & Gamble Digital Advisory Board, the Pfizer U.S. Health Advisory Board, and as an advisor to MyEdu and UserVoice. Previously, he was vice president of Communities and Conversations at Dell and head of communications at Novartis. Bob is a frequent blogger, speaker, and columnist. He holds degrees from the University of North Carolina at Greensboro and Fairleigh Dickinson University. He lives in Austin, Texas, with his wife and two daughters.

INDEX

Benchmarking, 258
Benioff, Mark, 6, 7, 8, 184
Bennett, William, 242
Berners-Lee, Tim, 4
Best Buy, 2, 3, 190
Best practices, 258
Beta communities, 95
Beta forums, 199–200
Beta sites, 150, 200–201
Beverly, Paul, 170
Bienaime, Jean-Jacques, 279
Big Idea marketing, 123–124, 137
Bigadda Web site, 178
Biip.no community, 179
Bing search engine, 161–162
Bishop, Bill, 239
Blogs, 166–168; business council on, 34–35;
   company-created, 133, 167, 253–254,
   255–257; employee connectivity via, 247,
   254; finding influencers involved in,
   107–108; language issues for, 177;
   mainstream popularity of, 44; news
   obtained from, 167; origin of, 166;
   political, 241
Blomquist, Bob, 171
BP oil spill, 227–228, 229–230
Brand meme algorithm, 108–111, 131
Brands: active sharing about, 131–132;
   available content about, 134–135;
   company-created networks about, 133;
   criteria driving results for, 126; customer
   support for, 9, 61; delivering messages
   about, 116–117; impact of influencers
   on, 115; importance of topics vs.,
   105–106; online protection of, 289; peer
   influence on, 129–130; search position
   of, 127–129
Brazilian online habits, 268
Brin, Sergey, 157
Bristol-Myers Squibb, 62
Broadband penetration,
   261, 262
Brown, Becky, 194
Buffett, Warren, 1, 204
Bull Durham (film), 97
"Business class" customers, 206
BusinessWeek, 9, 78, 115

Business-to-business (B2B) interaction, 21;
   idea generation and, 193–194; sharing
   information via, 195–196
BuzzMachine.com, 42, 117, 146

C
CafeMom community, 179
Cave Man marketing, 16
Cawthorn, Rob, 279
Cellular phones: e-commerce via, 84. *See
   also* Mobile devices
Charland, Bernie, 6
Chawla, Sona, 137–138
China: Internet use in, 266–267; social
   media sites in, 179–180
CIBA-GEIGY, 58, 107, 152, 218
Cirangle, Paul, 56
Clarke, Jeff, 193
Clinton, Bill, 224
Cloob.com community, 179
Cloud computing, 8, 10–11, 264
CNET reviews, 2
CNN.com, 111
Coca-Cola, 114
Collaboration, 13–15
Communities, 265–267; accepted solutions,
   220–221; beta, 95, 150, 199–201;
   customer-support, 212–213; social
   media, 178–180
Community forums, 165–166, 178
ComScore research firm, 51
Congressional Research Service, 239
Constituents: core needs of, 226, 229;
   empowerment through listening to,
   241; grassroots access to, 243–244;
   information filtering by, 227–228;
   Pre-Commerce politics and, 223, 239–240;
   social media interactions with, 241–242
Consumer Product Safety Commission
   (CPSC), 236
Content about brands: availability of, 126,
   134–135; creation of, 195, 289; customer
   consumption of, 128; distribution of,
   104, 108, 289; optimizing for search
   engines, 160
Content distributors, 104, 108
Control, culture of, 248–249, 258